T0305204

MULTIMETHOD RESEARCH, CAUSAL MECHANISMS, AND CASE STUDIES

MULTIMETHOD RESEARCH, CAUSAL MECHANISMS, AND CASE STUDIES

An Integrated Approach

GARY GOERTZ

Princeton University Press
Princeton and Oxford

Published by Princeton University Press, 41 William Street,
Princeton, New Jersey 08540
In the United Kingdom: Princeton University Press,
6 Oxford Street, Woodstock, Oxfordshire, OX20 1TR

Cover image courtesy of Shutterstock

ISBN 978-0-691-17411-2
ISBN (pbk.) 978-0-691-17412-9

British Library Cataloging-in-Publication Data is available

This book has been composed in Sabon

Printed on acid-free paper. ∞

press.princeton.edu

Typeset by Nova Techset Pvt Ltd, Bangalore, India
Printed in the United States of America

1 3 5 7 9 10 8 6 4 2

CONTENTS

TABLES

FIGURES

ACKNOWLEDGMENTS

FIRST I would like to acknowledge Charles Ragin, friend and colleague. Without QCA (qualitative comparative analysis) this book would not have been conceivable. I could have (and maybe should have) cited his work many more times than I have. His influence runs throughout the book in countless ways. Thanks Charles.

Similarly, Harvey Starr's work on the opportunity and willingness framework underlies much of chapters 2, 4, and 5. While I have used somewhat different terminology, the core is linked to the opportunity and willingness framework. Also, his classic, Most and Starr (1989), *Inquiry, logic, and international politics*, is one of the few books to think seriously about the larger issues of theory, logic, and research design, and certainly helped me when starting on the research path.

Thanks also go to many students of the IQMR (Institute for Qualitative and Multi-Method Research) and Notre Dame qualitative methods and research design classes. Over the years they have suffered and contributed greatly, as a single paper grew to become this book.

Steve Samford did a massive amount of work systematically surveying and analyzing journal articles 2005–2016 that used case studies. The discussions of research practice were significantly influenced by his reflections and thoughts.

The discussions of causal mechanisms, and notably the figures, were inspired by the work of a number of great scholars. In addition, without extensive discussions about their work, the figures you will see would not have been possible. So thanks to Anna Grzymała-Busse, Patrick Mello, and Dan Slater.

Special thanks go to Steph Haggard, Bob Kaufmann, and Marc Trachtenberg. Extensive email exchanges fundamentally shaped chapters 7 and 8.

Several people read the whole manuscript and deserve special acknowledgment: Jim Mahoney, Steph Haggard, Benoît Rihoux,

Hillel Soiffer (heroic work reading the whole manuscript twice), and one anonymous Princeton reviewer.

IQMR organized an author's workshop in June 2015 that proved invaluable. Without the unison about the importance of causal mechanisms, chapter 2 would probably not have been written. So thanks to all participants in the workshop.

Other people and workshops deserve thanks as well, including Jørgen Møller, Svend-Erik Skaaning, Carsten Schneider, David Waldner, and the University of Michigan Social Movement Workshop.

Sean Branff did much copyediting work on a couple of versions of the manuscript. There would be many more errors without his detailed checking.

Thanks to Eric Crahan and his staff at Princeton University Press. Eric was a sounding board for many aspects of the book, and came up with the final title.

MULTIMETHOD RESEARCH, CAUSAL MECHANISMS, AND CASE STUDIES

CHAPTER 1

Introduction

Singular causal claims are primary. This is true in two senses. First, they are a necessary ingredient in the methods we use to establish generic causal claims. Even the methods that test causal laws by looking for regularities will not work unless some singular causal information is filled in first. Second, the regularities themselves play a secondary role in establishing a causal law. They are just evidence—and only one kind of evidence at that— that certain kinds of singular causal fact have happened.

— *Nancy Cartwright*

T HIS book addresses some of the core issues in doing (1) multimethod research, (2) causal mechanism analysis, and (3) case studies. Multimethod research has become very popular and almost a requirement for book-length studies. Multimethod can mean many things, but here it means combining case studies with statistics, qualitative comparative analysis (QCA), experiments, or game theory models. The purpose of case studies is to explore causal mechanisms at the heart of theories. One does case studies because cross-case methods give little purchase on the causal mechanisms (M_i) by which X produces Y. For multimethod researchers, showing a significant causal effect in a cross-case analysis is not sufficient; one needs to provide a causal mechanism and evidence for it. Demonstrating a causal effect is only half the job; the second half involves specifying the causal mechanism and empirically examining it, usually through case studies.

Causal mechanisms, cross-case analyses, and case studies form the *research triad*; see figure 1.1. This volume rests on the proposition that commitment to multimethod research is commitment to the research triad. Multimethod research

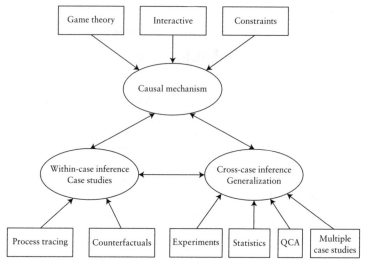

Figure 1.1: The research triad: causal mechanism, cross-case inference, and within-case causal inference.

typically is conceptualized as qualitative—within-case inference —along with quantitative cross-case inference. The research triad adds a third dimension to that, i.e., causal mechanisms. The research triad is an integrated approach because a commitment to multimethod research is also a commitment to a causal mechanism approach to explanation and social science research.

One way to see the integration is by looking at research that focuses, e.g., 90 percent of the research effort, on just one corner of the triad. For many experimentalists most of the effort is devoted to determining *the treatment effect*. They usually do not talk about causal mechanisms per se. While they usually have theories and hypotheses, these all boil down to the one treatment effect. Game theorists provide an nice example of those who focus a lot of attention on the model, i.e., causal mechanism. It is quite possible to publish articles where essentially the whole article is the model (this is very true in economics). Often historians focus on single events and the whole focus of the article is explaining some individual historical event. They are not interested in generalization and maybe only very implicitly interested in causal mechanisms.

The integrated approach rests on a central claim:

> As you move away from one-corner-only research you embrace the research triad.

For example, as a game theorist moves away from exclusive interest in the model, she begins to be involved in multimethod research, cross-case analyses, and within-case analyses. As soon as a case study researcher moves from one case to more cases, he is asking about generalization. Finally, as the Cartwright epigraph forcefully states, all statistical, experimental analyses and generalization imply individual case causal inference.

Good multimethod and causal mechanism research means a relative balance between the three corners of the research triad. If 90 percent of the effort is in demonstrating significant causal effects via cross-case analysis then the research is not serious multimethod or serious about the investigation of the causal mechanism. If the case studies are only "illustrations," then there is little commitment to multimethod research. Conversely, research using case studies—e.g., the popular paired comparison—is weak on generalization. Doing five or six case studies—as is common in security studies books—deals poorly with cross-case analysis and generalization. The ideal is a fairly balanced effort on all three points of the triangle.

Case studies are often considered of questionable inferential value. Clarke and Primo illustrate this view of case studies. When they refer to case studies they almost always describe them as "exploratory": "one can also design exploratory models with an eye toward explaining the events surrounding a specific case" (2012, 92). By "exploratory" they strongly imply the endeavor is not about causal inference. For example, their discussion of the analytic narratives project (Bates et al. 1998) falls into this category. When they talk about "empirical models" they mean statistical models. So a model of the US Senate—statistical or formal—is not exploratory, but a case study of the American Civil War in analytic narratives is exploratory. In contrast, the research triad emphasizes that case studies are about causal inference.

In everyday life—along with virtually all natural sciences—people successfully make individual-case causal inferences, e.g., origins of the universe, origins of the human species, why a given person died, why the Challenger shuttle exploded. None of these inferential successes relies on randomized treatments assigned to subjects, nor do they depend on conditional probabilities.

A core philosophy motivating this study is that we want to explain individual outcomes. Statistical analyses do not provide explanations: "There is little argument in political science that statistical models cannot serve as explanations in and of themselves. This belief manifests itself in the relegation of statistical models to devices for *testing* explanations" (Clarke and Primo 2012, 154).

The research triad assumes that one accepts the importance and value of causal mechanism analysis. One can find statistical methodologists who do not believe this is possible or important: "The importance of searching for causal mechanisms is often overestimated by political scientists, and this sometimes leads to an underestimate of the importance of comparing conditional probabilities. We do not need to have much or any knowledge about mechanisms in order to know that a causal relationship exists.... In general, as our understanding of an issue improves, studying individual cases becomes less important" (Sekhon 2004, 288–89; last sentence of the article). Gerring illustrates the skepticism about whether causal mechanism analysis is essential: "To clarify, this is not a polemic against mechanisms. It is a polemic against a dogmatic interpretation of the mechanismic mission. I argue that the analysis of causal mechanisms is best regarded as an important, but secondary, element of causal assessment—not a necessary condition" (Gerring 2010, 1500).

I do *not* survey or discuss how one goes about doing within-case causal inference in this book. There is a booming literature on the topic, e.g., Bennett and Checkel (2014), and Beach and Pedersen (2012; 2016) on process tracing, Mahoney (2012) on hoop and smoking gun tests, Goertz and Levy (2007), Levy (2008), and Harvey (2011) on counterfactuals. One can do statistical within-case causal inference. I take no position on how one does within-case inference. Similarly I do not cover how to do observational statistics, experiments, or QCA. As illustrated in figure 1.1 these methodologies provide input for the research triad but are not covered here.

"Qualitative" and "quantitative" are not very useful in describing or analyzing multimethod research. Instead of multimethod research as qualitative and quantitative, the research triad contrasts *within-case* causal inference (case studies) with *cross-case* causal inference (comparative case studies, statistical models, experiments, or QCA). This produces some surprising methodological bedfellows. Standard usage puts statistics in the quantitative category and set-theoretic approaches (e.g., QCA) in the qualitative. Experimenters spend a lot of time stressing the differences between experiments and observational research: here they are both cross-case methodologies. Similarly *comparative* case studies are cross-case analyses. I consider these all as versions of cross-case causal inference. In contrast, single case studies by their very nature are about what happens in individual cases. Case studies are fundamentally about within-case causal inference. The research triad means that multimethod research is multicausal inference analysis.[1] The causal inference techniques, procedures, and methodology of each type, cross-case and within-case, serve different but complementary goals.

The research triad works from a basic principle:

Multimethod work involves cross-case causal inference AND within-case causal inference.

Multimethod in this book means complementary causal inference methodologies. How one does cross-case inference or within-case inference is less important than the causal inference goals.[2]

---

[1] Thanks to Hillel Soifer for this point.

[2] Multimethod research can have other roles. Within the potential outcomes framework many of the core assumptions about treatments, randomization, selection, effect heterogeneity, noncontagion, etc. could be examined by looking closely at some individual cases. For example, Harding and Seefeldt (2013) stress that case studies can be extremely useful in understanding selection processes. Particularly, in the context of field experiments where "nature" does randomization, one needs to closely investigate via case studies the extent to which this assumption holds. For example, core to John Snow's famous natural experiment about cholera was an extensive analysis of who got water from the

To connect cross-case and within-case analysis means having a methodology for choosing cases for causal mechanism analysis. The practical problem of choosing cases runs as a bright red thread throughout the book. These decisions face all who connect case studies to other methodologies. In particular, I offer much specific guidance about case selection. This means a systematic set of guidelines for case selection including a list of criteria for getting to a final decision about which cases to choose.

McGuire (2010) illustrates typical multimethod research involving a statistical analysis and case studies. His dependent variable is health outcomes. The second chapter of his book is a large-N cross-national statistical analysis, which is followed by eight country case studies. These case studies focus on explaining outcomes in those countries, for example, the following:

> What needs to be explained, then, is why Costa Rica's infant mortality rate was so low in 2005 (why it attained a certain level); why it fell so fast from 1960 to 2005 (why it achieved a certain amount of progress), and why it fell faster during the 1970s than at other times within this period (why it evolved at a certain tempo). The sustained and effective public provision of basic health services to the poor, this chapter finds, goes a long way toward explaining why Costa Rica from 1960 to 2005 achieved a rapid decline (and, eventually, a low level) of infant mortality. (McGuire 2010, 66)

McGuire is making claims about what happened in Costa Rica and why it happened, i.e., within-case causal inference.

The standard rationale for multimethod work involves looking at causal mechanisms via case studies: "Despite some claims to the contrary in the qualitative methods literature, case studies are not designed to discover or confirm empirical regularities.

---

two different water companies. He showed that there was no obvious bias since both companies delivered to the same neighborhoods and there seemed to be no particular bias (e.g., wealth) among their clients. This volume does not deny the usefulness of case studies for these purposes. I am not trying to survey all possible uses of case studies or qualitative information in multimethod research. Rather I focus on using case studies to explore causal mechanisms. However, in my extensive survey of existing practice—articles and books—I have almost never seen case studies or qualitative methods used to check core assumptions of statistical models (this might be more common in sociology, which has a longer multimethod tradition).

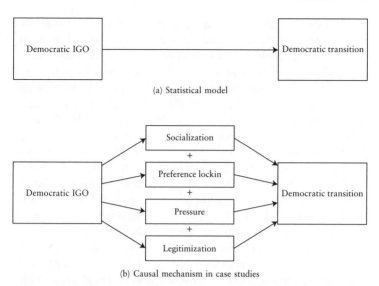

(a) Statistical model

(b) Causal mechanism in case studies

Figure 1.2: Causal mechanisms and statistical multimethod research: democratic IGOs and democratic stability. Source: based on Pevehouse (2005), table 5.1.

However they can be quite useful—indeed, essential—for ascertaining and assessing the causal mechanisms that give rise to empirical regularities in politics" (Fearon and Laitin 2008, 773). This is exactly what the research triad proposes: cross-case analyses for "empirical regularities" and case studies for causal mechanisms.

McAdam and Boudet give a similar rationale in their study of environmental social movements: "We conceived of the project as an attempt to develop an alternative to the methodological conventions of social movement research. Equally dissatisfied with 'thin,' large-N studies of protest events and rich but nongeneralizable case studies of this or that movement, we sought a middle ground between these two modal 'poles' of social movement scholarship" (2012, 52).

Pevehouse (2005) provides a nice example of why people want to do multimethod research. He argues that democratic IGOs (intergovermental organizations) can help establish democracy, make it more robust, and encourage transitions to democracy. As illustrated in figure 1.2a, there is a causal connection proposed between democratic IGOs and democracy in states.

He shows that there is a significant correlation between democraticness of the IGO and democracy in its member states. Multimethod research comes into play because he thinks there are multiple—and not mutually exclusive—causal mechanisms that explain this significant correlation. Figure 1.2b adds the causal mechanisms that produce this statistical effect: (1) acquiescence effect, (2) legitimization, (3) pressure, and (4) financial assistance (Pevehouse 2005, table 5.2, 153). Here one sees Pevehouse going around the research triad, from the statistical analyses to case studies to causal mechanism analysis.

Many hypotheses, experiments, and the like propose multiple causal mechanisms connecting the treatment to the outcome, as illustrated in figure 1.2. For example, Helfer and Voeten list three causal mechanisms whereby the European Court of Human Rights influences state policy: (1) preempting future international court litigation, (2) persuasive authority, and (3) agenda-setting at the national level. They argue—like Pevehouse—that "these three mechanisms may work separately or in tandem" (Helfer and Voeten 2014, 82). Hence, one role of case studies is to explore which of these mechanisms is actually at work.

A central role of case studies is combining within-case causal inference with analyses of causal mechanisms. These two in fact cannot be separated. To do process tracing, for example, means to make causal claims about the case. Usually it means that the causal mechanism in question can explain or contributes to the outcome in the individual case. Some researchers offer case studies as "illustrations"; this is disingenuous. Good multimethod research means that one must be serious about the within-case causal claims and make sure that they stand up to scrutiny.

Why after all is one doing a case study in multimethod research? The answer is almost always "to explore causal mechanisms." This is why the research triad is integrated and tightly linked. Doing multimethod research means doing case studies, which means exploring causal mechanisms. Once you have started down the multimethod path you have to pass by causal mechanisms.

Causal mechanism by definition means causal complexity (see chapter 2). A commitment to multimethod research and the research triad is a commitment to causal complexity. Causal mechanisms involve causal complexity. The contrast is with those who are almost exclusively interested in the effect of X_1 on Y. As the various figures in chapter 2 illustrate, causal mechanisms are complex entities. Most often the easiest—and maybe the only practical—way to empirically explore mechanisms is process tracing in individual cases.

One variable, single treatment analyses are by contrast causally simple. The classic examples are single-variable hypotheses empirically investigated via statistical analyses or experiments. At the other extreme are game-theoretic models, which often have numerous assumptions and complex features. Even simple game-theoretic models involve multiple assumptions about individuals, their beliefs, rules of the game, etc.

A quite popular move for game theorists is to move to the cross-case corner of the research triad. There have been extensive efforts—with substantial NSF (National Science Foundation) funding—to connect game theory and statistics, hence game theory and statistical cross-case inference. Notably the EITM program (Granato and Scioli 2004) has held summer workshops for a number of years where the central component has been connecting statistical methods with game-theoretic models.[3] However, there has been very little done to connect game-theoretic models with qualitative methods and case studies (though see Lorentzen, Fravel, and Paine 2016), hence game theory and within-case causal inference.

Chapter 6 argues that there is a very natural connection between game theory and within-case causal inference. In addition to the cross-case analyses, one moves in the within-case inference direction. Many—if not almost all—of the crucial theoretical entities in game-theoretic models are hard to observe and measure in large-N settings. Factors like beliefs, information, uncertainty, and preferences are hard to determine even in one case, not to mention dozens or hundreds. As a result, statistical tests are virtually always indirect. For example, in the audience costs literature and debate (discussed in some detail in chapter 7) the usual proxy of audience costs is democracy. "Democracy" is

---

[3] Other modeling techniques are presented, such as agent-based computer models, but the core is game theory and statistics.

some distance away from the theoretical mechanism developed by Fearon (1994). In contrast, there is some hope of assessing core model features in one or a few individual cases.

Case studies naturally link up with game theory because the game-theoretic model itself is a causal mechanism. A game-theoretic model thus calls out for an empirical analysis in individual cases to see if the causal mechanism works in real life as advertised in the model. In practice many formal game theory articles—where the focus is on the model—include historical examples. Fortunately for this volume, Peter Lorentzen and his colleagues have surveyed the use and nonuse of case studies in formal work in international relations and comparative politics.

While formal modelers may be less interested in testing their models against individual cases, their critics have not been hesitant in recent years to do so. A number of the prominent critiques of game-theoretic work are discussed in chapter 7 including critiques of audience costs theories and Acemoglu and Robinson's work (2006). These examples involve using case studies to evaluate the empirical usefulness of formal models.

Causal complexity can take other forms. What one might call "simple complexity" involves causal heterogeneity and interaction theories and hypotheses. In figure 1.1, above the causal mechanism ellipse, I have "game theory" as well as "interactive" causal mechanisms. This volume explores some general kinds of causal mechanisms. Particularly of interest are those that can also appear in cross-case analyses. Interaction terms are not uncommon in statistical analyses. QCA is built from complex interaction terms. To develop hypotheses about interactions of various sorts is to start down the road from the cross-case analysis toward the causal-mechanism corner. Much of this volume then is how to connect these two corners to the case studies in the third corner.

Within the potential outcomes framework there is tension between the individual-level counterfactual, which allows for a great deal of causal heterogeneity, and the overall goal, which is the estimation of average treatment effects (ATE). The ATE can contain a great deal of heterogeneity. Much of current methodological research involves looking at this causal heterogeneity.

For example, a famous experiment—a HUD-funded study (Department of Housing and Urban Development, USA)—looked at the hypothesis that the neighborhood in which an individual was raised (poor versus wealthy) has important impacts on social mobility, educational achievement, etc. Households were assigned randomly to poor versus wealthy neighborhoods (obviously the design was more complicated than this). These poor households contain heterogeneity of subjects: one of the findings was that girls benefited from better neighborhoods, but boys were perhaps worse off. In this case the average causal effect is meaningless, since it depended on the gender of the person in interaction with neighborhood.

By interviewing boys, girls, and parents in the housing study—i.e., doing multimethod research—the reasons for the differences between boys and girls became clearer:

> Girls in more advantaged neighborhoods also made friends at school and work rather than in the community, exposing them to a different set of peers. Among boys, a different set of social processes occurred. Boys who moved to more advantaged neighborhoods were separated from male role models left behind in their former neighborhoods, engaged in public leisure activities like hanging out and playing sports that put them at greater risk of contact with police, and lost the opportunity to develop "street smarts" that they would be more likely to need to navigate dangerous streets when they returned to poor neighborhoods. (Harding and Seefeldt 2013, 98)

This means that there is an interaction between the treatment and gender.

Interaction terms or mediating variables are a simple kind of complexity. QCA paths typically involve two to four factors and thus embody, as a matter of course, causal complexity. Cross-case methods can incorporate some modest complexity, but then one needs to think about how that links up with case studies and causal mechanisms. For example, how does one do case selection when there is an interaction term or a path with INUS (Insufficient but Nonredundant parts of a condition which is itself Unnecessary but Sufficient for the occurrence of the effect) variables?

Chapters 2 and 4 explore constraint causal mechanisms. These are inherently complex because constraints have causal effects only when there is motivation to violate the constraint (this is the core idea of Starr's 1978 opportunity and willingness framework). Nuclear deterrence does not explain the peace between the USA and Canada. For example, the impact of veto players (Tsebelis 2002) depends on the degree of ideological divergence among the veto players. Case studies must be chosen so that the causal mechanisms embodied in these constraint theories can be seen, i.e., not USA–Canada for the mechanism of nuclear deterrence.

Chapter 5 explores multimethod in the context of statistical interaction hypotheses or set-theoretic models. The X_1 and X_2 interaction raises the question about how they work together in a causal mechanism. In the QCA context there is the additional claim that within the path, X_1 and X_2 are necessary conditions. This means that the material in chapter 4 is critical. The causal mechanism analysis must focus on how X_1 and X_2 together produce Y. At the same time one needs to look at how the absence of X_1 or X_2 prevents Y from occurring.

One can start at the within-case case study corner of the research triad. This links easily to the causal mechanism corner because that is typically why one is doing the case study to begin with. Much more problematic is the link to the generalization ellipse. From the causal mechanism corner one asks about the scope and generalizability of the causal mechanisms.

Salmon (1998) refers to two grand traditions within philosophy of science, the first related to the hypothetico-deductive approach. The second tradition is that of causal mechanisms. The hypothetico-deductive approach is based in philosophy of science where the science in question is physics. The issue of scope and degree of generalization does not really arise. In contrast, in the philosophical literature on causal mechanisms, scope is a core consideration. Biological sciences—particularly biochemistry—become the sciences of analysis. In these sciences the scope of the causal mechanisms and theories is typically open and up for discussion. Causal mechanism ideas describe much better what biologists do than the covering laws of physics.

So instead of talk of testing causal mechanisms, one can reformulate the question in terms of the scope of the causal mechanism. Causal mechanisms with wide scope pass tests of importance and significance, while causal mechanisms of limited scope are empirically less important.[4]

In principle, theoretical and empirical scope are important research questions. However, they are rarely discussed in applied research and rarely appear in methods and research design textbooks. For statistical work, empirical scope is implicitly defined by the limits of the data set. The scope of game theory models is typically unclear since it is rarely made explicit.

Usually, case studies of the classic qualitative sort are not seen as good tests of a theory, hypothesis, or causal mechanism.[5] Chapter 7 discusses how a variety of scholars are beginning to do what I call "large-N qualitative testing." "Large-N" here is somewhat ironic because the testing uses many instances of within-case causal analyses to explore the scope and validity of some prominent game theory models or statistical analyses.

In large-N qualitative testing one starts with, say, a game-theoretic model. Then one moves within the research triad to individual cases and within-case causal inference and then to the generalization part of the triad. Finally, one draws some general conclusions about the empirical validity of the game-theoretic model.

Particularly in the case of game theory models, large-N qualitative testing begins by determining the scope of the case study population. For game theory models, constructing the case study population is a challenge (see the discussion of the audience costs debate). As discussed in chapter 7, a key part of the methodology is constituting the population.

The large-N qualitative critics of statistical studies almost never use *all* the cases in a statistical analysis for their within-case analyses, in fact the cases chosen form a relatively small

---

[4] As we shall see, however, they might apply to historically important cases, so in that sense they are substantively important.

[5] Sometimes an author will claim that a case study can disconfirm a deterministic hypothesis (e.g., Gerring 2012). Such strict falsificationism has long been discredited in the philosophy of science literature, and one can find little evidence for it in scientific practice.

subset of the statistical population of observations. At the same time, researchers claim that they have looked at all the relevant cases. Chapter 7 analyses this tension in some detail. All this is part of determining how empirically generalizable the model is.

Critics sometimes find that the game-theoretic analysis has narrow empirical scope. In discussions of statistical analyses, they find that while there might be a statistically significant correlation in the large-N analyses, there is little evidence for the causal mechanism when doing within-case causal inference.

Chapter 8 proposes rethinking how scholars do *multiple* case studies (i.e., not comparative case studies) and the connection between statistical analyses and within-case causal inference. It attacks directly the standard question:

> How generalizable is a successful within-case causal inference of a causal mechanism?

This means thinking about moving from the case study ellipse in figure 1.1 to the generalization ellipse.

In the "medium-N paradigm" outlined in chapter 8, additional case studies are designed and implemented in order to evaluate how generalizable the causal mechanism is. To investigate the empirical scope of a causal mechanism means deciding how many cases to explore and which specific cases to include.

The medium-N paradigm has important implications for case study research generally. For example, it implies that popular designs like paired comparisons have little to say for them. Similarly, the popular book format of one theory chapter and five or six equal case studies can be improved upon significantly.

Hence, chapters 7 and 8 form a pair. Consistent with the importance of exploring research practice in this book, chapter 7 looks at influential and controversial tests of prominent theories, such as Cusack, Iversen and Soskice (2007), Acemoglu and Robinson (2006), and Fearon (1994), by qualitative scholars, using the cumulation of within-case causal inference. Given that these large-N qualitative tests were published in major journals, e.g., *American Political Science Review*, the implicit methodology of these articles has convinced editors and reviewers.

Chapter 8 then systematizes and presents the logic of the medium-N paradigm. For example, most of the studies surveyed in chapter 7 attempt to look at *all* relevant cases. This might not be practical and might not be an efficient use of resources.

The relevance of the medium-N paradigm extends to experimental research as well. In both experiments and the medium-N paradigm, the emphasis is on high-quality within-case causal inference. For much of the discussion in chapter 8 one can substitute "experiment" for "within-case causal inference." For example, if you can do, say, four case studies of the same causal mechanism, which ones would you choose? Replace "case study" with "experiment" and you have the same basic methodological issue.

Jim Mahoney and I (Goertz and Mahoney 2012) argued that there were two cultures of methods research, one based on set theory and mathematical logic and the other based on statistical methods. Comparative case study and statistical multimethod research then lies at the intersection of the two cultures. Comparative-case-study methodology was, and is, strongly influenced by cross-case comparison ideas from statistics (see appendix A). Much case study methodology—notably Gerring (2006; 2017)—is explicitly based on statistical models.

One motivation for this volume is *integrating* and bridging these cultural divides. Often there is relatively easy and common linkage between two corners of the research triad, but a large gap to the third. This is because the two cultures cut through the research triad. For example, EITM builds strong linkages between game-theoretic models and cross-case analysis, but completely ignores the empirical exploration of game-theoretic causal mechanisms, which can only really be done in case studies. Classic qualitative research is the common link between case studies, within-case causal inference, and the causal complexity of causal mechanisms, but it has difficulties with cross-case analysis and generalization.

This tension appears in the statistical multimethod literature, which is strongly located in the cross-case statistical corner. Statistical concerns drive case study selection and at the same time downplay the importance of within-case causal inference and causal mechanism analysis.

One can see this cultural tension in Gerring's (2006) list of nine different case selection criteria. The causal mechanism type is number (7), the pathway case. This causal mechanism type is buried in the middle of Gerring's list. While he does not explicitly consider this list as ordinal, there is no doubt that the dominant and privileged types are those at the top: (1) typical and (2) diverse. The typical case is the average, representative case in the context of some population of cases.

Here we see the tension with practice. Since most researchers are interested in multimethod research for causal mechanism reasons, they rarely use Gerring's preferred case study designs.

Similarly, in recent years there has been a surge of articles, papers, and books looking at case selection for case studies from a potential outcomes perspective (Glynn and Ichino 2015; Herron and Quinn 2016; Seawright 2016; Weller and Barnes 2014). Since matching (e.g., Nielsen 2016) is almost always used for confounders, this leads naturally to pairs of comparative cases. This potential outcomes literature is an updating of the classic paired comparison–similar system design of qualitative methods.

In this book I think it is quite important to have a clear unified account of what case study research looks like when approached via statistical models and ways of thinking. In other words, if the cross-case statistical analysis were driving everything what would the methodology look like? In contrast to the integrated approach where each corner has its role to play, the statistical approach runs everything from the cross-case, statistical corner. Appendix A provides an account of a statistics-based methodology of case- and comparative-case-study research. For example, I discuss matching methods as the standard approach to confounders.

Appendix A is not a summary or a recap of this recent work, but offers its own account. It differs in important respects from the current literature. For example, it provides a pathway case selection procedure that is closer to the potential outcomes philosophy than Gerring (2017). I rely on the basic counterfactual of the potential outcomes approach while Gerring uses comparative statistical models to choose cases.

QCA provides a good example of an approach that stresses the corners of the research triangle. Ragin's groundbreaking book, *The comparative method*, proposed Boolean algebra as a means of doing cross-case comparisons. At the same time, he has continually emphasized that QCA is a *case-based* methodology. QCA results are closely connected to cases (unlike statistical multimethod research in general; see appendix A). Good QCA research always connects the paths of the cross-case analysis to the cases on those paths. The interactive nature of the paths in QCA points the researcher to a potential causal mechanism.

Individual scholars can maintain a balance between the corners of the triad. Bueno de Mesquita's research (see chapter 6) provides a good example. He develops game-theoretic models, does large-N statistical tests, applies the model to cases, and does predictions. Another example comes from the Robbers Cave experiment of Sherif et al. (1961), a classic in social psychology. Sherif and his colleagues explicitly discussed their combining of methods as a strength of the study; Donald Campbell in his 1988 introduction stressed its multimethod nature:

> One of the valuable slogans of the new emphasis on qualitative, contextual methodology is "thick description" (Geertz 1973). The Robbers Cave study provides such thick description. Moreover, the many ingenious subexperiments that are introduced, with their "natural" opportunities for quantitative measurement, add greatly to the "thickness," creating opportunities for participant action and qualitative observation that would not otherwise have existed, as well as providing quantitative measures. In this study, better than anywhere else I can think of, the proper synthesis of the qualitative-versus-quantitative dialectic is achieved. (Campbell in his introduction to Sherif et al. 1988, xxi)

It is common in sociology and psychology to do large-N analyses combined with interviews of individuals. For example, Louise Roth's book (2006) on the gender bias of Wall Street illustrates balanced qualitative and quantitative research. She had a clear large-N sampling strategy, did questionnaires and regression analyses. Yet much of the book comes from her interviews, which helped her understand how the structures and practices of Wall Street produced significant gender bias.

John Snow, Cholera, and the Research Triad

In his methods debate with Brady and Collier, Neal Beck asked the question of who owned the Snow–cholera example: "Who gets to claim John Snow?" (Beck 2010, 500).

In many respects, John Snow is a model of the research triad. He conducted a famous natural experiment, hence he is firmly located in the cross-case, empirical corner. At the same time, a lot of his research fits with the within-case and causal mechanism emphasis of the other two corners, as illustrated by his analysis of the Broad Street pump.

Snow is also a good choice because medical and drug examples are common in the social science methodology literature, and in particular, the multimethod literature. The well-known statistician David Freedman introduced the Snow–cholera example to social scientists in an often-cited chapter with the nice metaphor of "shoe leather" in the title. Freedman's Berkeley colleagues in political science picked up this example and it appears regularly in Brady–Collier–Dunning–Seawright publications, hence it is well known in the qualitative as well as statistical methods literature. Snow is a major figure in the history of epidemiology, sometimes considered the founding father for his various innovative methods for studying the causal mechanism whereby cholera is transmitted (Hempel 2007; Vinten-Johansen et al. 2003).[6]

It is useful to think of medical research in the context of the research triad. Modern drug developments start in the causal mechanism corner. For example, depression drugs are based on biochemical analyses of how the brain works. The cross-case analysis comes much further downstream in terms of testing whether a drug actually works. Medical doctors are located at the end; they hope that the drug works on individual patients and they have to decide whether generalizations about the effect of the drug apply to patient X.

Traditional medicines start from the individual case corner. Over time, societies discover that some plant works for some

---

[6] When considering this cholera example, it is critical to understand that Snow could not really get at the causal mechanism of cholera. This would require virus theory, Pasteur, and developments in biochemistry.

disease: this is generalization from individual cases. Modern medicine kicks in when it tries to find the "active ingredient" and mechanism. The history of medicine is full of examples of things that worked (e.g., penicillin). Often the elaboration of the causal mechanism came much later. Here the route is thus from individual case to generalization to causal mechanism.

As is often the case, these examples, such as Snow–cholera, get a life of their own. It is useful to go back to the sources and look at what kinds of analyses Snow conducted to convince himself— at the time he was not too successful at convincing others—that cholera was transmitted via drinking water.

Snow is justly famous for his natural experiment involving two water companies that competed in the same neighborhoods to deliver water to residents. The shoe leather Freedman referred to was Snow's extensive work going through the neighborhoods to show that the treatment—which water company used—was an "as if" randomized treatment. This involved showing that there was no bias by income, profession, education, etc. in the choice of water source. Hence, it is not surprising that in Dunning's (2012) book on natural experiments this example receives an extended discussion.

However, Snow conducted two other extensive shoe leather analyses. The one most interesting for this volume is "the case of the Broad Street pump," which illustrates many features of the arguments made in the chapters to come.[7] Most discussions of process tracing methodology employ the detective metaphor. Finding the cause is like Sherlock Holmes discovering the murderer. Collier (2011) has pushed this to its natural conclusion by publishing a methods article using an extensive analysis of a Holmes story. The Broad Street pump case has many features that illustrate Snow's detective work at its best.

In 1854 there was a very severe, but localized, outbreak of cholera in London. Within the area of a few square kilometers there were numerous cases of cholera. Snow as detective set out to discover the cause of this outbreak. It occurred at a time when he had convinced himself that infected drinking water was

---

[7] The third involves an important rule for dealing with confounders or alternative explanations and will be discussed in chapter 3.

the source. With his causal mechanism in mind he looked to link the cases of $Y = 1$ (cholera) with an $X = 1$—closeness to the source of bad water. Eventually his attention focused on the Broad Street pump, which seemed to be at the geographic epicenter of the outbreak; almost all victims were closer to the suspect pump than any other public water source.[8] He paid particular attention to the $X = 1$ cases of people who lived close to the pump but who did not get cholera ($Y = 0$). These cases could seriously challenge or disconfirm his causal mechanism. He tried to verify as much as possible his hunch that they got their water elsewhere, hence in fact they were $X = 0$ cases. Snow was eventually able to convince local authorities to shut down the pump.

In her biography of Snow and cholera, Hempel (2007) entitles the chapter devoted to the Broad Street pump "Proof definitive," and entitles her book *The strange case of the Broad Street pump: John Snow and the mystery of cholera*. In her analysis of Snow, this seems to be more or as important as the "Grand experiment" (one of her chapters) in demonstrating the mechanism of cholera transmission. In many ways the Broad Street pump became the symbol of Snow's work. For example, during the annual Pumphandle Lecture in England, members of the John Snow Society remove and replace a pump handle to symbolize the continuing challenges for advances in public health. At the US Centers for Disease Control in Atlanta, when an epidemiological problem requires a rapid, straightforward solution, staff have been heard to ask, "Where's the handle to this Broad Street pump?" (Vinten-Johansen et al. 2003, 392).

Snow's natural experiment and his detective work on the Broad Street pump were *both* brilliant pieces of scientific research. This volume argues we have much to learn from the Broad Street pump example. In fact, most multimethod work involving case studies fits with the Broad Street pump model. We shall see, for example, that most multimethod scholars when doing within-case causal inference regarding a causal mechanism

---

[8] The idea of drawing a map based on distance to the nearest water source eventually became Voronoi tilings, which are part of the mathematical theory of tessellation (how to fill up a space with tiles).

focus on what I call the $(1, 1)$ cases. This is a natural choice if you want to connect a causal mechanism $X = 1$ to the outcome $Y = 1$. The key to the Broad Street pump analysis was showing that almost all cases of cholera $(Y = 1)$ were within the area where the pump was the closest public water source $(X = 1)$.

In short, this book claims Snow by exploring his Broad Street pump methodology, how and why he selected the cases he did to explore a particular causal mechanism.[9]

Research Practice, Exercises, and Bibliographies

The approach developed in chapters 3 to 5 is essential to understanding multimethod *practice* in statistical, QCA, and game theory multimethod research. This volume features a strong interest in research practice. Most statistical research cites methods articles as justification. For research involving case studies this is far from standard practice. It is quite common for statistical multimethod articles and books to choose cases and do case studies without any reference to the methodology literature. Apparently, these practices are not too objectionable since they appear in major journals—e.g., *American Political Science Review*, *International Organization*, and *World Politics*. One goal of this volume is to make explicit the implicit methodology used and give it a critical examination. All of the chapters have significant pages devoted to research practice, as evidenced by publication in top-ranked journals and university presses.

Steve Samford and I have conducted an extensive and systematic survey of case study research practice in comparative politics (his field) and international relations (my field). We have systematically examined all articles that involve case studies— single case studies, comparative case studies, game theory, QCA,

[9] Dunning (2012, 18) appears to claim the Broad Street pump as well by using its famous map of cholera occurrence as the cover of the book. However he says that "Snow's strongest piece of evidence, however, came from a natural experiment that he studied during the epidemic of 1853–54." Dunning's main discussion of the pump case appears in the chapter "The central role of qualitative evidence" in the context of a discussion of causal mechanisms. In short, Dunning himself sees the pump analysis as a causal mechanism one.

and statistical multimethod in the top journals that publish articles using this kind of research (i.e., not *American Political Science Review*, *American Journal of Political Science*, and *Journal of Politics*, which only rarely publish research with a significant case study component). To explore the book context I have surveyed three top publishers: Cambridge, Princeton, and Cornell University Presses. This is particularly important because books give the opportunity to select more than two or three cases, which is critical for chapters 7 and 8.

This volume describes quite well most statistical multimethod research practice. Game theory multimethod practice—chapter 6—follows the logic outlined in this volume. Appendix A shows that very few scholars actually use the estimated statistical model to choose cases; instead they follow the logic of chapter 3. For example, in multimethod statistical work people almost never choose cases where $X = 0$ and $Y = 0$. This is puzzling from a statistical perspective but makes complete sense when the focus is on causal mechanisms via within-case causal inference.

For all my methods books (2005; Goertz and Levy 2007; Goertz and Mazur 2008; Goertz and Mahoney 2012) I have provided exercises for classroom and individual use. This book is no exception. I have gathered the exercises for all my books together in one file and about once a year I email an updated set of exercises (email ggoertz@nd.edu to be put on the list). The exercises are divided by topic, which means that they might cover more than one book, e.g., counterfactuals. The 2015 edition has about 350 exercises.

Some of the exercises have answers (provided for instructors), some are for discussion. Often they include extensions of the books into new but related areas. Typically the exercises refer to existing research that I am reading or teaching. They often contain the seeds of future papers and books.

I have found that they are very useful for students looking for paper topics for methods classes. Since they rely on published research, they have a strong applied flavor.

Because understanding research practice is core to this book, I have created several bibliographies. These will also be updated and available from me on request or via the Princeton University Press web page for the book.

The discussions of research practice are based on the following bibliographies:

1. Case study article bibliography. Established by Steven Samford, this includes all articles in *World Politics, International Organization, Comparative Political Studies,* and *Perspectives on Politics* in the period 2006–2015 that include one or more case studies. This includes game theory or statistical multimethod work with one or more case studies.
2. Game theory multimethod. Based on the larger bibliography by Lorentzen, Fravel, and Paine (2016), these are articles and books that have formal or game-theoretic models and one or more case studies. This bibliography is not complete or systematic but starts from Lorentzen, Fravel, and Paine and adds references as I discover them.
3. Medium-N designs. This includes books or articles with 10 or more case studies. These may or may not include other methodologies such as statistical analyses or game theory.

Statistical multimethod—statistical analyses with case studies—are very common, so there is little need for a bibliography. For example, most books with statistical analyses also include case studies (based on my incomplete survey of publications in international relations and comparative politics by Cambridge, Princeton, and Cornell University Presses, 2006–2015).

Hopscotch

Just as multiple causal paths may lead to an outcome, so too are there multiple paths through this book. Julio Cortazar published a famous novel entitled *Hopscotch*. While a traditional novel has a linear structure of chapters that are read in order, in *Hopscotch* the reader can jump around, reading the chapters as in the game hopscotch. This volume is a hopscotch methods book.

In this section I give an overview of each of the chapters, followed by some hopscotch suggestions.

Chapter 2 explores the concept of a causal mechanism and its connection to multimethod and case study research. It presents the standard motivation for multimethod research where there is significant cross-case evidence for $X \to Y$ and the researcher wants to explore the causal mechanisms by which X produces Y, i.e., $X \to M \to Y$.

The standard $X \to M \to Y$ view of causal mechanism significantly misses the way many researchers think about causal mechanisms. First of all, typically it is not one M that is present but rather multiple M_i (see figure 1.2). Second, these multiple M_i are occurring at the same time. Third, these M_i are substitutable and combinable. Hence, to think of causal mechanisms in terms of simple causal chains in time does not capture many theories and hypotheses.

Another weakness of the $X \to M \to Y$ view is that many mechanisms involve interaction terms, such as INUS causes and constraint causal mechanisms. Minimally, we have $X_1 * X_2 \to Y$. The theory of the interaction term must be at least a sketch of a causal mechanism. Chapter 2, as well as chapters 4 and 5, explores in some detail more complex causal mechanisms involving interaction terms.

So while the standard $X \to M_1 \to M_2 \to \cdots \to M_n \to Y$ captures some theories and causal mechanisms, there are other popular setups. This becomes clearer once one draws figures representing the theories (e.g., Waldner 2015).

I use examples from international relations and comparative politics to illustrate and discuss the connection between what constitutes causal mechanisms and cross-case and within-case analyses. They involve game-theoretic, statistical multimethod, and comparative case studies. They are prominent works that have defined debates in their fields.

Examples of actual research are useful in exploring some basic varieties of causal mechanisms. They help, in particular, to illustrate the constraint causal mechanism, which focuses on explaining why the outcome did not occur. Constraint causal mechanisms almost always imply an interactive causal mechanism between motivations and constraints, i.e., constraints have no causal effect absent motivations to be constrained.

Chapter 3 argues that the central goal of case studies is analyzing causal mechanisms. Does the theorist's causal mechanism work in individual cases? How does the causal mechanism produce the outcome? This chapter explores the basic logic of case selection when one wants to investigate how and if a causal mechanism produces the outcome.

Much work on case selection in qualitative work (e.g., King, Keohane, and Verba 1994) stresses the importance of variation on the independent and dependent variables. In contrast I focus on the various combinations of the two, e.g., $(X = 1, Y = 0)$ or $(1, 0)$. Some combinations are central to the analysis of causal mechanisms, e.g., $(1, 1)$, while others such as $(0, 1)$ are not very relevant. As such it is not a question of variation on X or Y separately as usually argued, but the various roles that the *combinations* of X and Y play in the multimethod enterprise.

The second half of the chapter adds complications in the form of confounding variables (or control variables) and alternative explanations. Analyses of causation have always stressed the importance of confounders; how is one to incorporate these concerns into the choice and analysis of individual cases?

Chapter 4 discusses constraint causal mechanisms. Here causal mechanisms are not about how X *produces* Y, but rather how X prevents Y from occurring or *constrains* Y. In many causal mechanism diagrams the $\rightarrow$ needs interpretation. When the arrow means "produces Y" is different from when the arrow means "prevents Y": they are different causal mechanisms with different methodological properties.

Constraint causal mechanisms are closely associated with necessary conditions. A strong constraint must be satisfied—i.e., is a necessary condition—for the outcome to occur. Necessary conditions are most useful in explaining why the outcome *did not occur*. At the same time, necessary conditions form part of the explanation for why events do occur, i.e., part of sufficient condition causal mechanisms.

Chapter 5 focuses on simple causal complexity in the form of statistical interaction terms or set-theoretic ANDs. It follows naturally from chapter 4 on constraint mechanisms. For constraints to have a causal effect there must be a motivation to break the constraint. Glass ceilings do not have an impact unless women want to move up the professional ladder. This means that constraint causal mechanisms must involve interaction terms. This chapter also contrasts interaction-term analyses with simple additive or contributing factors models. It addresses the relatively common situation where there are two or more causal variables in the cross-case analyses.

Outside of a couple of QCA articles (Rohlfing and Schneider 2013; Schneider and Rohlfing 2013), there is almost nothing on multimethod research for more complex hypotheses. As such, chapter 5 takes a look at these issues in the simplest complex QCA model, X_1 AND $X_2 \rightarrow Y$. In addition, it focuses on various QCA-related issues such as multimethod research in the context of fuzzy logic variables and fuzzy logic falsifying cases.

Chapter 6 applies the methodology developed in chapter 3 to "game theory multimethod" research, defined as a formal model combined with case studies. The game-theoretic model provides a causal mechanism that can be empirically explored via case studies or cross-case analysis. The EITM project has focused on the game theory–statistics connection; chapter 6 looks at the game theory–case study connection. The game theory–statistics multimethod research explores the generalization question, but fails to deal with the extent to which one can find the causal mechanism of the model in individual cases. As such, game theory–statistics focuses on two corners of the research triad but not the empirical analysis of the causal mechanism corner. In terms of practice, the methodology in chapter 3 describes well what game theorists do when they include case studies in their books and articles.

Chapters 7 and 8 flip this way of thinking on its head by supposing one starts with successful causal inference in a case study and then worries about how generalizable the causal mechanism is. These chapters discuss core parts of the *multiple case study* methodology that scholars have already begun to implement. There are some central ideas: (1) Do we find the proposed causal mechanism in individual cases? (2) How often, or within what scope, do we find the proposed causal mechanism? These are questions about generalization. For example, Copeland (2015) explores individually all major power crises and wars 1790–1991 to examine how generalizable his trade expectations theory is.

Chapter 7 explores some influential articles that have used case studies and within-case causal inference to test some prominent theories or to reexamine statistical tests of theories. These have appeared in top journals and have provoked a wide-ranging debate (for example, see the special issue of *Security Studies* (2012) devoted to audience costs theories of international conflict). These critiques have relied fundamentally on a set of within-case causal analyses that often contrast with findings of cross-case statistical analyses or challenge the empirical relevance of game-theoretic models.

Chapter 8 looks at what happens when one begins with intensive causal mechanism analysis and then moves to the selection and analysis of more cases. One might start with a convincing causal mechanism analysis in one or two cases. How should one move to include additional cases in the analysis? One answer—the classic one—is to do a statistical analysis. But what about doing more case studies? How can selecting cases lead to making a strong argument about the generalizability of the causal mechanism?

Regarding hopscotch, since you are reading these lines you have begun on square 1, with chapter 1.

One possibility would be to continue with chapter 3, which outlines core arguments of the book.

The causal mechanism chapter (chapter 2) can be read at any time.

For those particularly interested in causal complexity, the causal mechanism chapter (chapter 2) followed by chapters 4 and 5 is recommended.

For those interested in two cultures arguments, read chapter 3 followed by appendix A.

Chapter 6 on game theory multimethod is available for a hop anytime after chapter 3.

One could hop to chapters 7 and 8, which form a pair, to see the new medium-N paradigm proposed in this volume.

Those interested in QCA should jump at some point to chapters 4 and 5, where I discuss necessary conditions, fuzzy logic, and interaction terms.

As in the hopscotch game and novel, there are multiple paths through this volume. Some chapters can comfortably be skipped if not of interest, and the order can easily vary from person to person. Beyond reading chapter 3 very early on, the sequence can vary. While not a writer of Cortazar's skill, I have tried to make the various hopscotch readings of this volume work.

CHAPTER 2

Causal Mechanisms

Introduction

This volume contends that multimethod research means a commitment to the causal mechanism approach to social and political research, which itself means a commitment to case studies as the methodology for exploring causal mechanisms. If one expresses skepticism about the causal mechanism approach then multimethod research and case studies will hold relatively little value.

King, Keohane, and Verba (1994) famously adopt a statistical perspective for doing qualitative work. It is therefore not surprising that they are skeptical about causal mechanisms. They devote a section (3.2.1) to "causal mechanisms" (scare quotes are theirs). While seeing some utility in the idea, they emphasize how secondary the concept is and how problematic it is in practice:

> To portray an internally consistent causal mechanism requires using our more fundamental definition of causality offered in section 3.1 for each link in the chain of causal events.... Furthermore, there always exists in the social sciences an infinity of causal steps between any two links in the chain of causal mechanisms.... This approach quickly leads to an infinite regress. (King, Keohane, and Verba 1994, 86)

However, many quantitative researchers strongly support causal mechanism analysis:

> Social scientists have recognized for decades that the best explanations for how causes bring about their effects must specify in empirically verifiable ways the causal pathways between causes and their outcomes. This valuation of depth of causal explanation applies to the counterfactual tradition as well. Accordingly, it is widely

recognized that a consistent estimate of a counterfactually defined causal effect of D on Y may not qualify as a sufficiently deep causal account of how D effects Y, based on the standards that prevail in a particular field of study. (Morgan and Winship 2015, 325)

The emphasis on causal mechanism leads naturally to stressing the importance of case studies and within-case causal inference: "any cross-national empirical regularity or causal effect that cannot be meaningfully verified on the basis of country studies should be regarded as suspect" (Rodrik 2003, 10). A strong commitment to multimethod research means that statistical and experimental analyses are incomplete and quite suspect if the regularity cannot be found in case studies.

Causal mechanisms, case studies, and cross-case inference together form the research triad. To adopt the causal mechanism approach to research design and causation means to reject mono-method approaches (e.g., statistical analyses or experiments only). Causal mechanisms are about regularities, and hence about generalization. The investigation of causal mechanisms occurs via process tracing and counterfactual analysis within cases. Hence there is a tight methodological linkage between the corners of the research triad (figure 1.1).

What Is a Causal Mechanism?

There are various literatures regarding the concept and definition of "causal mechanism." The biggest islands are philosophy and sociology. This section does not intend to survey these literatures; already by 2001, Mahoney had found a couple of dozen definitions of the concept. Rather, the purpose is to explore the issues directly connected with multimethod research practice, along with a sense of where the literature on causal mechanisms situates itself in the larger methodological discussion about causation and explanation.

From the beginning, those who stressed causal mechanisms—usually in philosophy or sociology—emphasized the contrast between a mechanism view of causation and science and (1) covering-law approaches, e.g., Hempel, and (2) statistical,

Figure 2.1: Conceptualizing causal mechanisms.

probabilistic, or Humean views of causation. The analysis—utilizing a covering-law or statistical approach—could provide convincing evidence linking X to Y, but *could not explain how X produces or causes Y*. As Demeulenaere states,

> The introduction of the notion of mechanism was initially intended as an alternative to the inductive regularity thesis (Little 1991). It was moreover understood to be an attack on Hume's conception of causality as well as on Hempel's covering-law theory of explanation. Both theories are naturally very different; and the covering-law approach is not properly speaking a theory of causality, since it criticizes this notion. Nevertheless, a theory of mechanisms has been regarded as an alternative to both of these accounts of what causality is and what causality represents in the social sciences. (Demeulenaere 2011, 12–13)

There are many examples of important scientific work that does not provide causal mechanisms. Many laws of physics describe a relationship between X and Y, but do not give the mechanism. For example, Boyle's law of gases—$PV = k$, pressure times volume equals a constant—gives a relationship between volume and pressure. This law does not say why this relationship holds. Classic examples from medicine are the fact that smoking causes lung cancer or penicillin has a significant impact on bacterial infections. These correlations, experiments, or laws of nature do not tell us the mechanisms by which X produces Y.

From the causal mechanism point of view there is little difference between observational studies (e.g., smoking and lung cancer) and experimental ones. In neither case do we have a causal mechanism. The role of these methods is to determine whether there is a causal relationship between X and Y, not how X produces Y.

Figure 2.1 gives the standard diagram used to conceptualize causal mechanisms, with some additional comments.

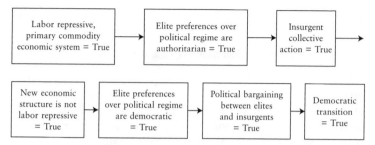

Figure 2.2: Causal mechanisms as causal chains: Wood's analysis of the democratic transition in El Salvador. Source: based on Waldner (2015).

The $X \to M \to Y$ figure is by far the most popular way (e.g., Hedström and Swedberg 1998, 9; Waldner 2015) to conceptualize in an abstract sense a causal mechanism. The explanatory variable X produces the outcome Y through some mechanism M. Given this figure, the metaphor of "causal chains" becomes very natural. However, it is relatively rare that authors give an interpretation of what the arrows mean.

One way to interpret the arrows is as two separate covering laws: "A causal mechanism has a finite number of links. Each link will have to be described by a general law, and in that sense by a 'black box' about whose internal gears and wheels we remain ignorant" (Elster 1989, 6). King, Keohane, and Verba (1994, see above p. 23) express the same idea, by arguing that one applies the basic idea of causation between X and Y to each link in the causal chain. In this approach, there is nothing special about the mechanism analysis: one applies the covering-law model at a finer scale.

Waldner (2015) illustrates the $X \to M \to Y$ idea of a causal mechanism using Wood's explanation of transition to democracy in El Salvador, figure 2.2. Wood (2000) argued that the economic system based on primary commodities with extensive inequality and labor repression generated preferences for an authoritarian regime. Repression generates insurgent action and eventually a civil war. New economic interests arise leading to preferences for democracy and then to bargaining with rebels to produce a democratic transition after decades of civil war.

In the general $X \rightarrow M \rightarrow Y$ causal chain there is an implication of temporal sequencing. However, in many causal mechanisms, factors are occurring at the same time. For example, the economic system—labor repressive, primary commodity—can certainly be a cause of elite preferences, as indicated in figure 2.2, although they are not neatly separated in time. In the middle of the causal mechanism, the economic system changes to not labor repressive, implying it was labor repressive until that change. So while the arrows may signal causal relationships, they often do not represent well the temporal relationships of the various factors.

Core to the causal mechanism analysis is drawing figures illustrating causal—and noncausal—relationships. The causal mechanism figure rarely can be drawn easily from theory discussions. Figures 2.3 and 2.4 show causal mechanism diagrams from Grzymała-Busse (2007). We had several caffeine-infused discussions regarding the drawing of the figures, with significant back and forth as I proposed a figure and she made recommendations for changes. For example, when I proposed a causal chain like figure 2.2, she objected because it implied a temporal sequence that was not correct. Similarly, I had an extended email discussion with Dan Slater regarding figure 2.8. In short, the drawing of causal mechanism figures is a nontrivial exercise (one I strongly recommend).

Another way to interpret figure 2.1 is with definitions of causal mechanisms:

> Mechanisms are entities and activities organized such that they are *productive* of regular changes from start or set-up to finish or termination conditions. (Machamer et al. 2000, 3; emphasis is mine)

> Mechanisms are generally understood as consisting of interacting components that *generate* a causal regularity between some specified beginning and end points. (Steel 2008, 40; emphasis is mine)

> The pathway or process by which an effect is *produced* or a purpose is accomplished.[1] (Gerring 2008, 178; emphasis is mine)

---

[1] This is why Gerring, in his typology of case studies, uses the term "pathway" analysis for causal mechanism case studies.

[A causal mechanism is] a complex system, which *produces* an outcome by the interaction of a number of parts. (Glennan 1996, 52, see also Glennan 2002; emphasis is mine)

The quotes above stress the core notion that causal mechanisms *produce* or *generate* outcomes.[2] This translates into the idea that causal mechanisms are sufficient for outcomes, or in a statistical interpretation that βs are positive and significant (see figure 2.1).

Sometimes causal mechanisms work to *prevent* outcomes from occurring. In terms of figure 2.1, we introduce negative coefficients into the figure. This presents a different class of causal mechanisms, discussed below as constraint causal mechanisms. In a set-theoretic context, these are often necessary conditions and they almost always involve interactive causal mechanisms. The default causal mechanism—often implicit only—is the generative mechanism illustrated in most of the figures of this chapter. The sufficient condition interpretation of figure 2.1 will play a key role in the next chapter.

An author's fundamental position on methodology often determines the interpretation of the $X \to M \to Y$ figure. An easy interpretation of M is as an "intervening variable." One way to interpret "$\to$" is as a significant parameter estimate or significant average treatment effect, as indicated by $\beta_X \gg 0$ and $\beta_M \gg 0$. Causal mechanisms interpreted in this statistical manner can be seen as invoking nothing new beyond the concatenation of two statistical analyses. Gerring nicely illustrates this position, as do Weller and Barnes:

This means that tools of empirical analysis usually associated with covariation (does one variable co-vary in a predictable pattern with another variable?) are, in principle, equally amenable to the investigation of intervening variables. (Gerring 2008, 172)

[Causal] Mechanism. Unobserved factors that lie between an explanatory variable and outcome in a causal chain. They are analogous to mediating or intervening variables that can, at least in theory, be manipulated. (Weller and Barnes 2014, 150 in Glossary)

---

[2] Another discussion would be the differences between these conceptualizations.

To *simultaneously* estimate β_X and β_M is quite a nontrivial matter. As Imai et al. (2011) show, it requires some strong assumptions and confident estimations of large-N counterfactuals to do the analysis. "Unpacking the black box of causality," their article's title, illustrates the statistical view of causal mechanisms as an intervening variable M. The causal mechanism is treated completely at the statistical, cross-case level. This implies that no multimethod research is necessary.

Experimental scholars typically use figure 2.1 if they use the causal mechanism idea. A survey of methodological works on experiments, such as Druckman et al. (2011), reveals very little explicit use of the causal mechanism term (an exception is Dunning 2012). However, there are discussions of mediating or intervening variables. This fits naturally with M in figure 2.1. The typical response of an experimenter is likely to be like Gerring or Imai et al.: one reapplies the statistical or covering law to each link in the causal chain. In the case of experiments, one ideally does experiments with M as the treatment.

> Analytically, a single random assignment ... makes it difficult, if not impossible, to isolate the mediating pathways of numerous intervening variables. To clarify such effects, a researcher needs to design several experiments, all with different kinds of treatments.... Indeed, an extensive series of experiments might be required before a researcher can make convincing causal claims about causal pathways. (Druckman et al. 2011, 20)

In the introduction I used Pevehouse's work on the impact of democratic IGOs on democracy within states, i.e., figure 1.2, to introduce causal mechanisms within multimethod research. This causal mechanism model with additive M_i is quite common, particularly in statistical multimethod research. Often there are multiple mechanisms by which X influences Y. Often they can be applied at the same time and have a cumulative (e.g., additive) effect. In short, the intervening M is often a set of M_i. The research triad means exploring the M_i in the case studies. For example, some M_i might be more influential or more common than others.

In the Pevehouse example, figure 1.2, I linked the M_i via addition. In my experience this is by far the most common way to think about the interaction of multiple mechanisms. There is no reason why this need be the case. For example, Weller and Barnes (2014) give an example where it is the exclusive OR. In figure 2.6, the M_i are linked by AND.

The Pevehouse figure also illustrates that causal mechanism figures generally need more than just $\rightarrow$ to connect parts. That figure uses "+" to connect two different mechanisms that work together to produce Y. The variety of causal, ontological (concepts), noncausal temporal relationships in causal mechanisms requires a much richer vocabulary of symbols. This is another reason why $X \rightarrow M \rightarrow Y$ proves inadequate for real-life causal mechanisms.

This section has focused on single causal mechanisms, but often some of the best research involves multiple causal mechanisms. For example, in chapter 3 I discuss Weinstein (2006) and Lange (2009), which have multiple causal mechanisms. Slater (2010) (see figure 2.8) also argues for multiple paths to the same outcome.

The $X \rightarrow M \rightarrow Y$ model, so popular in the methodological literature, does not fit well with multimethod research practice. Rarely is there only one M in the causal chain. As illustrated above, typically there are two or more links. The simultaneous M_i as in the Pevehouse example is a very common model. If it is hard to statistically estimate the simple $X \rightarrow M \rightarrow Y$ model, then anything more complex is, in practical terms, virtually impossible (the same applies to experiments). Case studies then become the only practical solution.

In short, causal mechanisms in multimethod research practice are almost always significantly more complex than the simple $X \rightarrow M \rightarrow Y$. The point of view that causal mechanisms are just intervening or mediating variables does not do justice to most of the causal mechanisms and theories that have proved influential.[3] The research triad comes into play because case

---

[3] See Goertz and Mahoney's (2005) causal mechanism diagram of Skocpol's *States and social revolutions*, which is far more complex than a simple intervening variable or interaction term. See also many of the causal mechanism diagrams in Waldner (2015).

studies are the only means for exploring these complex causal mechanisms.

. . .

An example serves to ground the preceding discussion and to connect methodological issues to concrete research. It also permits an ongoing analysis of the concept of a causal mechanism.

Chapter 1 used an international relations example: Pevehouse's analysis of the impact of democratic IGOs on democratization and democratic transitions. It is thus nice to use a comparative politics example here. Grzymała-Busse (2007) provides a good example because it is both high-quality research and it has features useful in this and future chapters.

Scholars often conceptualize causal mechanisms via causal chains. Figure 2.3 presents part of Grzymała-Busse's causal mechanism. She starts with the initial conditions where the crisis in Communist countries in 1989 led in some cases to the Communist Party leaving power and countries transitioning to democracy. The Communist Party in some of these democratic countries "reinvents itself" as a party and becomes a credible and "robust opposition" party. When this happens, it leads to "nonexploitation" of the state by political parties.

Grzymała-Busse's causal chain raises a core methodological–theoretical question about when the causal mechanism should start. The initial conditions for her study lie in the collapse of Communism and the democratization of some Communist countries. This forms the background and scope of her causal mechanism analysis. The top part of figure 2.3 plays the role of scope and initial conditions. One can see this already in the subtitle of the book, "Party competition and state exploitation *in post-Communist democracies.*"

The causal mechanism starts when the Communist Party reinvents itself and becomes a significant competitor in elections; this is the "robust competition" link. When this happens it leads to a situation where there is nonexploitation of the state by political parties. That these are the core links can be seen by the first two tables of the introduction to her book: table 1.1 is the dependent variable of state exploitation and table 1.2 gives

Initial conditions

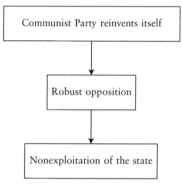

Figure 2.3: The causal mechanism leading to nonexploitation of the state. Source: based on Grzymała-Busse (2007, figure 1.1) and discussion with the author.

the degree to which Communist parties were robust competitors in post-Communist democracies.

A key issue in the conceptualization of causal mechanisms is the nature of X, which is often called the "initial conditions" or "trigger." There is a sense in which X occurs at a given time, setting the causal mechanism in motion. This is clearest in experimenters' view of causal mechanisms. The treatment, X, in an experiment sets the causal mechanism in motion. For Grzymała-Busse, the initial conditions are given in the top half of figure 2.3.

In much applied research, X is not a trigger or an event but rather a relatively unchanging *state*. As such, the implied temporal element of the causal chain can be misleading. In the

Pevehouse example, democratic IGO is not a trigger or an event, but rather a characteristic of IGOs that is typically constant or slow changing. It is not the democratization of the IGO that matters but its current democratic state. Similarly, Grzymała-Busse treats robust competition as pretty constant across time in her set of countries. Acemoglu and Robinson take a similar approach in their theory of democratization (see chapter 7); their causal mechanism starts with economic inequality, which is at best a very slow-moving variable.

In short, many of the X variables in multimethod research involve constant or slow-moving factors (e.g., mountainous terrain or ethnic fractionalization in the civil war literature). When choosing cases and doing process tracing, there are other factors that may be seen as triggering the causal mechanism, and that provide guidance for case selection and delimitation in multimethod research.

The M box of the causal mechanism figure is often called the "black box." This is because the causal mechanism is not known. There might be convincing evidence of the causal relationship between X and Y, but little might be known about how this works. Hence it is not uncommon for researchers individually or as a community to postulate multiple causal mechanisms to explain the relationship.

In Gerring's (2010) discussion of causal mechanisms, all the examples have this character: (1) economic development and democracy, (2) democracy and war, (3) resource curse and civil war, (4) geography and economic growth. In each case there is a long list of statistical studies that find a significant correlation between the two variables, but scholars have provided a variety of causal mechanisms to explain these statistical connections.

In most natural science and medicine examples, the laws of physics or causal effect of a drug does not end the discussion. Scholars always want to know the mechanism. What is the mechanism behind Boyle's law of gases? How does gravity described in Newton's law actually work? What is the mechanism by which penicillin reduces infection? There are usually competing mechanisms proposed, just as the political science examples.

The $X \to M \to Y$ view of causal mechanisms is often mis-leading or problematic when one gets to actual research: (1) it is often not clear where the causal chain should or does begin, (2) some early links in the causal chain function as scope conditions, (3) M is often a set of M_i and then there is the question of the relationship between these M_i (e.g., additive, logical AND), and (4) the temporal sequencing implied in the causal chain is often violated in various ways: some factors might be occurring at the same time, some might be state variables that change little or not at all over time. All of this means that the interpretation of M as an intervening variable is problematic. In most substantive research, one cannot decompose the causal mechanism into simple ones, i.e., $X \to M$ and $M \to Y$, and then apply standard statistical or experimental methods to each causal link separately. As a result, case studies are the only real research option, and one is thus in the research triad.

How Regular Are Causal Mechanisms?

Causal mechanisms are often described as being and containing "regularities":

> Mechanisms are *regular* in that they work always or for the most part in the same way under the same conditions. The *regularity* is exhibited in the typical way that the mechanism runs from beginning to end; what makes it *regular* is the productive continuity between stages. (Machamer et al. 2000, 3; emphasis is mine)

> Mechanisms behave in *regular* but not exceptionless ways. The washer could break; the eye could go blind; geologic changes could make Old Faithful less faithful. The behavior of mechanisms can be described by what Craver (2007) calls "mechanistically fragile *generalizations*." These are *generalizations* that are robust and non-accidental, but hold in virtue of the fact that they describe the behavior of the mechanism. (Glennan 2010, 257; emphasis is mine)

> To explain a social event therefore means to describe the various causal chains linking all the elements involved ... in constituting a social fact. This also means identifying the relevant elements between

which causal relationships exist, and determining their nature. From this perspective, a mechanism is the set of elements and their causal links that *regularly* lead from an initial social state to a subsequent one. (Demeulenaere 2011, 12; emphasis is mine)

Waldner (2012) describes causal mechanisms as "invariant," suggesting that when the initial conditions are present they lead almost without exception to the outcome. As the quotes above illustrate, causal mechanisms are typically thought to involve relatively high degrees of regularity. The Grzymała-Busse example illustrates a causal mechanism with a high degree of regularity. In all her cases, where there is robust competition there is no state exploitation.

Figure 2.1 gave one possible interpretation of the causal mechanism chain as involving statistically significant effects. The emphasis on high levels of regularity often does not fit well with the statistical interpretation of causal mechanisms. For example, in an experimental setting, a treatment might have large effects for a small number, e.g., 20 percent, of the subjects, and zero effect for the other 80 percent, resulting in a significant average treatment effect. However, few would say that the treatment regularly produces an effect.

In many cases of statistical multimethod research, the strong sense of regularity is unlikely to be present. The Pevehouse example illustrates this common situation. Sometimes democratic IGOs act to maintain democracies, but how regularly they do so is an open question. Statistical parameter estimates often do not directly address the regularity question. Average treatment effects, or estimated βs in statistical models, are not directly about regularity, they are about average causal effects. Large and statistically significant effects suggest regularity but are not direct evaluations.

Figure 2.1 gives a set-theoretic interpretation of a causal mechanism in terms of sufficient conditions (see Mahoney, Kimball, and Koivu 2009 for an analysis of sufficient condition causal chains). This is more in line with the regularity requirement. More or less explicit in the quotes above is that regularity means looking at when the causal mechanism is triggered and how often the outcome occurs. Triggering the causal mechanism means looking at $X = 1$ cases. So one is asking, "if $X = 1$ how often is $Y = 1$?" This is easily interpreted as a question about sufficient conditions. Typical standards in QCA practice require that a regularity must be found at least 70–80 percent of the time to be considered significant. QCA has established conventions about what constitutes an acceptable level of regularity. This is not Waldner's "invariant," but is usually higher than "statistically significant."

In the process tracing literature, scholars often think about causal mechanisms in sufficient condition terms. For example, Waldner (2015, 128) claims that "process tracing yields causal and explanatory adequacy insofar as: (1) it is based on a causal graph whose individual nodes are connected in such a way that they are jointly sufficient for the outcome." Beach and Pedersen state that "process-tracing case studies in their case-centric variant enable us to craft sufficient explanations of particular historical cases" (2016, 400).

In research practice, what counts as a regularity will be determined by the general standards for "significant relationships." Many cases of statistical significance will not satisfy the strong regularity requirements in the philosophical or methodological literatures. Set-theoretic and QCA standards come much closer by being statements of strong regularities.

This has important implications for case selection. If one chooses cases of $X = 1$ at random from a statistical analysis, it might be that the odds of seeing the causal mechanism in action are relatively low. In the experiment example above, it would be only 1 in 5. In multiple case study designs, e.g., comparative historical research, probably because the Ns are small, regularity requirements are much higher. In these settings, scholars work hard to produce almost exceptionless generalizations (see Goertz and Mahoney 2012 for a discussion).

The research triad, figure 1.1, includes generalization at one corner (along with cross-case analyses). Multimethod research means looking in detail at individual cases to explore causal mechanisms. At the same time, most social scientists want theories that travel; they want causal mechanisms that explain many cases. The methodological and philosophical literatures on causal mechanisms almost always include some requirement that the mechanism be a general one. To be a regularity means implicitly that the mechanism works within some, often unspecified, scope. Causal mechanisms are not different in this regard from experiments, which hopefully discover causal effects that are general.

Constraint Causal Mechanisms

Some readers may have already objected to figure 2.1 because the linkages were described as $\beta_X \gg 0$: Why not include negative causal effects? Discussions of causal mechanisms are full of language implying that the causal mechanism produces the outcome, which implies a positive relationship. Other common terms include that the mechanism "triggers" or "brings about" social outcomes. The definitions above by Machamer et al., Steel, and Gerring all include terms like *produce* or *generate*.

However, many mechanisms in the social sciences do not involve generating or producing an outcome, but in fact are about preventing something from occurring. I call these constraint causal mechanisms. Chapter 4 is devoted to constraint mechanisms, which are closely connected to necessary conditions. A strong constraint is a necessary condition, e.g., veto player models. I first became interested in necessary conditions because of their utility in explaining why something does not happen (Goertz 1994; see the "barrier models" section). For example, metaphors like ceilings or barriers—e.g., glass ceilings for women in labor markets—are often used for constraint factors.

Explaining nonevents poses some interesting and tricky theoretical, methodological, and philosophical issues. A common scenario is that there is motivation for change (X) but that produces no change because of the presence of constraint C. This means that there is no change in the value of Y from its initial condition. In statistical terms no change means no variation in Y, which obviously can pose problems (e.g., in differences-in-differences designs).

It is often the case that the $Y = 1$ event is well defined conceptually and is a relatively coherent state or event, but $Y = 0$

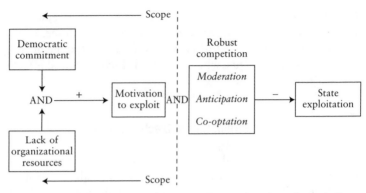

Figure 2.4: Constraint causal mechanisms. Source: based on Grzymała-Busse (2007) and discussions with the author.

can be quite a heterogeneous set. In the conflict literature, $Y = 1$ is often militarized disputes. So if one wants to explain the absence of militarized disputes, for example within the context of explaining "peace," one is confronted with the fact that "no militarized dispute" includes a variety of cases that are likely to have different explanations: (1) no dispute years between serious rivals, such as USA–USSR, (2) no dispute years between countries with very peaceful relationships, e.g., USA–Canada, (3) pairs with no relationship at all, e.g., Cameroon–Chile.

Figure 2.4 illustrates one general way to think about this. Again, Grzymała-Busse provides a nice example and substantive content. She argues that high democratic commitments AND scarce organizational resources generate motivations for political parties to exploit the state. In figure 2.4, these two factors together generate, produce, and are sufficient for state exploitation in the absence of any constraints. Hence the "+" above the causal arrow.

However, the presence of robust competition in the form of a reinvented Communist Party acts as a constraint or barrier to implementing state exploitation. Hence in figure 2.4 there is a "−" above the causal arrow from robust competition to exploitation of the state.

The core mechanism for Grzymała-Busse is robust competition. There are three mechanisms whereby robust competition leads to nonexploitation of the state:

> Robust competition operates through three mechanisms of constraint on state exploitation, which can be summarized as moderation, anticipation, and cooptation, ... First, criticism leads to a moderation of governing party behavior—or, at the very least, greater subterfuge. As we will see, this informal mechanism was especially influential in curbing the expansion of state agencies and administration. Fearing exposure and subsequent punishment in both parliament and in elections, government parties curb their opportunistic extraction of state resources.
>
> Second, the incentives for formal constraints grow all the more compelling when governing parties fear that their successors will use existing discretion against them. As a result, robust competition both limits the capacity of governing parties to exploit the state and generates the incentives to create formal state institutions that limit discretion even before exploitation takes place.
>
> Third, robust competition induces governing parties to share power, and to coopt their critics as much as possible. As informal rules evolved in parliaments, the opposition gained further power, including representation on and leadership of important legislative committees and party financing laws that benefited all parties, rather than just the incumbents. Robust competition also prevented a government monopoly on resources by leading potential donors to "insure" themselves by donating to multiple parties. (Grzymała-Busse 2007, 16–17)

These mechanisms *constitute* robust competition. They are not *causes*, but rather what robust competition is. To unpack the robust competition mechanism means looking in detail at moderation, co-optation, and anticipation.

Grzymała-Busse interprets the three factors on the left of figure 2.4 as a scope condition (personal communication). She stresses that all three variables on the left-hand side of the figure are present (have a value of 1) for all cases in her analysis. This is exactly what happens with scope variables. What is varying in her analysis is the degree of robust competition.

It is worth stressing the role of motivation when proposing constraint causal mechanisms; without motivation, the constraint causal mechanism makes no sense. If women had no desire to obtain high-level positions in institutions, firms, and government, then glass ceilings would have no causal effect. In the conflict literature, deterrence theories have exactly this feature. The deterrence mechanism assumes that there is some motivation to attack or to use military force; it is not useful for explaining lack of conflict in cases like USA–Canada.

Necessary conditions and scope conditions blur in many instances (see Mahoney and Goertz 2004). However one woman's scope condition is another man's causal variable. Critical in the constraint causal mechanism is that all the factors on the left are present. For example, in figure 2.4, if there is no motivation to exploit then robust competition has no causal effect. Many set-theoretic, QCA models can be interpreted in this way because causal configurations include the presence of motivation variables and the absence of constraint ones. The influential opportunity and willingness framework (see Cioffi-Revilla and Starr 2003 for a discussion and formal model) in international relations has exactly this structure. Opportunity is the constraint factor, while willingness is the motivation. Bara's (2014) QCA application of the opportunity and willingness framework to civil war illustrates the linkage of motivation and constraint.

In figure 2.4, the constraint causal mechanism involves an interaction between the motivation to exploitation and the constraint posed by robust competition. Chapter 5 addresses exactly this scenario where the core causal mechanism involves interaction terms. As such, the constraint causal mechanism will appear as a topic in both chapters 4 and 5.

Integrating Motivation and Institutional Constraints

Constraint causal mechanisms can either assume motivation—as seen above with Grzymała-Busse—or interests, preferences, and motivations can be incorporated into the model. This will be a central concern of chapters 4 and 5; the discussion in this section thus is an introduction to what follows in more detail below.

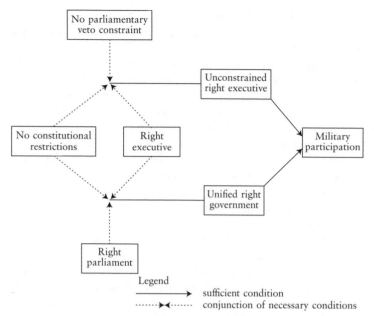

Legend

——————→ sufficient condition

·······►◄······· conjunction of necessary conditions

Figure 2.5: Institutional constraints AND ideology: decisions to participate in the 2003 Iraq War. Source: based on Mello (2012). With permission of Springer.

Perhaps the most empirically and theoretically important motivation consists of ideology. Ideological diversity is central to veto player models (Tsebelis 2002; see the discussion in chapter 4). A natural interaction term is thus ideology AND institutional constraints. For constraints to matter, there must be a drive to violate them; ideology provides just such a reason.

To give substance to the discussion, I use the excellent study by Mello (2012; 2014) about decisions by western democracies on whether or not to participate in the 2003 Iraq War. Mello used QCA as the methodology to explore the interactions between institutional constraints and ideology. QCA is a natural methodology to use in these settings because it focuses on inter-action terms and avoids many of the nontrivial methodological problems posed by multiplicative interaction terms in statistics.

Figure 2.5 reproduces Mello's basic causal mechanism for participation in the Iraq War. It is quite complex. It would be virtually impossible to estimate this model with statistics. QCA is really the only plausible cross-case methodological option.[4]

The causal mechanism is relatively complex for a couple of reasons. First, there are multiple institutional constraints on leaders. These include constitutional constraints on war participation. The most well known is perhaps the German constitution. Article 24(2) of the German Grundgesetz prohibits military operations outside "the sufficiently dense political and organisational framework of an international treaty-regime." A second constraint is the degree to which parliament has significant powers, e.g., veto, over war participation.

Ideology comes into play in terms of the executive as well as the parliament. Right-wing executives were in favor of participation in the Iraq War while the left was opposed. So there are four ideological combinations of left–right and executive–parliament.

Putting the institutional constraints together with executive and parliament ideology means the theoretical mechanism is quite complicated. Nevertheless, the basic logic is quite straightforward. It involves taking various combinations of constraint and motivation: (1) Unconstrained right executives lead their countries to war. (2) If the executive is left then institutional constraints do not matter because it does not want war participation to begin with. (3) Constitutional constraints are strong enough to prevent participation. (4) Right executives in parliament veto systems also need a right parliament.

This example illustrates that in some contexts one must include both motivation and constraint factors. To focus on only parliamentary and institutional vetoes—i.e., constraints only— is fundamentally an incomplete analysis. Unlike the Grzymała-Busse example where it is reasonable to assume high levels of motivation, in the Iraq War variation on motivation is critical.

To explore the causal mechanism of figure 2.5 requires a number of case studies. To explore constraints one needs, for example, a constitutional constraint with a right-wing executive. Japan would be a possible case study for this part of the

---

[4] Agent-based models can explore the theoretical logic of the model, but are not an option for empirical data analysis.

mechanism. To explore a parliament constraint we need a case where the parliament is left while the executive is right. Ideally, it would be good to have case studies for all the causal combinations of motivation–institutional constraint in figure 2.5.

Case studies and within-case causal inference come into play in these motivation–constraint analyses. Mello does a cross-case analysis of his causal mechanism using QCA. The research triad becomes involved because the two together make within-case causal claims. Mello implies that his theory explains each of the individual cases that are consistent with the QCA results. He does not do case studies, but to complete the research triad he would need to explore the cases in detail. Looking at the case-specific literature, does his model explain why Germany did not participate, why Australia did?

Even if the researcher is really interested only in the constraints, motivation must be included in the case selection. While not a principle articulated in methods books, it is something that case study scholars have known and practiced for decades.

Chapter 5 discusses how complex, interactive causal mechanisms typically require multiple case studies. Multimethod metaphors such as "on-line" or "off-line" are woefully inadequate, because there is much more going on in the theory and causal mechanism than an estimated statistical line.

Causal Mechanisms and Within-Case Causal Inference

The role of case studies in multimethod research is to make within-case causal inference via process tracing, counterfactuals, etc. The central purpose of process tracing is to find, verify, or disconfirm hypotheses about causal mechanisms.

Figure 2.6 takes a prominent example that will reappear at various points in this volume, notably in chapter 7. Haggard and Kaufman (2016) use multimethod research to explore a prominent set of theories—notably Acemoglu and Robinson, and Boix—that see economic inequality as driving a causal mechanism resulting in democratic transitions. The top of figure 2.6 gives the standard statistical analysis linking inequality

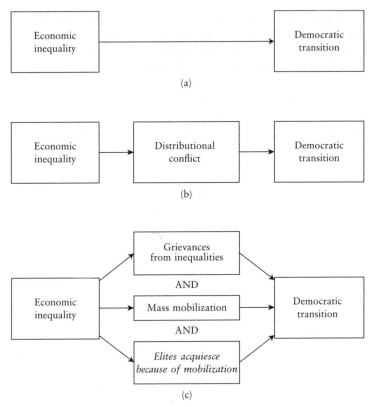

Figure 2.6: Inequality and democratic transition: the distributional conflict causal mechanism. Source: based on Haggard and Kaufman (2016).

to democracy; figure 2.6b gives the standard $X \rightarrow M \rightarrow Y$ view of the causal mechanism; figure 2.6c gives a more elaborate version, the Haggard and Kaufman analysis of the "distributional conflict" path to democracy, i.e., their interpretation of Acemoglu and Robinson (2006).

A couple of features make this causal mechanism significantly different from the Pevehouse example. Notably, the M_i are linked with an AND. So they are not substitutable as in the case where there is an OR between the M_i.

The cross-case statistical analysis in figure 2.6a could confirm the linkage between inequality and democracy. However, there is no guarantee that when one does the within-case causal analysis of figure 2.6c that the causal mechanism will be found in the cases. Conversely, it might be the case that there is no statistical relationship in the figure 2.6a analysis, but within-case analysis does reveal some cases of distributional conflict leading to democracy.

One could interpret this figure from a statistical point of view with distributional conflict as the mechanism or intervening variable. Figure 2.6c could be how distributional conflict variables are coded. In terms of case selection, we could select then on M_i, since in this case there are systematic data on them. The M_i become independent variables and democracy the dependent variable. Particularly the use of terms like "independent variable" and "coding" make this seem like a reasonable interpretation, but in fact it is not. Causal mechanism analysis is about within-case causal inference: *the causal inference in this case is already present in the causal mechanism M_i*, i.e., hardwired into M. To emphasize this point I have put a key causal inference in italics in figure 2.6c. The key causal inference signal here is "because of." So the interpretation of M_i as "independent variables" is incorrect because the "coding" involves a causal inference about Y.

This causal chain differs significantly from the Pevehouse example where arguably the links between X and M_i are not causal. These mechanisms are means that democratic IGOs use to increase the likelihood of democratic transitions. They are part of the causal mechanism, but there is no causal relationship between X and M_i. While the "$\rightarrow$" is usually interpreted in a causal sense, there are theories and causal mechanisms where the some of the linkages are not causal.

There is no guarantee that there will be consistent causal inference evidence for all the arrows in figures 2.6a–2.6c. For example, there might be cases where distributional conflict leads to democracy, but little evidence that inequality is driving the distributional conflict. In addition, there are alternative paths to democracy beyond the distributional one. Haggard and Kaufman also explore a causal mechanism where international actors play a central role, and another mechanism where transitions to democracy are driven by elite bargaining.

So the statistical analysis of figure 2.6a might link inequality to democratization, but the within-case analysis might find that the case is one driven by elite bargaining (i.e., correlation without causation).

This example illustrates that all the causal inferences in figures are up for grabs. First one needs to verify that $\rightarrow$ is causal within the proposed mechanism. Within the same figure there might be evidence for one causal arrow but not another. There might be cross-case evidence for $X \rightarrow Y$ but not for the causal mechanism proposed in the theory. Chapter 7 discusses the debate about audience costs where the causal mechanism is democracy $\rightarrow$ audience costs $\rightarrow$ crisis behavior. There is cross-case evidence for democracy $\rightarrow$ crisis behavior, but some deny that the audience costs causal mechanism is doing the causal work.

Equifinality and Causal Mechanisms

Equifinality is a critical feature of any methodology, including multiple case study and multimethod research. In the statistical culture, one does not talk about equifinality, but rather about confounders. In the context of causal mechanisms, this means that there are potentially multiple causal mechanisms that produce the same outcome. In addition, equifinality also appears in the causal mechanism itself. As illustrated by the Pevehouse example, within the causal mechanism M there are multiple paths to the outcome Y. As a general principle, both statistical and qualitative scholars view equifinality as omnipresent. Not only are there multiple Xs that lead to Y, but there are multiple Ms within each mechanism.

Figure 2.7 illustrates that equifinality can be present in multiple forms. Here there are two causal mechanisms and multiple paths within each mechanism, i.e., M_i. In addition, M_3 is in each causal mechanism. For reasons that will become clear, it is important to allow for the possibility of overlap between causal mechanisms.

Sometimes it is not clear whether something is a separate causal mechanism (i.e., a different X_i) or whether it is part of some larger causal mechanism, i.e., an M_i factor. For example,

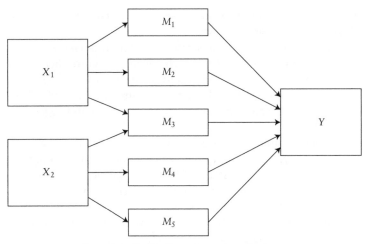

Figure 2.7: Equifinality and causal mechanisms.

Simmons and Elkins (2004), in a widely cited article, discuss various mechanisms of policy "diffusion."[5] They contrast three theories about why states adopt liberal economic policies. The first is via market competition, if competitor nations are adopting liberal policies and states adopt new policies to compete in markets. A second mechanism is global norms about economic policies. A third is learning from networks, successful states, or culturally similar states. There are independent variables in their statistical model representing each of these mechanisms. So should these independent variables be considered separate mechanisms, e.g., separate X_i, or M_i, within a larger theory of diffusion?

In this particular case they have separate mechanisms. One way to determine this is to look at the mechanisms for each of the variables. When they belong to different theoretical traditions then it is almost certain they are separate mechanisms. If one mechanism is basically market competition and the other is conforming to global norms then we are talking about different

---

[5] I use scare quotes because it is not clear that they are all diffusion mechanisms rather than other kinds of mechanisms, e.g., market competition.

mechanisms. In the abstract of the article itself they refer to "broad classes of mechanisms."

Simmons and Elkins illustrate a common scenario where there are multiple *competing* mechanisms. They are theoretical competitors. The social constructivist mechanism of diffusion via norms competes with the market competition model. These mechanisms also compete with the power politics and hegemony mechanism of realists.

Of course, multiple mechanisms can be at work in any given country. Economic policy can be the result of multiple mechanisms operating at the same time (i.e., collinearity). So while the mechanisms compete at the theoretical level, in practice they might complement each other.

In short, one must determine in many instances whether the scholar is exploring alternative mechanisms X_i, or whether they are factors M_i, within a single mechanism.

Since M is often a black box, the extent to which a confounder or alternative causal mechanism overlaps or not is not clear. Overlap is often explicit in set-theoretic models, where different paths may contain the same variables; for example, the paths ABc (where factors A and B are present and C is not present) and BDC (where factors B, D, and C are all present) may both be sufficient conditions for Y; B overlaps between the two causal mechanisms. As such the equifinality in figure 2.7 is quite common in QCA analyses because of overlapping variables in causal paths.

If overlap gets great enough then M_i becomes a necessary condition. By definition a necessary condition must be in all causal mechanisms leading to Y. Necessary conditions overlap in all causal mechanisms.

Slater (2010) is a nice example where there are four paths to "fragmentation," a type of counterrevolutionary state. Each path is unique in that it contains factors that are not on the other paths, as illustrated in figure 2.8. Unlike the Elkins and Simmon situation, these paths are not really theoretical competitors.

QCA as a matter of course generates overlap between causal mechanisms. In other settings, such as comparative historical research, I suspect that most of the time scholars work hard to avoid overlap between causal paths, as illustrated by Slater.

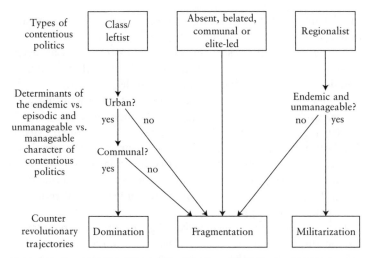

Figure 2.8: Causal mechanisms and equifinality: paths to fragmented counterrevolutionary states. Source: based on Slater (2010).

This is obviously a question about theory, but it is not obvious that mutually exclusive mechanisms are a good idea or a good reflection of how the world works.[6]

In the next chapter, alternative causal mechanisms and equifinality are key aspects of the methodology of multimethod research. Case selection depends on knowledge of alternative causal mechanisms. It means that the absence of one causal mechanism does not necessarily mean that Y will not occur, because other causal mechanisms might also be present.

Conclusion

For the purposes of this book, I take a generous view of causal mechanisms. These can be the mechanisms given for hypotheses in statistical analyses, they can be game-theoretic models, they

---

[6] This is related to the idea that typologies should have mutually exclusive categories. See Mahoney and Goertz (2012) for an argument for overlapping conceptual categories.

can be interpretations of causal effects found in experiments, they can be configurational paths in QCA.

As the various figures in this chapter illustrate, causal mechanisms take a variety of forms. The one form that is rare in practice is the one mediating variable model: $X \to M_1 \to Y$. As such, one of the first and most important steps in working with the research triad is to draw causal mechanism figures.

By using the Grzymała-Busse, Haggard and Kaufman, Mello, Pevehouse, Slater, and Wood examples, I presented the methodological issues closely tied to practice in actual research. These examples illustrate nicely the connection between multimethod research, causal mechanisms, and case studies. I shall return to these examples as appropriate.

The various causal mechanism figures in this chapter resemble directed acyclic graphs (DAGs) in some respects. The DAG approach has been extremely influential in the literature on causation (Pearl 2009; Pearl et al. 2016; Morgan and Winship 2015). Waldner's interpretation of Wood's causal mechanism (figure 2.2) is intended as a DAG. DAG figures are probabilistic models of conditional dependence that are given a causal interpretation. When scholars provide figures to describe their theories, they are probably not thinking in terms of DAGs (applied work using DAGs is quite rare). Nevertheless, it is always a good exercise to see whether a given figure does work as a DAG, or what needs to be done to make it a DAG. The relationship between DAGs and causal mechanism figures far exceeds the scope of this chapter, and remains an important topic of research regarding causal mechanisms.

This chapter does not pretend to cover all the issues in the philosophical and methodological literatures on causal mechanisms. For example, in the sociological literature a very large part of the discussion involves whether a commitment to causal mechanisms implies some kind of methodological individualism. Often the debate is framed in macro–micro terms, where X and Y are macro factors and M is the micro mechanism. Similarly, for some authors, whether the mechanism is observable is an issue. I think some mechanisms are observable while others are not.

At the same time, this chapter does serve to survey the core issues surrounding the philosophy and methodology of causal mechanisms that are relevant to empirical multimethod work. A commitment to multimethod research is a commitment—often implicit—to a causal mechanism view of explanation, since the role of the case studies is exactly to explore causal mechanisms. The link between causal mechanisms and within-case causal inference is very tight.

CHAPTER 3

The Basic Logic

Introduction

The goal of this chapter is to provide the logic of case studies in multimethod research, including statistical, game-theoretic, and qualitative comparative analysis (QCA) multimethod. If one is thinking about doing case studies in a multimethod context—say one to ten cases—the problem arises of which cases to choose. There must be a logic or rationale for the cases chosen and this rationale must be linked to the goal of exploring causal mechanisms. This chapter provides that logic.

Statistical researchers typically have well-developed procedures for case selection; they randomly sample for surveys; they use conventional populations—e.g., all advanced industrial societies; they analyze data sets collected by others—e.g., Correlates of War (COW) data sets. In contrast, the multimethod researcher faces the issue that since significant resources are going to be committed to a case, it is important to choose the right cases. The problem lies in that there may be dozens, if not thousands, of cases to choose from. For example, in the statistical multimethod context, McGuire (2010) has a large-N cross-national chapter looking at various health outcomes such as infant mortality. In the case studies, he asks a within-case causal question about what explains Costa Rica's performance. He had dozens of countries in the statistical chapter; why focus on Costa Rica?

The main reason for the rise of multimethod research has been the desire to combine the advantages of cross-case large-N research with the advantages of intense within-case causal analysis. Hypotheses of the form "X has an effect on Y" are often quite vague on the details of the causal mechanism. It is not uncommon for a researcher to provide several causal mechanisms to explain the effect of X. For example, there are various

TABLE 3.1
X–Y configurations

	$X = 0$	$X = 1$
$Y = 1$	$(0, 1)$	$(1, 1)$
$Y = 0$	$(0, 0)$	$(1, 0)$

mechanisms that attempt to explain the strong effect of democracy on war. A variety of mechanisms have been proposed to explicate the relationship between GDP/capita and democracy.

Within the research triad, case studies and causal mechanisms are closely linked:

> The central goal of the case study is to investigate *causal mechanisms* and make causal inferences *within* individual cases.

This goal underlies the vast majority of multimethod research and informs many discussions of case study methodology. This core goal must be placed front and center in the analysis of case study methodology.

Table 3.1 frames much of the discussion. Each cell of that table has a specific role (or nonrole) to play in doing case studies for multimethod work. Much case study work talks about variation on X or Y. Here, it is the specific configurations of X and Y that are important.

In addition, one must consider the role of additional variables, be they scope, confounders, control variables, alternative causal mechanisms, what are generically called Z variables in this chapter. In cross-case work one often is very aware of the problems confounders play in causal inference. This must be taken into consideration when connecting case studies for the analysis of causal mechanisms.

This chapter lays out the basic logic of case selection in service of this goal. Most of the chapter assumes that there is an X variable in the cross-case analysis for which one wants to choose case studies to examine causal mechanisms. The second part adds confounders, i.e., Z variables, to the mix to see how they influence the selection of case studies. The rest of the volume rests on the core methodological principles developed in this chapter. So, if one is hopscotching around, this chapter is a square to visit soon after chapter 1.

Defining Scope and Population

Statistical analysis typically relies on existing data sets, which implicitly define a scope. QCA data sets are much more the result of active choices by the researcher. Experiments often involve some relatively narrow scope, e.g., students in the same class, university, or town. Typically, the cross-case set of observations provides an initial definition of the scope of the analysis.

However, as Ragin has stressed (2000; 2008), the population and scope of the analysis must be constructed and defended. It is also something that can change as the result of case study analysis. In the multiple case study and game theory settings there is no preexisting data set, so scope is often not specified in the research. For example, Waltz's (1979) theory of structural realism has an unclear scope; for example, does it require anarchy? Formal theories might have a scope defined by the assumptions of the theory. Does the bargaining model of war apply only if states and leaders are rational? For example, Fearon states, "Toward this end, I am arguing that when one looks carefully at the problem of explaining how war could occur between *genuinely rational, unitary* states, one finds that there are really only two ways to do it" (1995, 382; emphasis is mine).[1]

Scope lies at the heart of the research triad. Each corner has implications and relevance for scope decisions. Ideally each corner of the triad contributes input to the final scope. Case studies can play a particularly important role in this four-way dialogue.

As such, the first step in selecting a case study is to define the potential scope of the causal mechanism:

One must provide a list of all possible case studies or the criteria for such a list.

This should be an obligatory part of any multimethod research project. If it is a statistical or QCA multimethod project, then the cross-case data set is a natural place to start. If there is no such data set, then theory or the causal mechanism can provide a starting point.

---

[1] This is a real issue, as can be seen by Lake's application (2010) of the bargaining model to the 2003 Iraq War.

It is not uncommon for graduate students to announce that they are comparing, say, Venezuela and Colombia. However, it is not obvious that these are the best cases for a given causal mechanism. I have found that demanding from students a complete list of possible case studies almost always raises a lot of issues, theoretical and methodological, and generates a useful discussion about the proposed project as a whole.

The scope of the theory or causal mechanism could well, and probably should, change as the case study analyses proceed, but it is almost always a good idea to start with the complete, if provisional, list. The list could easily be dozens of countries or thousands of country–time periods. Producing such a list should be considered an indispensable part of good methodological practice in all types of multimethod research.

Case Selection with No Causal Mechanism

When scholars have connected qualitative and statistical work, they have often used Snow's investigation into the transmission of cholera as a canonical example. First introduced into the methodological literature by Freedman (1991), it appears regularly in statistical textbooks and methods publications.

This multimethod literature has almost exclusively focused on the beautiful natural experiment that Snow used to demonstrate that cholera was transmitted via water (e.g., see Dunning 2012). This literature focuses on the end game of Snow's empirical investigations, where he had already become convinced that cholera was transmitted via drinking water.

It is useful to explore the earlier period in Snow's work, before he had a clear working hypothesis about the role of drinking water, and how he got to that theory to begin with. The natural experiment could occur only once Snow had a clear hypothesis. What does one do and how does one choose cases when the researcher has no real, clear causal mechanism, when one has only hunches, guesses, and intuitions?

At the early stages of his investigation Snow did what all medical scientists do when confronted with a new disease (e.g., AIDS), they violate the advice of King, Keohane, and Verba and select on the dependent variable. At the early stages of research, one focuses one's attention—often for long periods of time—on people with the disease, i.e., the $Y = 1$ cases.

This is often very much a *descriptive* and *conceptual* investigation. What *is* cholera? Usually the investigation of diseases begins with a set of symptoms that seem to characterize the disease. In the case of cholera, it is diarrhea and vomiting, which may result in dehydration and in severe cases, gray-blue skin. An untreated person with cholera may produce 10 to 20 liters of diarrhea a day. Often the diarrhea has a distinctive "rice water" look.

In the nineteenth century, it was not always obvious—just as it is in the twenty-first century for many diseases—whether the person really had cholera. For example, there are many paths to diarrhea, which almost all produce dehydration. Many of these diseases are unlikely to cause death, a feature of cholera which of course made it a much more serious health problem.

If one looks at much of Snow's early research, it involved systematic data gathering about Y: who had the disease, when, and where. This systematic knowledge of Y almost immediately generated hypotheses about the causes or transmission of cholera. For example, it seemed to be concentrated in poor areas of cities. The Broad Street pump investigation illustrates the focus on the occurrence of cholera. The first step was to map out the occurrences of $Y = 1$.

This is not very different from what happened 125 years later with AIDS. Much of the initial epidemiological work focused on the patterns of those with the disease. These data led to great controversy, as homosexual men were obviously under a much higher risk of AIDS than other populations. At the early stages it was not clear—but very politicized—what it was about being a male homosexual that put someone at high risk. It was a classic correlation without causal mechanism.

The famous democratic peace empirical finding illustrates the same pattern. When Singer and Small discovered the democratic peace (1974), all they had was a list of wars. Systematically looking at this list, they discovered that none were between democracies.

Almost all of these wars were clearly a war. Later large-N research used "militarized disputes" as the dependent variable. Some of these are not good examples of war or serious militarized conflict. So, for example, almost all large-N studies consider the militarized disputes between the USA and Canada over fishing in the 1970s to be tests of the democratic peace. Whether these should be considered as cases for testing theories of war remains controversial, however these would not be the cases one would start with. In fact, many of the counterexamples (see Ray 1993 for a nice discussion of them) are either not clearly wars, such as the fishing disputes, or not clearly democracies, e.g., Spain in the Spanish-American War. Looking at these cases is important once a causal mechanism has been proposed, but they are not likely to be helpful in generating an initial one.

In summary, when case studies are conducted in this exploratory way—which can also be done systematically—the focus is on the phenomenon Y and the examination of good cases of $Y = 1$.

The Logic of Case Selection for Exploring Causal Mechanisms

Table 3.1 provides a framework for thinking about case studies and multimethod research. Often the concern—in the methods literature and in practice—is on variation on X or Y *individually*. The focus in this volume is on the various *combinations* of X and Y. By the end of the chapter it will be clear that variation on X or Y per se is irrelevant. Each cell of table 3.1 plays a distinct role in case studies and multimethod research. In fact, I label each cell according to its role.

The subsections to follow explore the role of each cell in table 3.1. Not only do they vary in their role, they vary significantly in how important they are in multimethod research.

THE CAUSAL MECHANISM CELL, (1,1)

If the central goal of the case study is the exploration of a causal mechanism, then one should look at a good example of that causal mechanism in action. This means looking at cases where the causal mechanism should be present according to the cross-case analysis, i.e., $X = 1$, and where it produces the outcome, i.e., $Y = 1$. This is the $(1, 1)$ cell of table 3.1, which thus receives the causal mechanism cell label:

A focus on causal mechanisms leads to choosing cases from the $(1, 1)$ cell.

The connection between the cross-case and within-case analyses is verifying that when the cross-case observation falls into the $(1, 1)$ cell, the within-case analysis confirms that the proposed causal mechanism is in fact working for this observation.

Recall that qualitative researchers have been frequently accused of selecting on the dependent variable. This accusation is often somewhat misplaced. For example, take Geddes's (2003) discussion of selection bias in the qualitative literature on the causes of high economic growth. The causal mechanism involves the key role of labor repression in producing high economic growth. With this causal mechanism in mind, one would naturally look at $(1, 1)$ cases, such as South Korea, Singapore, i.e., high growth–high labor repression countries. This is exactly what one should do if the concern is with the causal mechanism X and how it produces Y.

Geddes's critique is purely cross-sectional; one does causal inference across cases. In the research triad, within-case analysis is critical: Do the authors make a convincing case that labor repression was critical to producing high growth in each of these countries? This is a within-case causal inference issue.

It is useful to consider the continuous analogue of table 3.1, which is figure 3.1. The four cells of the table map onto the analogous spaces in the figure. This means that the causal mechanism cell is the upper-right corner of figure 3.1.

With continuous variables we can be more specific in stating that one should look at *good* cases of the causal mechanism. "Goodness" is essentially distance from the $(1, 1)$ corner of the figure. This makes natural sense from a conceptual point of view. As one moves toward 1.0, the observation becomes a better instance of the underlying concept of X or Y. For example, good democracies are those near $X = 1$ at the extreme of the scale. Particularly if one is doing only one or two case studies, one needs to choose good cases on both X and Y.

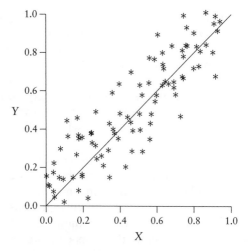

Figure 3.1: Case study selection: continuous *X* and *Y*. Reprinted by permission of the publisher, Taylor & Francis Ltd http://www.informaworld.com.

For the purposes of illustration and discussion I have put an OLS line in figure 3.1. One often reads in the multimethod literature about "on-line" versus "off-line" cases. The causal mechanism cell is not usefully thought of in these terms: there are off-line points in the upper right that could be good causal mechanism cases; there are on-line cases near (0, 0) that are not causal mechanism cases at all.

Ziblatt (2009) provides a nice example in a statistical multimethod context. He does one case study following a statistical analysis in which the main *X* variable is economic inequality and the dependent variable is electoral malpractice. The statistical analysis is limited to Germany in the late nineteenth century. For his case study, Ziblatt chose a region of Prussia: "This was a region where feudalism lasted longer than anywhere in Germany (into the nineteenth century), landholding inequality was higher than anywhere in Germany, and elections were marred by a greater incidence of electoral fraud than anywhere in Germany" (2009, 15). Clearly Ziblatt is choosing a (1, 1) case, and an extreme one at that, in terms of *X* ("landholding inequality was higher than anywhere in Germany") and *Y* ("greater incidence of electoral fraud than anywhere"). So in terms of figure 3.1, he chose a case in the extreme upper-right corner.

In a multiple case study context, to see whether the hypothesized mechanisms actually existed, Ross (2004) selected 13 "most likely" cases, which he defined as a civil war having occurred and in which his reading of secondary source material suggested that primary material exports played a role in the origin of the conflict. Clearly he selected cases from the (1, 1) cell.

It might well be the case that an observation falls into the upper-right corner of figure 3.1, but when the case study is conducted, the within-case causal inference does not find the causal mechanism to be working as theorized. This possibility will be a central part of chapter 7. If multimethod analysis is working well—i.e., connecting the cross-case analysis with the within-case—then cases near the (1, 1) corner are also confirmed by the within-case causal analysis. This is, after all, the idea behind multimethod research to begin with: combining different causal inference strategies that can provide independent support for a causal mechanism. There is no reason why the methodologies should always agree. If they did then multimethod research would be pointless.

Among the four cells of table 3.1, the multimethod researcher has a very clear preference for the (1, 1) cell. If the main goal is exploring how a causal mechanism works, then one chooses cases of the causal mechanism in action. These are located in the (1, 1) cell.

THE FALSIFICATION–SCOPE CELL, (1,0)

What about the other cells in table 3.1? Is there a priority among them? What about the "off-line" cells, (1, 0) and (0, 1)? Are these equally disconfirming cases (see appendix A)? The (1, 0) and (0, 1) cells are not of equal value and in fact serve different empirical and theoretical purposes.

The (1, 0) cell is of particular importance. These are disconfirming or falsifying cases. The causal mechanism hypothesis suggests that when X is present then the mechanism produces Y. Cases in the (1, 0) cell imply that the mechanism is not working.

They offer potential evidence against the causal mechanism hypothesis. Hence the presence of cases in this cell is of great concern. While most researchers avoid, for obvious reasons, case studies that tend to falsify their theories, their opponents obviously focus their attention on this cell.

Lipset, Trow, and Coleman's (1956) classic analysis is an example of a falsifying case study. It analyzed a union organization characterized by a high level of democratic procedures. The authors highlight how the organizational politics of the union cause it to deviate from the predictions of Michels's iron law.

Ideally the $(1, 0)$ cell has very few observations. The QCA methodology focuses on this cell in particular and the goal is to have zero cases in it. Typically, a QCA analysis will not proceed unless this cell has 20–25 percent or fewer of the cases in the $X = 1$ column. It is worth stressing that the key percentage is not based on the total number of observations, but rather the set of cases where the causal mechanism should be working, which is the $X = 1$ column.

One should face these falsifying cases head on. In good comparative work, scholars take very seriously the disconfirming cases. For example, Ertman (1997) has a couple of cases where his theory does not work and he spends more time discussing these than the confirming cases.

One response to cases in the $(1, 0)$ cell is to refine the theory. Ragin and Schneider (2012) describe a number of techniques for reducing the number of observations in this cell. One of these techniques is to adjust the scope of the causal mechanism. Thus the $(1, 0)$ cell has a very important positive use: it can be useful in finding the scope limits to the causal mechanism. Realistically, causal mechanisms do not work in all time periods and in widely different political, economic, or cultural situations. The positive use of falsifying cases is the *construction of the scope of the causal mechanism.*

Goertz and Mahoney (2012, chapter 16) illustrate the scope use of this cell. In a scatterplot of the classic GDP/capita and democracy relationship, there are a few observations in the lower-right quadrant, i.e., wealthy nondemocracies. Naturally one looks at these cases in some detail. It turns out that almost all of them are heavily oil-dependent states (e.g., oil monarchies). If one limits the scope of the GDP/capita and democracy hypothesis to exclude oil-dependent states then there is only one case (Singapore) in the (1, 0) cell. The benefits of almost no cases in the falsifying cell are often worth the price of reduced scope.

If one can do only a couple of case studies, then naturally they should be chosen from the causal mechanism cell (1, 1). Next on the agenda for case studies are observations from the (1, 0) cell. These case studies might be more superficial, depending on the nature and number of cases in the cell. If they all have a common feature—e.g., oil-dependent states—then the scope limitation is relatively easy to implement. Nevertheless, an intensive case study or two is often useful to explore why the causal mechanism does not work. This can be very informative about the causal mechanism itself and how it works.

Hence, the cases in the (1, 0) cell play two complementary roles: they disconfirm the causal mechanism, but at the same time they can aid in laying out the scope of the causal mechanism.

THE EQUIFINALITY CELL, (0,1)

The (1, 0) cases play a falsifying and scope role: What about the other "off-line" cases in cell (0, 1)? These are cases where the causal mechanism is absent and the outcome occurs. What is their methodological role?

Causal mechanisms usually have the form "when X occurs then the causal mechanism produces Y." If X is absent then there is no reason why we should or should not see Y. There might be other causal mechanisms that produce Y: there are alternative paths to Y. This notion is known as equifinality and hence the (0, 1) cell is the equifinality cell.

In a large-N setting, the $X = 0$ cases produce probabilistic hypotheses. If one of the causal mechanisms is absent then we would expect that Y is less likely to occur. These probabilistic hypotheses are the subject of cross-case analyses in the research triad. When doing large-N cross-case analyses, $X = 0$ cases have an important role to play. Where they are not very useful is in causal mechanism analysis in case studies.

Lijphardt's analysis of pluralism (1969) is a classic case of the (0, 1) cell. Lijphardt's key insight was that there were other paths to political stability beyond the classic Anglo-American one. Hence his analysis did not invalidate the relationship between pluralism and political stability, but rather showed that there are other ways to achieve it.

Equifinality does not exist in the conceptual vocabulary of scholars who use statistical methods. A search through the index of research design textbooks like Babbie (2001), discussions of popular statistical methods books such as Angrist and Pischke (2015), and econometric textbooks reveals that equifinality is not something that gets taught to students in statistical methods classes. In contrast, it is central to qualitative methods. For example, George and Bennett (2005) discuss the concept. It is absolutely central to QCA methods where the main goal of a QCA—what is produced by the software—is to determine the multiple paths to the outcome. Why this difference between statistical and qualitative methods?

Part of the answer is that equifinality is so deeply built into statistical and experimental models that it is not worth mentioning as an explicit concept. The problem of confounders has driven much statistical thinking over the decades. By definition, a confounder is another factor[2] that produces Y. Almost all statistical methods and discussions assume that the problem of confounders is very serious. Most statistical models used in applied research are additive in the link function, such as OLS and logit. Addition implies there are multiple combinations of the independent variables that can produce the outcome, i.e., equifinality. Experiments explore the effect of the treatment on the outcome: implicit—say in drug research—is that other treatments can have a positive impact on the outcome. In short, virtually all statistical approaches—experiments, potential outcomes, matching, general linear models—assume equifinality.

So why do qualitative scholars make a special point of equifinality? The answer to this question requires looking at the role of confounders, alternative explanations, and control

---

[2] Constraint causal mechanisms, factors that prevent Y from occurring, are discussed in chapter 4.

variables in multimethod and case study research. I discuss this extensively below in the form of additional Z variables, confounders or causal mechanisms.

Unlike the $(1, 0)$ cell, which is absolutely central because it falsifies the causal mechanism, equifinality is not necessarily a serious threat to a scholar's theory. It certainly could be part of a research agenda to investigate alternative causal mechanisms, but not to do so is equally acceptable. So the choice of observations from the $(0, 1)$ cell is completely optional.

For example, Fuhrmann looks at cases where there was nuclear cooperation that did not fit his causal mechanism. He examines cases from the $(0, 1)$ cell to discover whether there is another causal mechanism at work:

> One of the primary purposes of this chapter is to determine whether there is a variable that is important in explaining nuclear cooperation that I omitted from my initial statistical analysis. The examination of outliers reveals a novel explanation for atomic assistance. In three of the cases analyzed in this chapter—Brazil-Iraq, France-Iraq, and Italy-Iraq—the supplier provided nuclear assistance to secure a stable supply of oil from the recipient country. These examples suggest an alternative hypothesis for nuclear cooperation: oil-producing countries are more likely to receive peaceful nuclear assistance than non-oil-producing states. (Fuhrmann 2012, 128)

THE (0,0) CELL

What about the $(0, 0)$ cell? Here the causal mechanism is not present and the outcome does not occur. For investigating causal mechanisms, cases in cell $(0, 0)$ have little or no role to play. If the causal mechanism is absent, there is no particular reason why we should be surprised if the outcome does not occur either.

John Snow, cholera, and the Broad Street pump illustrate why the $(0, 0)$ cell is of little use for case studies. In the context of the Broad Street pump, the $(0, 0)$ cases are people far away from the pump without cholera. What is to be gained by looking at people living far away from the pump and who do not have cholera: Would we expect them to have cholera? Clearly, cases of cholera near the pump are $(1, 1)$ cases. Cases of people near the pump without cholera are falsifying cases. The Broad Street pump illustrates that the central action for case studies is in the $X = 1$ column, i.e., people living near the pump.

In a large-N setting, one can learn some things from the $(0, 0)$ cell, but it often is not something that points to multimethod and causal mechanism analysis. While it is somewhat useful to know that old heterosexual white women are not likely to get AIDS, it is much more useful to know that young homosexual men are likely to get it. In general, there are probably lots of groups with a low likelihood of getting AIDS. AIDS illustrates that this is often a function of the asymmetry between $Y = 1$ and $Y = 0$, where often the numbers in these two sets differ radically, with $Y = 1$ being much less common than $Y = 0$.

The $Y = 0$ or $X = 0$ cases are often conceptually problematic (Mahoney and Goertz 2004). For example, we have a relatively clear idea about the occurrence of a social revolution, however there are millions of cases of a social revolution not occurring. If we have to choose one or two among them it could be quite difficult. The $(0, 0)$ cases just compound the problem.

In short, there are no compelling reasons to choose cases from the $X = 0$ column. In specific circumstances they can be quite useful (see chapter 4 where this cell plays a role for constraint causal mechanism and necessary conditions), but there is no strong reason to choose from the $(0, 0)$ cell in general.

SUMMARY

In short, the methodological logic of causal mechanism research creates a clear hierarchy of importance among the cells as shown in table 3.2. The $(1, 1)$ cell is clearly the most important because this is where we can see the causal mechanism in action. Since this is the central goal of case studies in multimethod research, this cell is the most important.

The $(1, 0)$ falsification–scope cell is second in importance. Obviously these cases pose potential threats to the proposed causal mechanism. These potential disconfirming cases can be either explained away (e.g., measurement error) or can be dealt with via scope conditions.

TABLE 3.2
Case study selection: rationales and roles of X–Y configurations

	$X = 0$	$X = 1$
$Y = 1$	Equifinality Importance = 3	Causal mechanism Importance = 1
$Y = 0$	Counterfactual Importance = 4	Falsification–Scope Importance = 2

Pevehouse illustrates the central importance of the $X = 1$ column. In his case studies he focuses on regions—Americas and Europe—with highly democratic regional IGOs. While his statistical analyses incorporate regional IGOs from all regions, including low democratic regional IGOs, the case studies naturally focus on where the causal mechanism is at work, which would be in Europe or the Americas, not in the Middle East or Africa:

> This last point is important for my argument. If democratically dense regional organizations are necessary for the functioning of the causal mechanisms, those regions with few democracies and few democratically dense organizations will not be particularly good tests for my theory. It is not surprising that there are few cases where regional organizations assist in democratization in Africa, the Middle East or Asia—this is exactly what the theory suggests. (Pevehouse 2005, 115)

The (0, 1) equifinality cell suggests that there are other causal mechanisms, a significantly less important problem. Cases in this cell lead to questions about the relative importance of various causal mechanisms. It raises questions about alternative causal mechanisms, confounders, control variables—which I call Z factors—that are discussed below.

Finally, the (0, 0) cell is the least important. It is often hard to choose good cases from this cell. As discussed below, one can get to the (0, 0) cell via within-case counterfactual analysis. In many situations this will be a more attractive option than a problematic cross-case choice.

The key overall theme is that if the causal mechanism is about how X produces Y, then $X = 0$ cases have a much diminished role to play. The key action lies in the $X = 1$ column.

Two Contrasting Causal Mechanisms

Sometimes scholars have two clear causal mechanisms. So instead of the situation where $X = 0$ means "not-X" or the absence of X, $X = 0$ is another causal mechanism, in other words a nominal typology of causal mechanisms with two types. Often these two causal mechanisms have contrasting or opposite effects on the dependent variable.

Lange's excellent multimethod book (2009) illustrates this situation. He is analyzing the effects of "direct" or "indirect" rule on former colonies. He describes these two types of rule, which are quite different in their characteristics:

> Direct and indirect rule were two fundamentally different systems of control used by the British in their vast overseas empire. Direct rule depended on an integrated state apparatus and resembled the form of state domination that developed in Western Europe over the previous five centuries. It required the dismantling of preexisting political institutions and the construction of centralized, territory-wide, and bureaucratic legal-administrative institutions that were controlled by colonial officials. Direct rule was therefore both transformative and intensive.
>
> Indirect rule, on the other hand, was a form of colonial domination via collaboration with indigenous intermediaries who controlled regional political institutions. It created bifurcated colonial states based on two radically different organizational principles.... Both patrimonial rulers and bureaucratic officials, in turn, depended on and collaborated with one another to maintain a decentralized and divided system of colonial domination. (Lange 2009, 4)

Not surprisingly, Lange devotes a separate case study chapter to each type. As is implicit in the terminology, these are the only possibilities. Each is a specific and clearly specified form of government. His book explores the effects of these two types of government on the postcolonial experience of former British colonies. So the coding of one or the other as $X = 1$ is completely arbitrary.

A nice example of multimethod research from international relations is Weinstein's book on rebel groups and their use of violence (2006). In his summary figure (p. 12) he outlines two organizational strategies. The first is based on economic endowments leading to an opportunistic strategy in which insurgents extract resources via coercion. The second organizational strategy is via social endowments, which leads to an activist strategy in which insurgents obtain resources via striking a deal with civilians.

In nominal causal mechanism typologies with only two types, the $(0, 0)$ cell is also a causal mechanism cell. Weinstein devotes equal attention to each strategy and has in-depth case studies of each type. The coding of 1 and 0 is arbitrary.

Given that there are two causal mechanisms in the statistical analysis, Weinstein could easily have had two separate independent variables. However, in the statistical analysis, he uses a variable tapping the coercion strategy (looting of resource wealth). The assumption is that when this is low, then the other strategy is being used. Ideally, each mechanism should have its own continuous variable, since the two mechanisms might be correlated or there might be hybrid cases with some features of each pure type.

One signal that there is only one causal mechanism and not two is the relative number of cases where $X = 0$ versus $X = 1$. When the number of $X = 0$ cases is huge, i.e., no social revolution, and the number of cases of $X = 1$ is relatively small, that almost always means that $X = 0$ does not represent a causal mechanism. A related second signal is when the $X = 0$ cases are quite heterogeneous, which usually occurs when there are a very large number of $X = 0$ cases.

Even clearer is when the $X = 0$ cases are explicitly conceptualized and coded as not-X. "Peace" in virtually all statistical work on conflict is defined as not-war. Przeworski and his group define "authoritarian" as the absence of democracy (Cheibub, Gandhi, and Vreeland 2010).

In short, some scholars explore two causal mechanisms in parallel and in contrast. In this situation the 0–1 coding of X can be misleading. This book assumes that X stands for one causal mechanism not two.

Counterfactuals and Longitudinal Analysis

The research triad means doing within-case causal inference. While it is beyond the scope of this volume to discuss how this is done, it almost certainly involves counterfactual analysis of some sort. So one can ask in broad terms what counterfactuals would look like for each cell of table 3.2. One could look for actual examples that exemplify the counterfactuals exploring cases over time, i.e., longitudinal analysis. Longitudinal case studies involve tracking the case over time. Usually this will be tracking a change in X and evaluating the impact of that change on Y.

One of the most central differences between a within-case causal inference approach to case studies and a statistical one is philosophy about within-case causal inference. The potential outcomes approach is based on an "impossible" counterfactual that a scholar cannot observe, both treatment and control on the same unit:

> *Fundamental Problem of Causal Inference.* It is impossible to *observe* the value of $Y_t(i)$ and $Y_c(i)$ on the same unit and, therefore, it is impossible to *observe* the effect of t on i. (Holland 1986, 947)

The fundamental counterfactual is what would have happened if subject i had received the control instead of the treatment. Because of this problem of causal inference, one must use cross-case evidence, ideally an experiment, where one compares the treatment group with the control group. This means in the statistical approach to case studies—see appendix A—one often chooses an $X = 0$ case to compare with an $X = 1$ case.

Almost all natural scientists believe that within-case causal inference is possible: their theories explain individual events. One cannot be a medical doctor without believing in causal inference about cases. When political scientists and economists leave their offices and move to Washington to do policy and consulting, they must believe in within-case causal inference. If an economist is making policy recommendations, it must be

TABLE 3.3
Case study selection: counterfactual analysis

	$X = 0$	$X = 1$
$Y = 1$	Not useful Equifinality	Important Causal mechanism
$Y = 0$	Important Counterfactual	Not useful Falsification–Scope

with the belief that they will work in the specific case. When political scientists advise politicians, they must believe that their experiments apply to a specific election. The research triad makes explicit this connection between cross-case analyses and specific cases.

Of course, within-case causal inference is not without problems, but no method of causal inference, including experiments, is without its own set of issues. If one thinks that within-case causal inference is possible, then one also believes that within-case counterfactuals are doable and have value.

There is a key methodological point:

One can do counterfactual analysis of cases in the cells of the 2×2 table, e.g., table 3.3, which generates observations in other cells.[3]

The obvious place to start is with the causal mechanism cell $(1, 1)$. The counterfactual question—and everyone agrees on this point—asks, if causal mechanism X had been absent then what would have happened to Y? Doing a within-case counterfactual moves around in the 2×2 table. Starting with the $(1, 1)$ cell, one asks what will happen when X counterfactually becomes absent. If the causal mechanism argument is supported by the within-case counterfactual, then one arrives at the $(0, 0)$ cell.

---

[3] It should be noted that much current statistical work involves constructing counterfactual observations or their equivalent, e.g., Abadie et al. (2015). These "counterfactual observations" are as good as the causal models and data used to generate them. For example, this means that R^2 considerations have come back from the methodological dead, because core to constructing good counterfactuals is not causal effect, but rather model fit.

Hence, there are two ways to have a $(0, 0)$ case. The first is to choose a different case with $X = 0$ and $Y = 0$, the statistical approach to case studies. The second option is via within-case causal inference, which produces a $(0, 0)$ case from counterfactual analysis of a $(1, 1)$ case. In short, we do not have to choose a separate case of $(0, 0)$ because counterfactual analysis generates these cases from the $(1, 1)$ cell. The $(0, 0)$ cell is critical to case study methodology, but not as a separate cross-case case study. It is critical because of the counterfactual analysis of the $(1, 1)$ cases.

One can think about counterfactuals from all cells of the table. I have focused attention on the causal mechanism $(1, 1)$ cell. But one can work the counterfactual from the other direction: take a case from the $(0, 0)$ cell and make $X = 1$. Does the counterfactual analysis lead to the $(1, 1)$ cell?

In table 3.3 I have listed this as a good cell for counterfactual analysis. This is a direct consequence of the overdetermination problem for the $(1, 1)$ cell. Since the outcome did not occur, i.e., $Y = 0$, when one does the counterfactual, i.e., making $X = 1$, there is not much risk of overdetermination.

The downside to the $(0, 0)$ cell is that there may be a lot of cases that would not be suitable for counterfactual analysis. Particularly when $X = 0$ is poorly defined, which is the case when it is explicitly or implicitly defined as not-X (as when peace is defined as not-war), the selection of cases from the $(0, 0)$ cell can be problematic.

What about counterfactuals from the $(1, 0)$ falsification–scope cell? Changing $X = 1$ to $X = 0$ seems less valuable since we have no reason to think Y would occur anyway. So this cell appears to have little utility from the counterfactual perspective.

What about the $(0, 1)$ equifinality cell? This seems like a bit of an odd counterfactual because if the other path is still present, we would still expect to have $Y = 1$, i.e., the counterfactual produces overdetermination. Counterfactuals from this cell seem to be of little value.

In short, counterfactual analysis is useful for cases in the $(0, 0)$ and $(1, 1)$ cells, while it has little relevance for off-diagonal cells. As such, in table 3.3 I have ranked the diagonal cells as important while indicating that the off-diagonal cells are not useful.

Longitudinal analysis provides a way to go in the other direction. Counterfactual analysis starts with $(1, 1)$ and ends with $(0, 0)$. Longitudinal causal analysis takes cases of $(1, 1)$ and goes back in time to when they were $(0, 0)$. The within-case causal inference involves exploring when X becomes 1 and why that had an impact on Y. In chapter 5, I discuss a nice example by Aktürk (2011), where he tracks three X variables over time. Sometimes these cases are somewhat hard to find. The democratic peace literature rests almost exclusively on cross-case analyses. Wars are rare events and countries rarely change regime type. Because the democratic peace is dyadic, one can find cases where the dyad went from not-democratic (i.e., one or both countries are not democratic) to democratic. There are a couple of dozen of these cases and Hensel, Goertz, and Diehl (2000) find, in almost all, that the occurrence of militarized disputes went dramatically down after the dyad became jointly democratic. Such cases would naturally be a part of a multimethod investigation of the democratic peace, in conjunction with the usual cross-case statistical analyses.

In general, multimethod researchers should see whether such longitudinal $(0, 0)$-to-$(1, 1)$ cases exist in the cross-case data set (or elsewhere for that matter). They mirror and complement the $(1, 1)$-to-$(0, 0)$ counterfactuals.

Avoid Overdetermination Guideline

The counterfactual in the $(1, 1)$ cell can be ambiguous because of equifinality. The counterfactual conclusion of $(0, 0)$ implies that there were no other causal mechanisms present that could generate Y. If the counterfactual analysis of $(1, 1)$ fails, then we have a situation of $(0, 1)$; Y would have occurred in spite of the absence of X. As we have seen, this means equifinality, what I call Z variables. Both X and Z are mechanisms that produce Y. Hence, critical to this counterfactual is the existence of alternative paths Z to Y.

Counterfactual analyses explicitly raise the question of overdetermination. It is quite common in QCA analyses for a single case to be on multiple paths. In a statistical context, collinearity among variables produces the same problem. This leads to an important guideline for selecting cases:

Avoid Overdetermination Guideline: avoid case studies that contain multiple causal mechanisms.[4]

One might not know this from the start, but if there are preceding statistical or QCA analyses, then these cases-to-avoid could be identified based on these results.

This guideline flows naturally from the emphasis on a specific causal mechanism. We want, at least initially, cases that are clear examples of the causal mechanism. Overdetermined cases are muddied waters, because of the existence of multiple causal mechanisms. This makes counterfactuals for $(1, 1)$ cases somewhat problematic, since the problem of overdetermination can be serious. This problem is exacerbated by the fact that because of high levels of correlation or limited diversity, there might be quite a bit of overlap between causal mechanisms.

When we consider Z as the presence or absence of an alternative causal mechanism, the case selection guideline is clear: choose $Z = 0$ cases. Cases where $X = 1$ AND $Z = 1$ are overdetermined. If the goal of the case study analysis is to investigate the causal mechanism X, then one clearly wants to avoid the overdetermined ones. The guideline is to not choose cases where $Z = 1$.

Snow's first (of three) extensive analysis of an outbreak of cholera (rarely discussed in the social science literature, e.g., not by Dunning 2012; see Hempel 2007 for a history) illustrates this guideline to avoid overdetermination. One thing that all had noticed was that cholera outbreaks were very often in poor neighborhoods. Naturally this led to speculation about the causal role of poverty. Snow was drawn to a localized outbreak of cholera because it occurred in a rich neighborhood. Since his

---

[4] Schneider and Rohlfing give the same principle in a QCA setting: "Selection must achieve control in the context of a counterfactual inference on INUS conditions by following what has been coined the unique membership principle" (Schneider and Rohlfing 2013, 563). "As the term suggests, the unique membership principle requires the selection of cases that are typical cases for one sufficient term only" (2016, 537).

causal mechanism was drinking water rather than poverty per se, he was able to hold a major confounder absent by looking at this particular outbreak.

Krook (2010) provides a nice illustration of the issues of overdetermination. Her QCA analysis produced the following two paths to high women's representation.[5] The first path (which might be considered the Scandinavian route) is women's status alone, which is sufficient for high levels of representation. The electoral system is potentially a strong confounder, because much evidence indicates that women's representation is higher in PR systems. The overdetermination problem is that Scandinavian countries are also proportional representation regimes. In fact, all the countries with high women's status are also proportional representation states. The key counterfactual is then that these states would have had high levels of representation even with a majoritarian system.

Tannenwald—a popular example in the qualitative methods literature—illustrates the Avoid Overdetermination Guideline in practice. She explains why the USA did not use nuclear weapons after 1945. As a social constructivist, her main alternative explanation (Z) is mutual nuclear deterrence. The choice of this confounder arises from the basic theoretical juxtaposition of social constructivism and realism:

> Most importantly, these are all cases [Japan 1945, Korea 1950–53, Vietnam 1961–73, 1991 Gulf War] in which mutual nuclear deterrence did not operate or operated only weakly. US leaders could have used nuclear weapons had they wished to, without significant fear of nuclear retaliation (and in one case they did so). I focus on non-deterrence cases here on the assumption that if we can explain non-use on the basis of mutual assured destruction (MAD), we need not care about a taboo. (Tannenwald 2005, 17)

She avoids cases where the main confounder is present, using the logic of the Avoid Overdetermination Guideline.[6]

---

[5] I exclude the path generated by one complicated case: Luxembourg.

[6] Lily Tsai's investigation of governance at the village level in China is another example of the application of the Avoid Overdetermination Guideline. She conducted several in-depth case studies of villages. Good cases are villages that

Suppose that one is unaware of the alternative causal mechanism Z until the case study is well under way, i.e., one has in fact chosen a case of $X = 1$ and $Z = 1$. Within-case causal analysis must confront this situation head on. The reality is that in any given case there are almost always alternative explanations of the outcome. These alternative explanations are functionally the same as Z. Blatter and Haverland (2012) place a large emphasis on the evaluation of various alternative explanations *within* the case. In addition, this is a core concern in the methodological literature on process tracing.

As such, the case study researcher has in fact two options: If the alternative causal mechanism is known then select cases of $Z = 0$. If alternative mechanisms are ambiguous, unclear, or unknown, then within-case causal analysis must be done to contrast the two mechanisms.

Scope Variables and Generalization

Above, Z was an alternative causal mechanism. However, additional variables can function as scope variables, i.e., S. If one thinks about the standard use of the most similar system design in comparative case studies, many variables often work fundamentally as scope variables. Scope variables are about generalization:

A scope variable S acts as a limit to the generalizability of the causal mechanism X.

Take a standard use of a region, say, Africa, as an additional factor. All the cases chosen are coded 1 on the Africa variable. Hence, if pressed, the researcher will claim to feel pretty confident about how things work in the African setting, but would hesitate to generalize to, say, Latin America.

---

evidence a high level of social solidarity but which, based on alternative causal mechanisms, would be judged unlikely to develop good governance, e.g., they are poor, isolated, and lack democratic institutions or accountability mechanisms from above.

Thinking about additional variables as a scope condition is very congenial to a causal mechanism view of case studies because it encourages the researcher to evaluate where and when the causal mechanism is likely to work or not. If the case study is more exploratory, then the researcher may choose S to be those instances where the causal mechanism is easy to see or more likely to have the predicted effect.

If the researcher feels pretty convinced of the validity of the causal mechanism then she might choose S to be as broad as possible. This makes sense of the "crucial" or "most difficult" case idea that occurs often in case selection justifications. The argument is that if the case study works for S near 0 (assuming for the moment that S runs from 0 to 1) then it is certain to work for cases of S near 1:

> Additional variables in much past and current work are scope variables, not control or confounding variables or alternative causal mechanisms.

More generally, generalization is often and usually should be a main concern when thinking about selecting multiple cases for analysis. To generalize is to expand scope and to include a wider variety of cases. This leads to the following conclusion regarding research designs:

> Multiple case study and multimethod research designs should embrace a most different system logic.

For example, Aktürk explicitly uses a most different systems analysis for exactly this reason: "State policies toward ethnic diversity are very different in these three countries [Turkey, USSR-Russia, Germany]. Therefore, the observation of an analogous process of transformation in state policies across these countries provides a robust confirmation of my argument that three elements are separately necessary and jointly sufficient for change" (Aktürk 2011, 117, see also table 1).

Causal mechanism analysis is the central goal of case studies in multimethod research. The presumption is often that statistical analyses have found that X is significant with the correct sign (e.g., Weller and Barnes 2014). The case study then looks to individual cases to confirm the causal mechanism.

Causal mechanism analysis starting with a case study works in reverse. The initial case studies explore the causal mechanism. The subsequent case studies then explore the limits of the causal mechanism: How general is it? In short, the case-study-first approach flips things. The statistical model starts with evidence for generalization then moves to mechanism. The case-study-first approach focuses initially on the mechanism then moves to generalization.

Exploring scope limits is absolutely central to all multimethod work. Ragin has often stressed (e.g., Ragin 2000) that populations are constructed. Central to case study work is thus constructing the population where the causal mechanism works or is likely to be seen. Since scope construction is not a standard part of statistical research practice—it could be, but it is not—it is not surprising that the central role of scope has been ignored. The issues of scope and generalization form a central part of the medium-N paradigm proposed in chapter 8.

One of the features of causal mechanisms is that their scope conditions are typically unclear. In almost all methodological and philosophical discussions of causal mechanisms, the contrast is with (universal) covering laws. Many of the examples in the philosophy literature come from biology (natural or micro), where the scope of the causal mechanism is an unknown. Ideally, scope should arise as an issue for all three corners of the research triad: it should be a part of theorizing and doing cross-case analyses, as well as case studies.

Choosing within Cells

The criteria discussed above do only part of the job. While one can have a clear sense of which kinds of cases are best for a case study, one must still choose within these criteria. There are potentially dozens, hundreds, and even thousands of cases within a cell.

Since the goal is to investigate causal mechanisms, we want good cases for this purpose. A careful look at the causal mechanism involves looking at good examples of X and Y; these are most often those at the "extremes" of X and Y. If the causal mechanism involves democracy then one chooses only among those cases that are clearly democratic; hybrid or competitive–authoritarian regimes would not be a good choice. In short, one chooses cases that have fewer conceptual or measurement issues.

The same applies to choosing cases in the $(1, 0)$ falsifying cell. If possible, one chooses cases that clearly falsify the causal mechanism hypothesis.

Data availability is a critical concern and often will be central in limiting the choices in a given cell. This follows naturally from a concern for within-case causal inference and causal mechanism research. It would not make much sense to include cases for which the information one needs is absent or poor.

Another relevant concern is policy applicability. If one has a choice between cases that occurred in 1800, 1900, and 2000, one might decide that it is more useful to choose the 2000 case to see whether the proposed causal mechanism works in the post–Cold War world, rather than whether it worked in 1800.

These are all legitimate reasons to exclude or include cases in a given cell. In particular, I think the quality of information is critical. This may itself remove a large percentage of possible cases from consideration. While a pragmatic concern, it is critical if the goal is to investigate causal mechanisms and do within-case causal inference.

Research Practice

Looking at research practice is quite useful in the context of multimethod and case study research and is a key feature of each chapter of this book. Unlike statistical methods, people doing multimethod or multiple case study work often *do not cite any methodological literature at all*. For example, North et al. (2013) and Rodrik (2003) have edited anthologies of case studies: there is no justification of case selection at all. This would be unheard of in statistical analyses, where practice is almost always justified by citations to methods textbooks and articles. Particularly in the case of statistical and game theory multimethod, researchers may well have never taken a qualitative methods course or any course dealing with case study methodologies. Hence it is of interest to examine what people do in practice with respect to case studies.

Steve Samford and I systematically examined all articles published in *Comparative Political Studies*, *International Organization*, *Perspectives on Politics*, and *World Politics*, 2006–15. These are the main international relations, comparative politics, or general journals that publish multimethod or case study research. It would be pointless to survey journals like *American Political Science Review* or *American Journal of Political Science* since they publish almost no research using case studies. To be included, the article had to include one or more case studies. This could be multiple case studies or case study plus some other methodology, typically statistical analysis.[7] A bibliography of all the articles fulfilling these criteria is available from me (ggoertz@nd.edu) or via this book's Princeton University Press web page.

I have also looked at multimethod and multiple case study research in books. This is a significantly different context. One major difference is that books offer the space for case studies that journals are less and less likely to give. The second is that books often are looking for wider audiences and case studies make them more attractive to a larger readership. I created a bibliography of all the international relations and comparative politics books (excluding anthologies) published by Cambridge, Cornell, and Princeton University Presses, 2006–2015. It is beyond my resources to read all these books; however, as I shall discuss here and in future chapters, it is not necessary. Dominant patterns are very clear, and diminishing returns to reading more books set in quite fast.

This volume covers case studies as they intersect with four different research designs: (1) statistical multimethod, which is statistical analyses plus case studies, (2) game theory multimethod, which is a formal model plus case studies, (3) QCA multimethod, which is a QCA analysis with some case studies and (4) multiple case studies. The central question is the degree

---

[7] Excluded are statistical case studies of a given country, e.g., analysis of a national survey in Italy.

to which the methodology outlined above can be found, or not, in practice in these four designs.

Looking at statistical multimethod practice—articles and books—the methodology given here describes practice quite well. Without exception in the articles, and virtually without exception in the books I have surveyed, scholars conducting a statistical analysis (e.g., logit, OLS) with a few case studies choose their case studies from the $(1, 1)$ cell. The justification is exactly that given here: they want to explore the causal mechanism in individual cases because the statistical tests are only indirect.

Within the $(1, 1)$ cell, researchers generally follow the analysis above and choose good cases. They almost always choose cases in the upper-right corner of figure 3.1. While the metaphor of on-line is sometimes used for this choice, it is likely that in fact the case studies are not actually on the estimated line (this is discussed at some length in appendix A).

Similarly, statistical multimethod scholars almost never choose cases from the $(0, 0)$ cell. They are almost always implicitly following the notion that these cases do not illustrate well the causal mechanism.

Since the purpose of the case studies in the statistical multimethod context is to support or illustrate the causal mechanism or hypothesis, scholars rarely explore falsifying cases. Not surprisingly, they choose cases that illustrate well the causal mechanism in the hypotheses and ignore the cases that do not fit well.

The exceptions are those who are criticizing a given hypothesis or causal mechanism. Much of chapter 7 will be devoted to examples where the author is using case studies to test some well-known empirical finding or game-theoretic model.

When one moves to Z variables as alternative causal mechanisms and the Avoid Overdetermination Guideline, my discussion finds little reflection in practice. Whether the case was overdetermined vis-à-vis alternative causal mechanisms was not a question researchers asked.

In a statistical multimethod context, this might well be because equifinality is not part of the methodological repertoire. Often confounders are not alternative causal mechanisms, but generic variables like population, region, etc. In general, there is almost no discussion of avoiding case studies that are overdetermined (see appendix A for some discussion of this issue).

Overall, the discussion above describes quite well statistical multimethod practice. The major difference is in the lack of attention to the overdetermination guideline. With this caveat, the methodology outlined in this chapter describes pretty well the implicit methodology of most statistical multimethod researchers.

I cover game theory multimethod research in some detail in chapter 6. Suffice it to note here that the logic of choosing cases from the $(1, 1)$ cell remains extremely valid in this context as well.

QCA multimethod research quite consistently follows the logic outlined here. Unlike statistical multimethod, QCA always associates cases with causal mechanisms and paths. Cases that lie on multiple paths are signaled by the software, so the overdetermination problem is presented by the methodology to researchers.

What is relatively rare in articles is QCA multimethod research. It is not common to have a QCA analysis along with case studies. This might be because QCA software generates multiple paths, hence the need for a case study for each path.[8] It is really only in books that one can explore QCA multimethod practice.

Because QCA focuses attention on the $(1, 0)$ cell, these falsifying cases often receive attention. This is aided by the fact that often there are not too many of them, so it is not too hard to explore them.

In short, the methodology proposed here fits well with QCA practice.

More problematic are comparative case studies as a cross-case methodology. As discussed in appendix A, these often mimic statistics. A common design is a paired comparison—$(0, 0)$ and $(1, 1)$ cases—along with a most similar system design for the Z variables. One can find numerous examples of this research design. However, it is usually applied in a quite loose and not very systematic way. Authors will often provide a list

---

[8] It might also be that articles devoted significant space to explaining the QCA methodology, which limits the space available for case studies.

of variables—often 5 to 10—where the cases match. Typically, these are not really alternative causal mechanisms, for example, region or language variables.

One can find examples where case studies are used to explore the causal mechanism. Diez (2013) provides an example of this approach, arguing that in two $(1, 1)$ cases (Mexico City and Buenos Aires) that same sex unions were a consequence of "the ability of well-organized activists [i.e., nonstate actors] to present an effectively framed policy within rare political opportunities that provided the ideal conditions for the policies to be adopted" (Diez 2013, 213). He makes the case that the causal mechanism is the same in the capital cities of Mexico and Argentina.

Ornston (2013) is another example; he offers a three-case study in which each case is located in the $(1, 1)$ cell. The primary case (Finland) is geared toward developing "creative corporatism" as a new causal mechanism, and the other two, similar but less-developed, case studies (Sweden and Denmark) are aimed at assessing the role of this kind of corporatism as the primary causal factor in the development of the high tech industry.

In conclusion, the methodology outlined here does quite a good job of explaining practice in the statistical multimethod, game theory multimethod, and QCA multimethod contexts. The Avoid Overdetermination Guideline is generally not used when considering alternative causal mechanisms. In paired comparative case studies, the statistical approach to qualitative research (see appendix A) does a good job of explaining practice because the two cases are chosen to mimic statistical cross-case analyses.

Conclusions

The analysis in this chapter works from the assumption that underlying X in a cross-case analysis is a causal mechanism that produces Y. The logic of the various 2×2 table cells is basically a sufficient condition logic. This corresponds to the way most scholars implicitly think about causal mechanisms and case studies.

Nevertheless, there are certainly situations where the causal mechanism is more closely related to necessary conditions than sufficient conditions, or more generally, when the causal mechanism involves constraints. This will lead to somewhat different conclusions about the relative importance and logic of the cells in a 2×2 table. This is a central topic of the next chapter.

Multimethod research strives to achieve a balance between cross-case testing and within-case causal analysis. The multimethod scholar wants to get the individual cases right, while at the same time being interested in causal mechanisms that travel and have widespread relevance. We have seen that constituting populations and scope is critical in the selection of cases.

A core question for the causal mechanism logic of case studies is the generalizability of the causal mechanism. This is related to, but significantly different from, the representativeness criterion of the statistical logic (see appendix A). To ask whether an X–Y relationship in a given case is representative of that relationship in a population is different from asking how general a causal mechanism is. To discuss generalizability means asking, how regular is causal mechanism X? How many falsifying examples are there? How important is it vis-à-vis other causal paths? How large is the scope? These are not questions about representativeness.

In the logic of causal mechanisms and multimethod research everything starts with the $(1, 1)$ cell. Here is where one examines the causal mechanism and does within-case causal inference. The other cells often have a scope role. Potentially falsifying examples are ways to examine scope limits. Other causal pathways are another kind of scope condition, suggesting alternative causal mechanisms. The point of the case studies is not to mimic cross-case causal inference, but to provide a different kind of causal inference based on the detailed examination of causal mechanisms in individual cases.

CHAPTER 4

Constraint Mechanisms and Necessary Conditions: Explaining Nonoccurrence

Introduction

Chapter 2 introduced the basic framework for analyzing constraint causal mechanisms. Constraint causal mechanisms are intimately related—both theoretically and methodologically—to necessary conditions. Both constraint causal mechanisms and necessary conditions are fundamentally about explaining why Y does not occur or the failure of some process.

The basic causal logic of necessary conditions relies on the core notion that the absence of X is the cause of the absence of Y. This occurs often in the single-case counterfactual: if not-x_i, then not-y_i. Hence the causal mechanism must involve explaining why the absence of X results in the absence of Y. A very strong constraint means that the outcome does not occur in its presence: the absence of the constraint is necessary for Y.

Goodwin (2001) provides a nice example in his discussion for why Honduras did not develop a revolutionary movement. His overall framework stresses how necessary very exclusionary authoritarian regimes were for the emergence of revolutionary movements: "I suggest in this chapter that revolutionary movements became strong *only where* militarized yet infrastructurally weak states were consistently exclusionary, antireformist, and more or less indiscriminately repressive of their political opponents (moderates and reformists as well as revolutionaries) throughout the 1960s and 1970s" (Goodwin 2001, 143; emphasis is mine).

One strategy for explaining the absence of revolutionary movements in Honduras is the absence of this necessary condition:

> Even imperfect and poorly consolidated democracies tend to diffuse revolutionary pressures.... During the 1980s, violent conflicts raged in neighboring countries, but Honduras remained relatively quiescent. No significant revolutionary movement challenged the Honduran state, despite social problems and inequalities that rivaled those of its neighbors.... Still, trade unions and peasant organizations were generally tolerated and occasionally won concessions through militant protest. Dissident intellectuals and human rights activists spoke out against the government. And, perhaps most important, the armed forces in Honduras never indiscriminately attacked peasant villages or popular organizations in the manner of their Salvadoran or Guatemalan counterparts. As a result, Hondurans never felt the need to join or support revolutionaries in order to defend themselves or to improve their welfare. So while Honduras's quasi-democracy did few things well, it was remarkably effective at preventing the emergence of a popular revolutionary movement. (Goodwin 2001, 303)

Goodwin's analysis of Honduras also illustrates a key theme in this chapter. Honduras is a good case because there were all kinds of reasons why one might expect revolutionary movements. These kinds of reasons are Z variables and are critical to the selection of good cases in the necessary condition version of the Avoid Overdetermination Guideline.

Necessary conditions, like constraints, can vary in their strength. Scholars often resort, for both constraints and necessary conditions, to metaphors such as ceilings. A glass ceiling is a constraint on the mobility of women in the labor market. Institutions and norms are often thought of as constraints on behavior.

There is an issue of orientation and language in moving back and forth between necessary conditions and constraints. I shall use the following principle:

As the necessary condition X decreases in value—i.e., moves toward zero—the constraining effect of X increases.

When we get to fuzzy logic figures in the second of half of the chapter, this is visually quite clear. The ceiling metaphor illustrates the basic intuition: as the ceiling gets lower—X decreases—the constraint of the ceiling is increasing.

Constraint and necessary condition theories are inherently complex and multivariate. For a constraint to have a causal impact, there must be a motivation to violate the constraint. Hence this chapter and the next, which discusses interactive causal mechanisms, are intimately connected. This chapter focuses on the necessary condition or constraint causal mechanism. But at critical points—for example, case selection—one must include the motivation variable into the analysis.

This chapter argues that QCA and mathematical logic in general provide a framework to think about the methodology of constraint causal mechanisms. This means that the logic of multimethod research for necessary conditions extends to constraint theories, which might not be formulated explicitly in set-theoretic or mathematical logic terms. This chapter thus does double duty: it works out the set-theoretic logic of multimethod work for necessary conditions and it shows how that applies to constraint causal mechanisms more generally.

This is critical because statistical multimethod researchers—statistical models plus case studies—implicitly adopt the sufficient condition logic described in the previous chapter. When scholars view constraints as just negative coefficients in a statistical model then it seems that the logic of the last chapter applies there as well. In a similar spirit, one might propose that the necessary condition methodology is just the mirror of the sufficient condition logic. If one looks at a 2×2 table, the necessary condition cell is the mirror of the sufficient condition cell. Hence, one might assume that there is nothing additional needed for a necessary condition case study methodology. Both these positions are incorrect. Necessary condition methodology is not the mirror of sufficient condition methodology. Negative statistical coefficients involve different multimethod procedures from positive ones. Here again the causal arrow, $\rightarrow$, is ambiguous, implying that there is no difference between necessary and sufficient conditions or positive and negative coefficients.

One can get some intuition about why necessary condition causal mechanisms might be different from sufficient ones from the metaphors and symbols scholars use. Sufficient causes use the arrows typical of causal mechanism discussions, $X \to M \to Y$. Necessary conditions are often written $Y \to X$ (e.g., Schneider and Wagemann 2012); however, this is a not a causal arrow but a formal implication arrow.[1] So a chain of necessary conditions looks like $Y \to M \to X$. This can look quite odd because one usually interprets the arrow as meaning causation, when here it means something about the data—i.e., Y is a subset of M, which is a subset of X (see Mahoney, Kimball, and Koivu 2009 for an extensive discussion of chains of necessary or sufficient condition arrows).

After discussing the relationship between constraint causal mechanisms and necessary conditions, this chapter introduces fuzzy logic into the mix. In many ways, the logic of necessary conditions comes out more clearly in 2×2 tables, but in general it is important that one looks at how things work in fuzzy logic (continuous variables) and how the dichotomous logic of a 2×2 table transfers to fuzzy logic. The fuzzy logic approach connects more intuitively with constraint causal mechanisms. Constraints are typically continuous, and graphically, the fuzzy logic version permits a visualization of the constraint.

In summary, this chapter continues the analysis of constraint causal mechanisms started in chapter 2. It explicitly links them to necessary condition causal mechanisms. Framed in this way, one can use the resources of the QCA literature—Boolean and fuzzy logic—to develop a methodology for case study and multimethod research.

Defining and Using Necessary Conditions

The basic idea of a necessary condition is clear, though this chapter will demonstrate it can be trickier than one might imagine. A necessary condition is one without which the outcome would not occur. In terms of logic, if not-X then not-Y. In set theory, Y is a subset of X; there are no occurrences of Y without X.

[1] This arrow also illustrates why selecting on the dependent variable is valid for necessary conditions.

TABLE 4.1

Necessary conditions: nondemocracy is necessary for interstate war

	Democratic dyad	Not-democratic dyad
War	0	36
Not-war	169	1045

Source: based on Russett (1995, 174). © 1995 by the President and Fellows of Harvard College and the Massachusetts Institute of Technology. Reprinted by permission.

Table 4.1 provides some cross-case data from the democratic peace thesis that could easily be interpreted in necessary condition terms. The data in the table support the claim that nondemocracy is necessary for war. The zero in the upper-left cell—often called the necessary condition cell in QCA—means that all wars occur between not-democratic dyads or that the wars dyads are a subset of the nondemocracy dyads.

While scholars typically discuss necessary conditions as bivariate hypotheses, necessary conditions involve additional variables, Z_i:

If X is necessary for Y, then when X is absent Y does not occur *no matter what the values of the other independent variables Z_i.*

For example, no matter how favorable other conditions are, if a veto player says no, then nothing changes.

This feature of necessary conditions is absolutely critical to the case study and multimethod analysis of necessary conditions. For example, case selection uses these Z_i values. In other words, one cannot treat X and Y as a bivariate hypothesis for exploring necessary condition causal mechanisms; the same is true for constraint causal mechanisms.

Table 4.1 also illustrates the typical way one does cross-case analysis of necessary conditions. One looks at the set of all interstate wars to see whether there are any between democracies. This is the $Y \rightarrow X$ version of a necessary condition. In fact, this is how Singer and Small (1974) discovered the democratic peace. They had a data set on wars and they looked to see whether there were any democratic dyads.

While most scholars have an intuitive understanding of dichotomous necessary conditions, which are part of basic Aristotelian logic, they usually have little idea what continuous necessary conditions look like. Fuzzy logic provides the extension from a two-value mathematical logic to an infinite-valued (typically all real numbers in the [0,1] interval) logic.[2] The continuous version of necessary conditions links up very nicely with constraint theories, which themselves typically model constraint strength in continuous terms.

Necessary condition hypotheses and causal mechanisms are quite common in political science and sociology. Over 10 years ago I (Goertz 2003) provided a list of 150 necessary condition hypotheses from all across political science, and the number has not decreased over the intervening years. Necessary condition hypotheses occur in all substantive areas of political science and sociology and across all theoretical perspectives. For example, they are quite common in game-theoretic and formal work; see chapter 6 for an extended discussion.

The discovery and analysis of necessary conditions lies at the core of the Boolean and fuzzy logic methodologies. Typically, these are discovered inductively in the data analysis. One of the first steps of a QCA analysis is to explore whether there are any necessary conditions. This must be done before the researcher moves to the analysis of sufficiency in the causal paths (see Schneider and Wagemann 2012 for a good treatment).

In summary, necessary condition hypotheses are relatively common and empirical data often support such hypotheses (see Goertz 2012 for many data examples).

Constraint Causal Mechanisms and Necessary Conditions

Necessary conditions and constraints meet because they both are about explaining why things do not happen or why a process fails. For example, "maximization under constraints,"

---

[2] This induces some important differences from the classical logic of the Greeks. For example, the law of the excluded middle no longer holds: something can be half-true and half-false.

as a basic part of applied calculus and part of the training of all economists, means a hard constraint. All solutions must satisfy the constraint. A necessary condition is a strong constraint in that all paths to the outcome must include it. For example, principals act as a constraint on agents:

> There is almost always some conflict between the interests of those who delegate authority (principals) and the agents to whom they delegate it. Agents behave opportunistically, pursing their own interests *subject only to the constraints* imposed by their relationship with the principal. The opportunism that generates agency losses is a ubiquitous feature of the human experience. (Kiewiet and McCubbins 1991, 5; emphasis is mine)

One way to think about necessary conditions is via constraints. A strong constraint cannot be violated. For example, in most veto player models, agreement of the veto players is a strong constraint that must be met:

> Strong constraints are necessary conditions.

Many see norms and institutions as constraints on behavior. International regimes prohibit a given behavior, for example, various regimes and treaties ban possession or use of certain kinds of weapons—e.g., nuclear weapons, chemical weapons, landmines. Many economists and rational choice scholars see institutions as constraints on behavior. Social constructivists meet rational choice scholars in viewing institutions and norms as constraints on behavior:

> Institutions ... are the humanly devised constraints that shape human interaction. (North 1990, 3)

> In general, I will have little to say about compliance with norms, because, in this theory, compliance or noncompliance is merely the result of the application of the principle of maximizing utility under different constraints. (Coleman 1990, 286)

> We define international institutions as explicit arrangements, negotiated among international actors, that prescribe, *proscribe*, and/or authorize behavior. (Koremenos, Lipson, and Snidal 2001, 762; emphasis is mine)

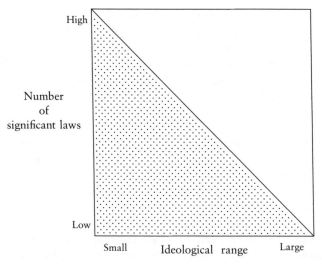

Figure 4.1: Constraint causal mechanisms, necessary conditions, and veto players: expected data scatterplot. Source: based on Tsebelis (1999). Reprinted by permission.

By *norm* I mean shared expectations about behavior, a standard of right or wrong. Norms are prescriptions or *proscriptions* for behavior. (Tannenwald 1999, 436; emphasis is mine)

Veto player theories (e.g., Tsebelis 2002) are a nice way to see how constraint causal mechanisms and necessary conditions link up together. The strength of veto player constraints depends on how far apart the veto players are ideologically:

In one dimension, policy stability depends on the maximum ideological distance between veto players, not on their number. (Tsebelis 1999, 595)

If the veto players all agree then there is little constraint. When they massively disagree—US politics over the last 20 years—then the constraints really kick in.

Figure 4.1 illustrates what data should look like when generated by a constraint causal mechanism, in this case veto players. This "triangular" scatterplot is familiar to QCA scholars, because that is what a fuzzy necessary condition produces. The diagonal line graphically illustrates the constraint: When veto players agree—narrow ideological range—there is little constraint on the number of significant laws that they can pass. But as their ideological differences increase, the constraints increase.

The Tsebelis veto player model is one where the theoretical framework generates the prediction of a triangular scatterplot. Often these scatterplots appear in descriptive analyses of data and one then might *infer* that X is necessary for Y. This is not fundamentally different from scatterplots where all the points lie nicely on a line and then the scholar fits a linear function to the data. In both cases the data are consistent with those models, but there are always other models that can produce the same scatterplot (i.e., the Quine–Duhem principle in philosophy of science).

In summary, constraint causal mechanisms and necessary condition causal mechanisms overlap to a large extent. These causal mechanisms can be generated from a wide range of theoretical and substantive perspectives, from social constructivism to game-theoretic models.

The Causal Mechanism Cell, (0, 0)

Necessary conditions and constraint causal mechanisms are particularly useful for explaining the *nonoccurrence* of Y, i.e., $Y = 0$. By definition the absence of a necessary condition ($X = 0$) means that the outcome cannot occur. In contrast, the presence of a necessary condition is consistent with both $Y = 0$ and $Y = 1$. Thus for necessary conditions, the key cell for causal mechanism analysis is the $(0, 0)$ cell; see table 4.2.

The problem is that picking from the $(0, 0)$ cell is often quite challenging. There are many cases that one would almost certainly not choose for a case study (see Mahoney and Goertz 2004 for a discussion). However, just because it is harder to find cases does not mean that one should not choose from this cell.

TABLE 4.2

Case study selection: X–Y configurations

	$X = 0$	$X = 1$
$Y = 1$	$(0, 1)$	$(1, 1)$
$Y = 0$	$(0, 0)$	$(1, 0)$

Note: $X = 1$ means necessary condition is present.

There is a key methodological point here:

The $(0, 0)$ cell is the causal mechanism cell for necessary condition and constraint causal mechanisms.[3]

One must distinguish the cross-case analysis of necessary conditions, where looking at the $Y = 1$ cases is completely acceptable, from the causal mechanism, within-case analysis of necessary conditions. The core usefulness of a necessary condition is explaining why the outcome did not occur. Its causal power is constraint and prevention, not sufficiency and occurrence.

A major issue with the $(0, 0)$ cell is that there are two potential explanations for cases that lie there: (1) absence of a necessary condition or (2) absence of all sufficient conditions. This is the necessary condition version of the overdetermination problem of the previous chapter. Overdetermination for sufficient conditions is when $Z = 1$. Overdetermination for necessary conditions is (1) when additional necessary conditions Z_i are zero or (2) when all the sufficient condition paths are absent (see below for an extensive discussion).

---

[3] This is the major difference between my approach and Schneider and Rohlfing's. They very heavily discount the value of cases in the $(0, 0)$ cell (or the equivalent region in fuzzy logic): "In contrast, cases in Zone 4 [basically the $(0, 0)$ cell] can play a role in comparative process tracing. This is why we label them as *individually irrelevant (IIR) cases*. They are formally in accord with a pattern of necessity, but are substantively irrelevant for explaining how the presence of Y requires the presence of X because they are neither members of X nor Y" (Rohlfing and Schneider 2013, 225). Where we agree is on the problems of choosing from the $(0, 0)$ cell, where many, if not most, cases would not be appropriate.

The causal mechanism cell for necessary conditions is the mirror of that for sufficient conditions, i.e., for sufficient conditions it is the $(1, 1)$ cell and for necessary conditions it is the $(0, 0)$ cell. The logic of the choice mirrors that for sufficient conditions: this is the cell where we should most clearly see the causal mechanism at work.

For sufficiency causal mechanisms, the notion of a good case is relatively simple: choose cases in the $(1, 1)$ corner. For necessary conditions and constraint causal mechanisms, the analogous rule is choose cases near $(0, 0)$. However, this is not enough by itself to determine the good cases. We must bring additional Z variables into play because of the ambiguity of the $(0, 0)$ cases.

The (1, 1) Cell: Counterfactuals and Trivialness

If the mirror image hypothesis were correct then the $(1, 1)$ cell would be of little importance when examining constraint causal mechanisms and necessary conditions, since the $(0, 0)$ cell is the least important for sufficient conditions. However, that is absolutely not the case: to explore necessary condition causal mechanisms one should choose cases from the $(1, 1)$ cell.

Rohlfing and Schneider stress the usefulness of $(1, 1)$ cases:

> In a QCA on necessity, the goal of process tracing is to investigate why the presence of the outcome requires the presence of the necessary condition. This focus yields the first insight for the choice of cases for comparative process tracing: *Every comparison must involve at least one case that is a member of the outcome.* (Rohlfing and Schneider 2013, 225)

We agree that the analysis of the $(1, 1)$ cell must be a counterfactual one:

> Hence, the focus of process tracing should be on within-case evidence that lends credence to this claim. In the analysis of single typical cases, this can only be a *counterfactual* because we only select cases with both X and Y present. (Rohlfing and Schneider 2013, 223)

As Rohlfing and Schneider stress, one reason to choose from the $(1, 1)$ cell comes from the importance of within-case causal inference. If X is necessary for Y then the within-case causal analysis should support the counterfactual that the absence of X would have resulted in the absence of Y. Hence, the $(1, 1)$ cell is a good way to test necessary condition hypotheses via within-case counterfactual analysis.

However, it is nevertheless very important to have real cases where the absence of X prevented Y from occurring, i.e., $(0, 0)$ cases. To see the causal mechanism in action is to choose cases from the $(0, 0)$ cell. The counterfactual analysis of $(1, 1)$ is a useful supplement, not a replacement.

Recall that counterfactuals from the $(1, 1)$ cell for sufficient conditions were seriously problematic because of equifinality. The working assumption in chapter 3 was that there were multiple causal mechanisms that produce Y. The fact that X is now a necessary condition causal mechanism means that it must be included in any sufficient condition causal mechanism analysis (a major topic of the next chapter).

An ideal real case mimics the counterfactual one. One of the big advantages of case studies is the ability to track events over time. The counterfactual changes X to 0, which then produces $Y = 0$. Sometimes it is possible to find real cases like this. Process tracing then explores why the absence of X generates the failure of Y. We shall see an example in the next chapter.

The $(1, 1)$ cell also plays a key role in evaluating the trivialness of the necessary condition causal mechanism. Take the simplest, one-path set-theoretic model, X_1 AND $X_2 \rightarrow Y$. Necessary conditions X_1 and X_2 contribute to the sufficiency of the combination. Necessary conditions also have a "sufficiency effect" (Goertz 2003). The closer a necessary condition comes to being sufficient, the more important and nontrivial it is.

A key difference in the methodology of case studies involving necessary conditions lies in the questions, oft-raised, about the trivialness of the necessary condition. The methodological principle involves the role of the necessary condition in producing the outcome:

To evaluate the trivialness of a necessary condition involves exploring its sufficiency effect in producing the outcome.

This is a reason to choose a case from the (1, 1) cell for intensive case analysis.

All these considerations lead to the following guideline:

Include (1, 1) case studies when exploring a necessary condition or constraint causal mechanisms.

Thus there exists a major asymmetry between the methodology for necessary conditions compared to that developed in the previous chapter for sufficient conditions. The methodology for necessary conditions is not the mirror of that for sufficient conditions. While (0, 0) cases were not important for sufficient condition causal mechanisms, the analogous (1, 1) cases are critical for necessary condition analyses.

The Falsifying–Substitutability (0, 1) Cell

There is a falsification cell for necessary conditions, which is (0, 1). These are situations where Y has occurred in the absence of X.

The issue of substitutability needs to be at the center of the analysis, therefore table 4.3 labels (0, 1) the falsification-substitutability cell. The key question that needs to be investigated in the case study is whether some new factor, X_2, substitutes for the proposed necessary condition X_1.

These substitutability analyses often have a very functionalist nature (see Goertz 2004 for an extended discussion). The new factor X_2 is playing the same role in the causal mechanism as X_1. This kind of discovery may constitute a relatively minor threat to the causal mechanism analysis, since the basic mechanism remains intact. Rohlfing and Schneider (2013) have a long examination of this point, along with a good empirical example.

Skocpol (1979) as usual serves as a nice example of the issues involved. One of her main hypotheses is that state breakdown is necessary for social revolution. Many noticed the causal mechanism: international pressure → state breakdown → social revolution.

Geddes (2003) explored the relationship between international pressure and social revolution via statistical analysis. She found at best a weak correlation between the two. What she failed to take into account is that state breakdown can occur via other mechanisms. Skocpol's actual model was (dominant class leverage OR agrarian backwardness OR international pressure) → state breakdown (see Goertz and Mahoney 2005; Goertz 2005, chapter 9). Hence, substitutability can transform falsifying cases into confirming ones.

The falsification–substitutability cell in some ways is in fact an equifinality cell. The equifinality takes place at a lower level of analysis. This generates what Mahoney (2008) calls a SUIN (a Sufficient but Unnecessary part of a factor that is Insufficient but Necessary for an outcome) cause and what I call (2005) a two-level theory. Mahoney's article describes in detail the logic of substitutability that must be considered when analyzing cases in the (0, 1) cell. The simplest one is $(X_1$ OR $X_2)$ AND $Z \rightarrow Y$; X_1 and X_2 are SUIN causes of Y. Neither is a necessary condition by itself, but one or the other is necessary. This kind of analysis might have major implications if the literature has treated X as necessary when it is in fact a SUIN cause.

In a larger context, SUIN causes in the falsifying cell are a form of omitted variable bias but of a different sort than in the usual linear statistical model. One not only finds a key omitted variable, but is also creating a new concept at the same time. The $(X_1$ OR $X_2)$ variable is typically some higher-level theoretical concept (hence the reason for calling them two-level theories).

The goal for the researcher then is to reformulate the theory so that these falsifying cases disappear (see Ragin and Schneider 2012 for a nice discussion). This means important conceptual and theoretical innovation.

The Irrelevant (1, 0) Cell

What about the (1, 0) cell? Cases in this cell do not disconfirm the necessary condition analysis; Y might not occur in the presence of X because X is only necessary, not sufficient. Cases in the (1, 0) cell are irrelevant to the analysis of a necessary condition causal mechanism.

TABLE 4.3
Case study logic: necessary conditions

	$X = 0$	$X = 1$
$Y = 1$	Falsification–Substitutability Importance = 3	Counterfactual Importance = 2
$Y = 0$	Causal mechanism Importance = 1	None Importance = 4

Note: $X = 1$ means necessary condition constraint is present.

In a large-N cross-case analysis, the number of cases in this cell gives information about the trivialness or the sufficiency effect of X (Braumoeller and Goertz 2000; Ragin 2008; Goertz 2006). However, for a causal mechanism analysis, it is not clear that anything can be gained by looking at cases in this cell.

In contrast, the mirror cell for a sufficient condition analysis has real potential payoff since one might discover a new pathway to Y. As such, that cell ranks third in importance in the context of sufficiency (the $(0, 0)$ cell being last). However, for necessary condition and constraint causal mechanisms, the $(1, 0)$ cell has no usefulness.

Summary

For necessary condition causal mechanisms, the ranking of cells in terms of importance is $(0, 0)$ in first position, then $(1, 1)$, followed by the falsification–substitutability cell $(0, 1)$, with the $(1, 0)$ cell in a very distant fourth position; see table 4.3.

While potentially tricky in terms of case selection, the key fact about necessary conditions is that they are better for explaining failure than success, hence the focus needs to turn to the $X = 0$ cases, which if the causal mechanism is correct, are also $Y = 0$.

The $(1, 1)$ cell is useful for examining the potential critique that X is a trivial necessary condition. This is done by showing that X has an important sufficiency effect on Y. In addition, within-case counterfactual analysis of $(1, 1)$ cases can provide evidence about the necessity of X.

Table 4.3 gives the methodological roles that the four cells play. One can contrast this with the analogous table generated

TABLE 4.4
Case study logic: sufficient conditions

	X = 0	X = 1
Y = 1	Equifinality Importance = 3	Causal mechanism Importance = 1
Y = 0	Counterfactual Importance = 4	Falsification–Scope Importance = 2

for sufficient conditions, given in table 4.4, with the associated rankings of the cells.

This chapter explores the question of whether the logic of multimethod work and case selection for necessary conditions mirrors that for sufficient conditions. Comparing tables 4.3 and 4.4 suggests that the causal mechanism cells are mirror images; the other cells play different roles. There are a number of significant differences between the two logics:

1. The $(0, 0)$ cell is quite unimportant in the sufficient condition logic, but the mirror $(1, 1)$ cell for necessary condition causal mechanisms is important.
2. For sufficient conditions the falsification cell also serves scope functions; for necessary condition causal mechanisms the falsification cell works with substitutability.
3. For sufficient conditions the least important cell is $(0, 0)$, while for necessary conditions it is $(1, 0)$.

In summary, necessary conditions and constraint causal mechanisms have important differences from sufficiency causal mechanisms. One is not the mirror or inverse of the other. In general, one needs case studies from both the $(0, 0)$ and $(1, 1)$ cells for necessary condition and constraint causal mechanisms, while that is not the case for sufficiency.

Avoid Overdetermination Guideline for Necessary Condition and Constraint Causal Mechanisms

The previous chapter discussed the overdetermination problem for sufficient conditions. Overdetermination in the sufficient condition setting is when alternative causal mechanisms are present (e.g., $Z_i = 1$). So what about overdetermination when Z is a necessary condition or constraint factor?

One way to think about this is via the metaphor of necessary parts for a machine to function (i.e., sufficiency). If one is interested in the role of a particular part as necessary then one can ask what kind of nonfunctioning machines, i.e., $Y = 0$, would be good choices. One would not choose machines that are completely broken down: ideally, one should choose a broken machine where all the other parts are functioning properly, i.e., all $Z_i = 1$. In this situation one can really see why X is necessary for Y.

For example, in Brady's influential analysis of the Florida 2000 elections (2004), there are multiple necessary conditions, aka hoop tests. If one were doing case studies of individual voters it would make no sense to select those who have failed on the first hoop test, for example, living in the wrong time zone. One would select only those that have survived the previous hoop tests, i.e., these are $Z_i = 1$ cases.

Soifer (2015) provides a nice example of how sequencing necessary conditions works in a causal chain analysis. He is looking at the creation of central state capacity in nineteenth-century Latin American countries. The first link in the causal chain is the broad and lasting consensus to build central state capacity. Some states—Colombia is his main example—decided instead to delegate to regional governments and institutions. The absence of central state capacity in Colombia was not because they failed to build a central state, but rather because they decided not to try. The second link in the causal chain—exclusion of local elites from the rank and file of the state administration—determined success among those that tried. To do within-case analysis of any given link in a temporal chain requires that the case has passed all the previous hoops.

One can generalize this into a principle that for exploring causal mechanisms for link Z_n in a temporal causal chain, one needs to choose cases that have $Z_i = 1$ for all $i < n$, i.e., all previous links. Often, permissive conditions are found in the first link and productive ones in the second. Some classics of comparative historical politics have this causal structure (see

Soifer 2012 for an extensive discussion with examples; see also the next chapter, "Interactive causal mechanisms").

Within the set-theoretic context, there are two kinds of confounders for necessary conditions: necessary condition confounders and sufficient condition confounders. The sufficient condition confounder for failure is less obvious. The failure of Y could be because *all* the sufficient conditions for Y are absent. The simplest form of multiple sufficient conditions is Z_1 OR Z_2 OR $Z_3 \to Y$. So cases in the $(0, 0)$ cell could arise because Z_1, Z_2, Z_3 are all absent.

Adding a necessary condition to the simple sufficiency models produces X AND $(Z_1$ OR $Z_2) \to Y$. If X is necessary but not sufficient for Y then X interacts with other factors to get over the sufficiency bar. So overdetermination of $Y = 0$ can occur (1) because X is absent (i.e., the necessary condition) or (2) because $(Z_1$ OR $Z_2)$ is absent.

This leads to the Avoid Overdetermination Guideline for necessary condition and constraint causal mechanisms:

Avoid Overdetermination Guideline: good $(0, 0)$ cases have $Z_i = 1$.

For sufficient conditions where we select on $Z = 0$, the confounders to avoid are the $Z = 1$ cases. For necessary condition causal mechanisms, we select $Z = 1$; the confounders to avoid are the $Z = 0$ cases.

More generally, the logic is that a good case is one where all the other factors suggest that Y should occur, but in fact it does not. This brings out why X is necessary. In contrast, if all factors Z_i point to failure, the role of X will be much harder to bring out.

Skocpol's *States and social revolution* illustrates this nicely. Her basic model is X_1 AND $X_2 \to Y$. She has six $Y = 0$ cases of no social revolution. If she is implicitly following the Avoid Overdetermination Guideline for necessary conditions then these would all be cases with $(X_1 = 1$ and $X_2 = 0)$ or $(X_1 = 0$ and $X_2 = 1)$. This is in fact what she did.

When put into a substantive context, it seems quite obvious that cases where both X_1 and X_2 are zero will be of little use for case studies. There are thousands of cases where the two variables are absent. Most of these probably have little value in exploring her necessary condition hypotheses. Skocpol's logic is that when one variable is present, social revolution might have occurred (what Mahoney and Goertz 2004 analyzed as the Possibility Principle).

Following the Avoid Overdetermination Guideline produces $Y = 0$ cases with a natural counterfactual: What would have happened if X had been present? This counterfactual is difficult to establish if other necessary conditions are also absent, or if there are few factors that push toward sufficiency. If all other conditions are favorable then the counterfactual is a core piece of the multimethod analysis for necessary conditions.

The best cases for causal mechanism analysis of necessary condition and constraint causal mechanisms involve choosing cases where all other variables Z_i point toward sufficiency. When those necessary conditions lie in a temporal causal chain, then one selects case studies that have passed each of the previous links.

The general problem with the $(0, 0)$ cell is that there are often a lot of cases in that cell to choose from. While it obviously depends on the theory and empirical setting, the Avoid Overdetermination Guideline will likely dramatically reduce the set of good $(0, 0)$ cases. Skocpol's *States and social revolutions* illustrates this: there are a huge number of cases where both X_1 and X_2 are absent, but relatively few where one is present. Including Z_i factors into the research design then facilitates the task of selecting appropriate cases for within-case causal mechanism analysis.

Constraint Causal Mechanisms

Constraint causal mechanisms were introduced in chapter 2. These must in some fashion include some *motivation* or *interest* variables for the constraints to act against. For example, a classic problem in the deterrence literature is interpreting successful deterrence. If there is no threat to begin with then deterrence is not a good explanation of the absence of war: nuclear deterrence does not explain why Canada has not attacked the USA.

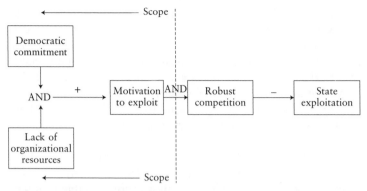

Figure 4.2: Constraint causal mechanisms: constraints on state exploitation. Source: based on Grzymała-Busse (2007).

International relations conflict scholars are familiar with Starr's influential opportunity and willingness framework. In that framework each concept—opportunity and willingness—is necessary and together jointly sufficient (see Cioffi-Revilla and Starr 2003 for a formal model). Opportunity is the constraint variable and willingness is the motivation or interest factor.

Grzymała-Busse illustrated nicely how constraints can be the focus of causal mechanism analysis. Figure 4.2 reproduces the figure from chapter 2. She is interested in robust competition as a constraint on state exploitation, so she takes the motivation to exploit as mostly given in her book. The left-hand side of figure 4.2 corresponds to the decision to build central state capacity in Soifer's model: if that is absent then the right-hand side of the figure becomes a moot point. Failure to build central state capacity is already explained by the first link in the causal chain.

The key point in all these constraint examples is that if you want to focus on the constraint factor X, one selects only cases where motivation Z is present. This is exactly what the Avoid Overdetermination Guideline says. As these and other examples illustrate, comparative-case-study scholars have often understood the logic of the Avoid Overdetermination Guideline in practice.

The principal–agent quote above (p. 96) illustrates the risks of *assuming* motivation to be present. Principal–agent models almost always assume that agents are motivated to act opportunistically. Depending on the setting, this may be a questionable empirical assumption for many agents. Brehm and Gates (1977) show that many government civil servants fail the assumption of the principal–agent model: they want to do their jobs well. Many employees of the US Forest Service want to manage and protect US forests.

In statistical research, motivation and constraint variables are often both included as variables in models. As such, there will be cases in the data set where the motivation variable is absent when the constraint is present. These are not good observations for causal mechanism analysis. For example, most statistical studies of nuclear deterrence include dyads where there is no motivation, e.g., they include cases like India–USA, or USA–Canada. Only a small percentage of the large-N observations are suitable for causal mechanism analysis, mostly enduring militarized rivalries.

If one does not want to look simultaneously at the constraint and motivation variables (the subject of the next chapter) then causal mechanism case studies must be selected where motivation or interest factors are present. These are the only ones that satisfy the Avoid Overdetermination Guideline.

Scope

Scope conditions are closely tied to necessary conditions. *By definition* all cases included have a value of 1 on the scope condition. So scope variables satisfy the definition of a necessary condition $Y = 1$ as a subset of $S = 1$. It is for this reason that Grzymała-Busse in figure 4.2 considers motivation factors as scope conditions; they all have value 1 on the motivation–scope variable.

Whether something is outside the model as a scope condition or inside the model as a motivation variable is a matter of emphasis on the part of the researcher. If the focus is really on constraints then it is quite reasonable to consider motivation as scope. Or, as illustrated by Soifer (2015), these can be separate aspects of some larger—book-length—analysis.

The disadvantage of the scope use of necessary conditions is that because they are used for case selection, they are almost always used as dichotomous variables. For pragmatic reasons, case selection is normally an all-or-nothing affair; it is hard to half include a case. If the constraint or motivation variable is included then naturally we can think of it as varying in strength.

As in most things there is a trade-off. Treating motivation–interest as a constant allows one to focus on the constraint causal mechanism. The trade-off is that treating motivation—e.g., grievance in civil war studies—as constant is often empirically problematic.

One can think of SUIN variables as scope-increasing variables (see Rohlfing and Schneider 2013; Ragin and Schneider 2012). In the context of necessary conditions, the counterexamples generate an *increase* in scope via substitutability. They are scope increasing because they convert counterexamples into consistent ones. The logic with sufficient conditions is usually to decrease scope to increase fit. For necessary conditions, one changes the model to increase fit and increase scope.

In summary, the logic of necessary conditions and the logic of sufficient conditions are opposite. For sufficient conditions, the falsifying examples generate a decrease in scope, while for necessary conditions they produce an increase in scope via substitutability.

Necessary versus Sufficient Condition Formulations

The methodology for necessary conditions differs in important respects from the standard, default, sufficient condition approach. One immediate problem lies in the fact that one can reformulate necessary condition hypotheses as sufficient condition ones and vice versa. To take a popular example, "nondemocracy of at least one state in a dyad is a necessary condition for war" versus "joint democracy is a sufficient condition for peace" (see table 4.1).

The research triad rests on the assumption that case study methodology is driven by concerns about causal mechanisms. Using the example of the democratic peace, one needs to go back to the main dependent variable under consideration: Is it "war" or "peace"? The dependent variable in virtually all large-N statistical studies is militarized interstate disputes (aka MIDs). This means that peace is conceptualized as "not-MID." This is problematic: for example, the USA and North Korea have not been at peace for most years since 1955, but rather they have been in a state of not-MID.

The sufficient condition version of the democratic peace—the most popular one—is problematic exactly because of the problematic conceptualization of peace as not-war. The sufficient condition version in practice is explaining "not-war" or "not-MID." This is a heterogeneous category. In many studies, "peace" includes (1) years of peace between the USA and Canada, (2) years of not-MID between serious rivals such as India–Pakistan or the USA–USSR, and (3) years of no interaction such as Chile–Cameroon (see Goertz, Diehl, and Balas 2016 for a discussion of the concept of peace). Arguably, the causal mechanisms producing these three "not-MID" zero cases are quite different. In contrast, the necessary condition version focuses on the dependent variable of militarized disputes and wars. Here, the concept and data for militarized disputes are clear.

The decision about how to formulate the democratic peace as a multimethod research agenda—whether to focus on sufficiency or necessity—then depends on whether one is developing a causal mechanism for peace or for war. If it is a causal mechanism for peace then the formulation "joint democracy is sufficient for peace" is the way to go. If it is a causal mechanism for war then the necessary condition version is appropriate. Given the way the democratic peace literature has worked, where the dependent variable is occurrence of militarized disputes, the appropriate formulation is the necessity of nondemocracy in the dyad.

Fuzzy Logic Necessary Conditions

We have already seen what a fuzzy logic necessary condition looks like above in Tsebelis's analysis of veto players, figure 4.1.

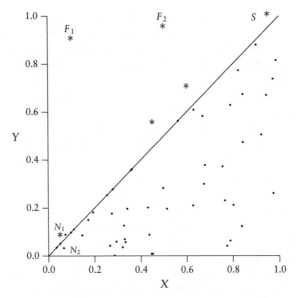

Figure 4.3: Fuzzy logic necessary conditions and case selection.

Figure 4.3 gives the same in the more standard fuzzy logic version.[4] A necessary condition in fuzzy logic is defined as $Y \leq X$. This equation generates points below the diagonal. Figure 4.3 illustrates the key issues involved in thinking about these issues, with some hypothetical data.

The data in figure 4.3 are pretty consistent with the necessary condition hypothesis, but not perfectly so. All cases above the diagonal are falsifying or counterexamples to the fuzzy logic necessary condition hypothesis. All cases on or below the diagonal are consistent with the hypothesis.

The fuzzy logic analogue of the $(0, 0)$ cell of a 2×2 table, e.g., table 4.1, are cases below the diagonal close to zero. The $(1, 1)$ cell is the causal mechanism cell for sufficiency and hence cases near $(1, 1)$ are good cases for sufficiency.[5]

---

[4] You can get the standard version of figure 4.1 by flipping the X-axis.

[5] If one overlays a 2×2 on figure 4.3 there are parts of the $(0, 0)$ cell that lie above the diagonal. This is a reminder that there are differences between fuzzy logic and Boolean algebra.

Following the logic of 2×2 tables, good constraint causal mechanism cases are located near $(0, 0)$ and below the diagonal. Cases such as F_1 in the upper-left quadrant are strong falsifying cases. The further above the diagonal, the stronger the counterexample.

The cases in the middle are gray because they are not good examples of X or Y. In general, one would not choose cases in the center of figure 4.3.[6] While some cases might be strongly falsifying, such as F_2, they might prove problematic for case studies because they are not good cases of X. As a general rule, good cases are at the corners of the fuzzy logic square. The notable exception is the $(1, 0)$ corner. As in the 2×2 table analysis, observations in this region have little to offer for causal mechanism analysis of necessary conditions.

With fuzzy logic one can see why cases near $(0, 0)$ are good for necessary condition analysis. If X is near 0 there is a strong prediction about Y. In contrast, if X is near 1 it is very easy to satisfy the necessary condition inequality. It is *impossible* to have a strongly falsifying case when X is near 1.

One is always concerned with trivialness (aka coverage) of necessary conditions, which means a scholar must analyze the sufficiency effect of X. This is one reason why cases near $(1, 1)$ are very useful, because they are the cases one would choose in the analysis of sufficient conditions.

Since one is looking for cases either near $(0, 0)$ for necessary conditions or near $(1, 1)$ for sufficient conditions, whether they are strictly below or above the line is of relatively minor importance. For example, there is not really a significant difference between points N_1 and N_2 in figure 4.3. There is a main rule for case selection:

Choose cases that are close—in terms of Euclidean distance—to $(0, 0)$ for the analysis of necessity and near $(1, 1)$ for the analysis of sufficiency.

I have illustrated this in figure 4.3 by putting the closest case to $(1, 1)$, point S, above the line. This falsifies the

---

[6] Standard QCA analysis removes cases exactly in the middle, i.e., equal to 0.50, from central parts of the methodology.

necessary condition hypothesis, but would be consistent with a sufficient condition hypothesis. There are no nearby cases that are consistent with the necessary condition hypothesis. The same logic means that we would prefer a case near $(0, 0)$ just above the diagonal to a more distant one that is consistent with the hypothesis.

In summary, the case selection for fuzzy logic necessary conditions in its general outline follows quite naturally—as it should—from the logic of 2×2 tables.

Cross-Case Analysis of Necessary Conditions

Multimethod research as defined in this volume means combining within-case analysis such as counterfactuals with cross-case analysis. Necessary conditions—and constraint causal mechanisms—raise a variety of questions about how to combine a case study of a necessary condition causal mechanism with some cross-case analysis. There are two quite distinct contexts within which a cross-case analysis can be conducted: (1) QCA and (2) statistical multimethod. To complicate things further, necessary conditions often involve selecting on the dependent variable, which is generally seen as bad practice (e.g., King, Keohane, and Verba 1994), but which is valid when analyzing necessary conditions. The subsections below treat each of these two contexts.

SELECTING ON THE DEPENDENT VARIABLE AND QCA

Perhaps the biggest lesson that comparative scholars took away from King, Keohane, and Verba was that selecting on the dependent variable was bad practice and essentially no good causal inference can come from such a research design. King, Keohane, and Verba were not alone: Geddes, in a frequently cited article (1990), attacked Skocpol on exactly this point.

A number of scholars in the years following the publication of King, Keohane, and Verba noted that selecting on the dependent variable was valid for necessary condition hypotheses. Not surprisingly, this became well known among QCA scholars (e.g., Ragin 2000), but others also made the same argument (e.g., Dion 1998; Braumoeller and Goertz 2000), and often used Skocpol as an example.

One way to describe a necessary condition is via the logical formula $Y \rightarrow X$. The $\rightarrow$ often is interpreted in a causal sense, but within set theory it means "if Y then X," which is noncausal in nature. For necessary conditions, this means that whenever we see $Y = 1$ then we should see $X = 1$, so Y is used to select cases.

Selecting on the dependent variable for necessary condition hypotheses is quite common, though not always recognized as such. For example, Milner's multiple case study work (1997) on international cooperation treaties illustrates this. She has a hypothesis: with multiple endorsers, the executive will have to obtain the endorsement of at least one endorser for ratification of an international cooperation treaty to occur. As Pahre notes, this hypothesis invokes a necessary condition:

> The final hypothesis, H4b, is more interesting on research design grounds. It states a necessary condition, since ratification will occur *only if* at least one endorser approves of the cooperation treaty. For this case, Milner's method of selecting on the dependent variable is entirely appropriate, although she needs only to examine cases of successful ratification to test her claim (Dion 1998). Her studies of TEU (Treaty on European Union) and NAFTA (North American Free Trade Agreement) are therefore entirely appropriate. (Pahre 2005, 135–36; emphasis is mine)

As part of standard QCA practice (e.g., see Schneider and Wagemann 2012) one searches for necessary conditions by focusing on the $Y = 1$ cases. The necessary condition analysis is part of the larger analysis exploring the sufficiency paths to $Y = 1$.

Since QCA focuses on the $Y = 1$ cases for analyses of sufficiency, it is natural to choose among those cases for looking at necessary condition causal mechanisms. The tension arises because the $(0, 0)$ cases do not form part of the QCA analysis of the sufficient paths to Y. This means that the best case studies of a necessary condition causal mechanism lie *outside* the data used to confirm that X is necessary for Y in cross-case analyses.

While some might find this problematic, it is a positive feature. Core to multimethod results is that case studies should complement the cross-case analyses. Using the cross-case analysis to see that a basic requirement of a necessary condition is fulfilled is different from analyzing the causal mechanism by which the absence of X causes the absence of Y.

STATISTICAL MULTIMETHOD

Treating necessary conditions in a statistical multimethod context is much more problematic than in set-theoretic and QCA analyses. Necessary conditions are logical and Boolean operations. Statistics, alternatively, is based on linear algebra. Boolean and linear algebras *are two different kinds of algebras with different defining properties.* Goertz and Mahoney (2012) give a more intuitive discussion of their fundamental differences, while Thiem, Baumgartner, and Bol (2016) give a mathematical treatment of them.

The most common practice using statistical methods is to treat the necessary condition just like any other variable. The key methodological and mathematical point is that whatever the results, *this is not a test of the necessary condition hypothesis.*

In a statistical model context one can think of negative parameter estimates as potential constraints and eventually necessary conditions. So in a linear, additive model context, when is a constraint so strong that it must be met? This occurs—in say a logit context—when the parameter estimate and the value of X are so large and negative that no possible combination of the other positive X values can overcome the negative effect of the constraint.

This happens most clearly when there is separation in the data. For example, when the dichotomous data fit perfectly a necessary condition—i.e., perfect separation—and when that variable is put into a logit analysis, the parameter estimate is basically negative infinity (Zorn 2005). Obviously, the weighted sum of all the positive factors will not outweigh negative infinity, so the model predicts failure when the necessary condition is absent (see Goertz 2012 for an extended discussion).

When there is no separation or near separation, it is hard to tell whether a given constraint is strong enough in a statistical analysis to merit being classified as a necessary condition. In part, this is because one needs a good model that, in particular, includes all the relevant positive factors to make sure the constraint overwhelms the sum of the positive effects.

Separation is a serious problem for statistical estimation. For example, the statistical software Stata typically just removes the offending necessary condition from the analysis. In addition, statistical methods cannot distinguish sufficient conditions from necessary conditions: you get the same parameter estimate in both cases.

However, from a multimethod point of view all the principles described above hold.

- One needs to verify via 2×2 table analysis that the potential necessary condition is not a sufficient condition. Statistical parameter estimates cannot do this.
- One does not use the estimated line (e.g., logit) to choose case studies.
- One can use the statistical estimates to decide which Z variables should have value 1.
- One should avoid overdetermination if there are multiple necessary conditions, though this is probably quite rare in statistical analyses.

Negative parameter estimates are in general not necessary conditions. One needs to look at scatterplots and 2×2 tables to determine how strong the constraint is and where it is. Strong constraints, such as veto players, are necessary conditions, but many substantively weak negative effects will not pass necessary condition tests.

The large-N data set will almost certainly include cases where the necessary condition is absent along with the positive sufficiency factors. These are overdetermined cases. Some of these are likely to be on-line cases for the statistically estimated model. However, these observations are not good candidates for causal mechanism case studies.

If X is a necessary condition then putting it in statistical models will almost always—trivial necessary conditions being the main exception—generate very significant results. In addition, omitted variables are generally not a big issue (surprisingly). The case of perfect separation illustrates this: one can add or subtract other independent variables and this will not (except in cases of massive collinearity) change the negative infinity estimate for the necessary condition.

My discussion in this subsection has generally assumed dichotomous variables. Once one has continuous independent and dependent variables, things get much more complicated. However, if the theory or causal mechanism is a constraint and if the data look like those in figures 4.3 and 4.1 then the basic requirements for a necessary condition causal mechanism are likely to be met. For example, Tsbelis's veto player data (1999) have the triangular form of his theory.[7]

To return to a previous example, the democratic peace started from the empirical finding that democracies do not fight wars with each other. However, almost none of the large-N statistical work uses war as the dependent variable. In part, this is the desire to see whether the basic empirical finding holds for lower severity conflicts. But if war–no war is the dependent variable, there is usually perfect separation (see table 4.1), and logit analyses become very problematic. What makes democratic peace analyses statistically possible is that there are militarized disputes between democracies—not many, not severe—but nonetheless there are some.

Research Practice

Research practice regarding necessary conditions and constraint causal mechanisms is complex and varied. In some areas, like comparative historical and formal models, it is quite common to find explicit necessary condition hypotheses. For example, Ragin (1987) was motivated to develop the "comparative method"

---

[7] See Goertz, Hak, and Dul (2013) for some specific suggestions regarding statistical methods for analyzing the strength of constraints with continuous variables; see also Dul's NCA (Necessary Condition Analysis) website http://www.erim.nl/nca for more, including R code.

by reading Barrington Moore and other comparative historical scholars. As we have seen here (e.g., Tsebelis) and as will be seen in chapter 6, necessary condition propositions are a normal part of game theory and formal modeling.

Necessary conditions appear naturally in case studies in the form of individual-case counterfactuals. Often the point of the case study is that the outcome would not have occurred without X. Hence there is a completely intimate relationship between necessary conditions, counterfactuals, and within-case causal inference. Fearon stresses the close connection between within-case causal inference and case studies:

> My impression, after reviewing literature for examples and evidence, is that counterfactuals are most likely to be found performing confirmatory work in case studies where the analyst is explicitly concerned with giving a causal explanation for some event or phenomenon. (Fearon 1991, 180)

One does necessary condition analysis at the cross-case level and then uses counterfactuals as a core methodology for within-case causal inference.

Stokke (2012) provides an excellent example of combining within-case counterfactuals with cross-case analysis methodologies in his analysis of the effectiveness of the Barents Sea fishing regime. It is a model to be followed by all doing multimethod work involving not only necessary conditions but any multimethod combination of cross-case analysis and counterfactuals for individual cases. For Stokke, core counterfactuals involve what the values of the various causal factors *would have been* in the absence of any fishing regime. He then uses the QCA analysis and model to evaluate the causal impact of various factors on the performance of the regime. He is able to evaluate how much impact any given factor had in any given year because (1) he has clear QCA models of success and failure and (2) he has the counterfactual values for the causal factors.

While Stokke does counterfactuals using QCA, the same principles apply if one uses a statistical model to evaluate the counterfactual impact of key causal variables (see appendix A). One needs the counterfactual values of the Xs and the estimated model to determine the counterfactual impact of any given variable in any given case. The basic methodological principles are no different from what Stokke did with QCA.

My systematic review of case-study and comparative-case-study research, as well as multimethod research, in major journals from 2006–15 revealed some, but not a large number, of explicit necessary condition hypotheses. Most often the scholar argues that X is a significant negative cause of Y but is not more specific than that. Probabilistic—and implicitly linear—negative hypotheses are quite common. These take the form "the larger X then the less likely Y is to occur or the lower the level of Y."

At the same time, constraint causal mechanism hypotheses are common. Any proposed negative relationship is a potential constraint causal mechanism. If the hypothesized constraint is very strong then one might interpret it in terms of the methodology of necessary conditions described in this chapter.

While the theory, hypothesis, or causal mechanism might be a constraint, there is a tendency to treat it methodologically as a sufficient condition. If the scholar is thinking in terms of negative parameters in a statistical model then the tendency is to treat the necessary condition as if it were a sufficient condition. This runs the risk of major research design errors because the logics of the two—while similar on some points—have different properties. Notably, the way Z variables are treated is exactly the opposite.

Necessary conditions have interesting theoretical and methodological characteristics. If one applies the default procedures—fine for sufficient conditions and positive causal mechanisms—one should not be surprised that there are issues. One can see this in the literature on selecting on the dependent variable, where following the default King, Keohane, and Verba advice is not useful. Rather, one needs to be very aware of the issues of case selection, and more generally the methodology for testing necessary condition and constraint hypotheses.

Conclusion

One paradox of necessary condition causal mechanisms is that their logic pushes the scholar to do case studies from the $(0, 0)$ cell. However, in practice this is relatively rare. This mismatch might arise for various reasons. The $(1, 1)$ cell is such a focal point that it drives everything. Scholars might not recognize the differences between a sufficient condition causal mechanism and a necessary condition one. They are both "causes" and sufficiency logic is applied by default.

Necessary condition causal mechanism methodology has some important differences from the methodology for sufficient conditions: (1) Equifinality plays a different role in the sufficient condition methodology from that in the necessary condition one. (2) The question of the trivialness, or conversely the importance, of a necessary condition plays a central role; the trivialness of a sufficient condition is rarely a concern. (3) The rankings and roles of the cells of the 2×2 table are somewhat parallel, but there are some notable differences. In particular, the $(0, 0)$ and $(1, 1)$ cells in the necessary condition analysis have high priority, while only the $(1, 1)$ cell has priority in the sufficient condition analysis.

While well beyond the scope of this chapter or book, necessary condition and constraint causal mechanisms raise some tricky questions about causation and the explanation of nonevents. Sometimes $Y = 0$ is well defined. At other times $Y = 0$ is very expansive and inclusive and doing case studies can be problematic.

On the explanatory side, often we follow the moral philosophy that sins of commission are worse than sins of omission (this is often true in legal systems). Necessary conditions are by definition about the absence of X so they can have this omission character.

While statistical models are virtually always symmetric, the existence of necessary condition and constraint causal mechanisms suggests that causal asymmetry is a significant methodological and theoretical issue. QCA embraces causal asymmetry in various ways; for example, the models for explaining failure might be different from those explaining success. The methodology for necessary condition and constraint analysis has its own character and it is not just a mirror image of the sufficient condition methodology.

CHAPTER 5

Interactive Causal Mechanisms

Introduction

This volume argues that in the research triad, causal mechanisms, cross-case analyses, and case studies go hand in hand. Chapter 2 considered causal complexity in terms of causal mechanisms. Chapter 3 discussed causal complexity in terms of alternative paths to the outcome, i.e., equifinality. We saw in the previous chapter that necessary conditions and constraint causal mechanisms imply interaction models.

Virtually nothing in the statistical multimethod or case study literatures analyzes case studies in the context of an interaction-term hypothesis. Usual suspects like Gerring (2007) or Lieberman (2005) either speak of individual variables X or the statistical model as a whole. Typical practice is to consider $(X_1 * X_2)$ as a single variable and apply the univariate procedures discussed in chapter 3. This is an incomplete analysis of the mechanism.

This chapter focuses on causal mechanisms that have two major component parts, X_1 and X_2, which work together to produce Y. The key assumption in the context of this chapter is that X_2 is *not* a control variable, contending theory, or scope variable. Instead, $(X_1 * X_2)$ denotes a causal mechanism that has two different core parts. The theory or causal mechanism is an explanation of how X_1 and X_2 work together to produce Y.

Univariate hypotheses are without a doubt the dominant form in quantitative political science and sociology, but hypotheses utilizing interaction terms are not uncommon (Brambor, Clark, and Golder 2006). While it is harder to tell definitively in qualitative studies, interaction-term hypotheses are probably more common than in statistical studies—this is certainly true for comparative historical research.

It is critical for both statistical and multiple case study research to work out explicit interaction-term case study methodology. By default, QCA generates logical AND results, thereby incorporating interaction terms into its framework. QCA has interaction analyses at its core: *it searches for causal combinations.* In contrast, interaction terms are optional in statistical analyses, have significant methodological challenges, and are hard to interpret. For example, three-way interactions are extremely rare in statistical analyses, but extremely common in QCA results. Given the difficulty of interpreting—particularly a continuous—three-way statistical interaction term, it is not surprising that they are very rare.

What one means by "interaction" models varies from linear algebra (i.e., statistics) to Boolean algebra (i.e., QCA). There are major differences between the set-theoretic AND and the multiplication "$*$" in statistical models. The simplest standard models look like

$$X_1 \text{ AND } X_2 \longrightarrow Y, \tag{5.1}$$

$$Y = \beta_0 + \beta_1 X_1 + \beta_2 X_2 + \beta_3 (X_1 * X_2) + \epsilon. \tag{5.2}$$

There are many differences between these two equations (see Goertz and Mahoney 2012 and especially Thiem, Baumgartner, and Bol 2016). For example, in equation (5.1) there is no intercept, along with the obvious absence of the error term ϵ. In equation (5.1), X_1 and X_2 together are sufficient for producing Y. That is certainly not always the case for equation (5.2). Furthermore, notational ambiguities between set-theoretic and statistical approaches can lead to confusion about how to interpret a notion like $(X_1 * X_2)$. As such, to refer to set-theoretic interaction terms I use X_1 AND X_2, for a multiplicative interaction term I use $X_1 * X_2$.

The core of this chapter focuses on the set-theoretic (QCA) approach to case studies and multimethod work. I focus my attention mostly on equation (5.1), but do consider some issues regarding the linear model with interaction term. There are analogies and similarities between the two and some of the same issues arise.

The set-theoretic interaction-term model X_1 AND $X_2 \rightarrow Y$ is in fact composed of three separate hypotheses:

1. X_1 is necessary for Y.
2. X_2 is necessary for Y.
3. X_1 AND X_2 is sufficient for Y.

Since the set-theoretic model contains necessary and sufficient condition hypotheses, the reader should be familiar with the preceding chapters (i.e., one should have hopscotched the previous two chapters before arriving here).

The statistical model—equation (5.1)—also has three core hypotheses:

1. X_1 has a significantly positive or negative causal effect on Y.
2. X_2 has a significantly positive or negative causal effect on Y.
3. $X_1 * X_2$ has a significantly positive or negative causal effect on Y.

Here the signs of all the terms can be all possible combinations of positive and negative. The statistical interpretation of continuous interaction terms is somewhat complex and the effects cannot only be positive or negative, but can change sign and/or significance depending on the range of X_i. All this makes it is very difficult to treat statistical interaction terms in the context of this chapter. As such I limit my discussion to dichotomous variables in the statistical model and assume the simple—but most common—case, which parallels QCA: X_i have a positive effect on the probability of Y and the interaction term also has a positive effect.

The multiplicative interaction term is zero—assuming dichotomous variables—except when $X_1 = 1$ and $X_2 = 1$. In contrast, QCA will consider all four possible interaction terms, ($X_1 = 0$ AND $X_2 = 0$), ($X_1 = 0$ AND $X_2 = 1$), ($X_1 = 1$ AND $X_2 = 0$), and ($X_1 = 1$ AND $X_2 = 1$). Many of these are *not* considered interaction terms in the linear algebra model. For example, for ($X_1 = 1$ AND $X_2 = 0$), equation (5.2) above becomes $Y = \beta_0 + \beta_1 X_1$. There are major differences between statistical models and set-theoretic ones; what "interaction term" means differs significantly between the two.

While there are fundamental mathematical differences between set-theoretic and linear algebra interaction models, there is one key parallel: each has three basic hypotheses that should be connected in multimethod research to case studies. In both models one needs to look at the "main effects," which are the individual terms. The set-theoretic model is quite different because X_1 and X_2 are necessary conditions, which they generally are not in the statistical model. Nevertheless, the basic parallel of three hypotheses makes some of the methodological issues analogous.

Causal interpretation issues come out, yet again, when interpreting causal mechanism figures. Take, for example, Slater's theory of counterrevolutionary trajectories, figure 2.8. One possible interpretation of part of that figure is (leftist AND urban AND not-communal) → fragmentation. Some of the arrows become AND and the last arrow becomes "is sufficient."

Waldner's causal chain figure of Wood's analysis, figure 2.2, is explicit that each node has value 1 (i.e., is "true") and one could apply the interpretation of → as a statistical interaction term between each box. Unlike Slater, whose has interaction terms including a mix of 0s and 1s, Waldner–Wood has all 1s, which makes it fit more easily within a statistical modeling context. Comparing this figure with Slater's, one notices that it is not specified what happens when a box is "not-true." Presumably the process stops and the outcome does not occur. This would lead to an interaction-term interpretation where if one variable is 0 then the whole interaction term is 0. However, in a statistical context one would still have the main effects contributing to increasing likelihood of the outcome.

In short, causal mechanism figures often imply specific interactions. The "→" can be interpreted as an interaction term between the two factors connected by the arrow. However, viewing → as an AND or as a "*" is an *interpretation*, though not necessarily the only one or necessarily the author's. The key point is that causal mechanism figures can easily be interpreted as interaction-term models.

Statistical Models: Multiplicative Interaction Terms

This section explores "simple causal complexity" in statistical models, which is a multiplicative interaction term. Additive models are not causally complex. While the statistical model might have dozens of variables, often the emphasis is on the effect of just one. Although one could define causal complexity in terms of the number variables, here it means a causal mechanism with interactions between variables: models that are linear in the link function are not complex as understood here.

When the hypothesis and theory in question involves two (or more) core theoretical variables, an immediate question (or at least it should be an immediate question) is which of the following models is being used:

$$Y = \beta_0 + \beta_1 X_1 + \beta_2 X_2 + \epsilon, \tag{5.3}$$

$$Y = \beta_0 + \beta_1 X_1 + \beta_2 X_2 + \beta_3 X_1 * X_2 + \epsilon. \tag{5.4}$$

When there are statistical analyses one can see whether the author includes an interaction term. While useful, it is not in fact conclusive, as theory and statistical models do not always match. If one were to read just the theory and hypotheses sections, one might expect to see interaction terms in the statistical model which are not there. Sometimes the author, e.g., Norris (2012), is quite explicit about the additive and noninteractive character of the hypotheses, but one wonders nevertheless about interaction terms.

In short, in studies with two or more core causal factors, it is sometimes not clear whether the variables interact and thus whether equation (5.3) or equation (5.4) applies. This is critical to multimethod work since how one does the case studies varies significantly between the two equations.

Take for example Ansell and Samuels's (2014) look at economic inequality and its relationship to democracy. Their analysis follows in the long tradition of the influence of economic factors on democracy. They have two core causal factors, income inequality (from rising middle classes and economic growth) and land-holding inequality, which have significant impacts on the likelihood of democratization. Economic development results in a larger middle class. It also produces more income inequality (at least in the early stages of economic development). Moore (1966) famously stressed the importance of the bourgeoisie for

128 • Chapter 5

TABLE 5.1
Income and land inequality: probability of democratization

	Low land inequality	High land inequality
Low income inequality	Moderate	Low
High income inequality	High	Moderate

Source: based on Ansell and Samuels (2014, table 1.1a).

democracy. High levels of land inequality, e.g., Prussian Junkers, mean powerful economic groups opposed to democracy.

Table 5.1 reproduces their basic hypotheses. A natural question is whether there is an interaction between these two forms of inequality or whether it is a straight additive model. Just looking at table 5.1 suggests that the additive model is the correct interpretation. If X_1 or X_2 were necessary conditions then the "moderate" cells would have "low probability." Instead, the presence of X_1 or X_2 increases the probability of democratization to "moderate" levels.

The interaction term here means an additional increase in the probability of democracy beyond the additive effect. To translate that into English would require terms like "virtually certain" or "extremely high" to describe the "high" cell.

Since Ansell and Samuels mostly use statistical analyses, one can check them to see whether there are interaction terms. In the statistical analyses (Ansell and Samuels 2014, chapter 5) there are no interaction terms in the model. So one can conclude on multiple grounds (including close inspection of the text) that they see no interaction between the two.[1]

When working with additive causal mechanisms, one needs little additional methodology beyond that of chapter 3 to think about causal mechanism case studies. Table 5.2 reproduces

[1] One could and should also examine the formal model. Since they use differential calculus modeling it is almost certain that there are interactive effects. This is because the partial derivatives involving the core causal factors are not constant, which they would be in an additive model.

TABLE 5.2

Income and land inequality: example cases

	Low land inequality	High land inequality
Low income inequality	Korea 1970	Germany–1900, China–1880
High income inequality	UK–1900, Sweden–1900, China–2010	Brazil–1985

Source: based on Ansell and Samuels (2014, table 1.1b).

Ansell and Samuels's "example" cases. Following the logic of chapter 3, one would explore the causal impact of each of the forms of inequality separately, choosing cases where the other form is absent, applying the Avoid Overdetermination Guideline.

However, their main case study—the United Kingdom—is one where both causal factors are present. The cases where one causal factor is present and the other is absent get minimal, one-page, case studies. If they had hypothesized an interaction effect then the UK case study would have been relevant. Looking just at the case study selection, one would conclude that there is an interaction effect being proposed.

There are three core hypotheses in equation (5.4), indicated by three βs. This normally then would require at least three case studies to explore each of these hypotheses. As discussed in appendix A, there is often a disconnect between the statistical model and the case studies. For Ansell and Samuels, ambiguity arises because the case study is an $X_1 * X_2$ case, which is exactly the case one would choose if the theory included an interaction term.

In summary, for statistical multimethod research it is important to be clear about whether one is including the interaction term or not. If there are statistical analyses with an interaction term then it is normally unambiguous. However, when there is no interaction term it is not so clear; the verbal formulation of the hypothesis and theory might strongly suggest one.

Good statistical multimethod research connects clearly the statistical model with the case studies. If there are two (or more) core theoretical variables then one should ask about interaction effects. If there is no theoretical reason why there should be an interaction then that needs discussion. The case studies then need to map onto the parts of the additive or interactive causal mechanism. The point of the $X_1 * X_2$ case study is *to explore how X_1 and X_2 interact, not the main effects of X_1 and X_2*.

Contributing Factor Model

Ansell and Samuels illustrate the common additive, linear model that dominates statistical analyses. It is useful to see the analogue of that within the set-theoretic world, which I call the contributing factor model, where the "+" in linear algebra becomes a set-theoretic OR.

While not discussed in the QCA literature, one can have a pure sufficiency model, one with no necessary conditions at all, i.e., no INUS causes and no necessary conditions in general. This is the direct parallel in the causal sphere of the family resemblance model in building concepts (Goertz 2005). By definition, family resemblance is a sufficiency, no necessary condition setup. For example, a simple family resemblance model is

$$((X_1 \text{ OR } X_2 \text{ OR } X_3) \geq 2) \to Y, \quad X_i \in [0, 1]. \quad (5.5)$$

The easiest way to implement the OR is by interpreting it as addition. While QCA uses the maximum for the OR, there are variants such as equation (5.5) that interpret OR using addition. This is analogous to a logit model, where the Y is predicted to occur if the weighted (by β) sum of the independent variables is greater than 0.50.

The X_i in equation (5.5) are "contributing factors": they contribute to sufficiency for Y, but typically they are neither necessary nor sufficient alone to produce Y. This is exactly the family resemblance concept model applied to causal equations. For dichotomous variables it is the "m-of-n" rule for objects to belong to conceptual sets; in equation (5.5) it is the 2 out of 3 rule.

In short, one should have two possible models in mind when thinking about the sufficiency effect of X_i:

INUS : $\qquad\qquad\qquad\qquad\qquad\qquad$ X_1 AND $X_2 \rightarrow Y$,

Contributing factor, family resemblance : $\quad$ (X_1 OR X_2 OR X_3) $\rightarrow Y$.

One can get an intuition about how the contributing factor model might appear in practice by considering X_i variables, i.e., (X_1, X_2, X_3). If almost all of the $(1, 1, 0)$, $(1, 0, 1)$, and $(0, 1, 1)$ cases are $Y = 1$ cases then the contributing factor model is likely generating the results. Notice that there are no necessary conditions, since Y occurs when $X_i = 0$. The results would be even stronger if the rows $(0, 0, 1)$, $(0, 1, 0)$, and $(1, 0, 0)$ were cases where Y did not occur. This would indicate that the sufficiency effect of X_i individually is not enough to produce Y on its own and that other contributing causes need to be present.

So what does all of this have to do with case studies and multimethod research? If our causal mechanism has two core components, X_1 and X_2, we need to be clear about how these work together to produce Y. The standard QCA model with necessary conditions has different implications for case study selection than the contributing factor model does. It is not surprising that the multimethod logic differs between a model with necessary conditions and another model without them. In both cases we want to analyze the sufficiency effect of X_i, but that is going to imply different choices because in one case the causal mechanism includes AND and in the other it has an OR.

Typological Theories

Two-way and N-way tables are common tools for presenting theories with multiple independent variables. Table 5.3 illustrates this from the well-known Downing study about the causes of early modern autocratic and democratic regimes. As with table 5.1, we have all of the four possible combinations of the independent variables and what Downing's theory says should occur.

TABLE 5.3
Interaction theories: Downing's theory of absolutism and constitutionalism

	High levels of warfare	
	Domestic economy necessary	Other finance available
Military–bureaucratic absolutism	Prussia, France	
Preservation for constitutionalism	Poland, Dutch Republic, Sweden	England (1688–1713)

	Low levels of warfare	
	Domestic economy necessary	Other finance available
Military–bureaucratic absolutism		
Preservation for constitutionalism		England (–1648)

Source: based on Møller and Skanning (2015, table 1).

Downing (1992) explains why some European countries became instances of what he terms "military–bureaucratic absolutism," whereas medieval constitutionalism survived in others following the onset of the sixteenth-century military revolution. To explain the different evolutions, Downing argues that the intensity of warfare after the military revolution was critical. Only high levels of warfare required the absolutist turn, as intense geopolitical pressure required significant financial resources. Some states, e.g., Netherlands, were able to use outside financing. Others, such as France, had to mobilize domestic taxation to pay for war. Military–bureaucratic absolutism was the requisite response only if warfare had to be financed by mobilizing the domestic economy.

Many famous and frequently discussed comparative historical works involve interactions between two or more variables. Here are a few examples of the core interaction hypotheses, starting with Downing. I do not go into detail because they are well-known examples, in both the substantive and methodological literatures:

- Downing (1992). High levels of warfare AND domestic war financing only is sufficient for the rise of a military-absolutist state.
- Ertman (1997). Party-centered politics before World War I AND strong civil society is sufficient for interwar democratic stability.
- Luebbert (1991). Liberal hegemony pre–World War I AND not red–green alliance is sufficient for liberal democracy. Not liberal hegemony AND not red–green alliance is sufficient for fascism.
- Skocpol (1979). State breakdown AND peasant revolt is sufficient for social revolution.

There are two interrelated issues in interpreting tables such as table 5.3. First, is there an interaction between the two core independent variables? Second, should the table be interpreted in set-theoretic terms of necessary and sufficient conditions?

If the answer to the second question is yes, the set-theoretic interpretation is correct, then the answer to the first must be yes as well, i.e., there must be an interaction. The Ansell and Samuels example illustrates that one can (1) reject the interaction term and (2) reject the set-theoretic interpretation of the variables and their relationships.

So how should one interpret table 5.3 and similar tables that could be made for the classics of comparative historical research? My answer, not surprisingly, is a two cultures one. Because we are talking about comparative historical analysis, the default interpretation is the set-theoretic approach, where each is necessary and together they are jointly sufficient (see Mahoney 2003).

Tables such as 5.1 and 5.3 thus are ambiguous and require additional interpretation. In comparative historical studies (see Møller and Skaaning 2015 for a nice discussion of many examples) these typologies receive the set-theoretic interpretation. In a statistical context there is no clear default when the theory has two or three core independent variables.

Theories expressed in tables such as 5.3 often form theoretical typologies, where the typology is all possible combinations of the independent variables. These typologies, however, require additional interpretation as to their causal structure. One can see the causal ambiguity of typological theories by asking about how one would conduct a causal counterfactual analysis. For example, in the critical (1, 1, 1) cell, where both causes and the outcome are present, we cannot formulate counterfactuals, e.g., for process tracing, without making further assumptions about the basic causal model.

George and Bennett (2005) presented "typological theories" as a tool for thinking about causal complexity (see also Elman 2005):

> We define a typological theory as a theory that specifies independent variables, delineates them into the categories for which the researcher will measure the cases and their outcomes, and provides not only hypotheses on how these variables operate individually, but also contingent generalizations on how and under what conditions they behave in specified conjunctions or configurations to produce effects on specialized dependent variables. We call specialized conjunctions or configurations of the variables "types." A fully specified typological theory provides hypotheses on all of the mathematically possible types relating to a phenomenon, or on the full "property space," to use Lazarsfeld's term. (George and Bennett 2005, 235)

"Conjunctions" are the interactions of *all* the independent variables. For each type—i.e., each cell in the table of all possible interaction terms—the typological theory predicts an outcome.

Typological theories require interpretation. It is clear that according to George and Bennett we do have interaction terms. In a statistical context what we *do not* have are (1) main effects and (2) lower-level interaction terms. So equation (5.4) is a poor interpretation of the structure of typological theories.

Typological theories also differ significantly from QCA. Typical QCA solutions (1) do not involve interactions of all the variables and (2) only contain a small number of combinations or configurations in the final solutions. The purpose of QCA is to use Boolean algorithms to reduce the complexity of all the combinations and the number of terms in each type or path.

It is not clear in discussions of typological theories whether they should be interpreted as necessary and sufficient conditions.

George and Bennett do not often use set-theoretic terminology. QCA is treated in a chapter that surveys a number of *other* qualitative methods. Møller and Skaaning treat typological theories as separate, though related, to QCA:

> Typological theory can in many respects be seen as a simpler version of Qualitative Comparative Analysis (QCA). However, there are also some important differences between the two methods. First, although typological theory includes a number of strategies of reduction originally devised by Lazarsfeld (Lazarsfeld and Barton 1951; see also Elman 2005), it does not employ the QCA manipulation tools, including Boolean minimization and the formalized use of logical remainders (i.e., unobserved configurations). Second, as opposed to QCA, explanatory typologies can simultaneously operate with more than one positive outcome. (Møller and Skaaning 2015, 24–25)

In contrast, Beach and Rohlfing (2015) tread a middle ground: "It is legitimate to focus on QCA, but this ignores TT [typological theory] *as another set-theoretic cross-case technique* that has recently received increasing attention" (Beach and Rohlfing 2015, 3; pre-publication, emphasis is mine). While it is quite possible to interpret typological theories as set theoretic, it is not a given.

Chapter 2 raised the issue of overlap between causal mechanisms. Each row of a typological theory table constitutes typically a separate causal mechanism, composed of differing values of the independent variables. So while Slater's causal mechanism, figure 2.8, contains no overlap between causal mechanisms, typological theories have massive overlap. Normally, each factor when equal to 1 appears in half the paths to success and half the paths to failure.

Whether a set of causal mechanisms has a little or a lot of overlap is something that must be determined on theoretical grounds (or in the case of QCA by the minimization algorithm). One cannot say a priori that high or low overlap is good. However the amount and the nature of the overlap do have important methodological implications.

In short, theoretical typologies and N-way tables require more specification. If the theory has more than two core causal variables, scholars will have to make decisions about how to combine them and which ones to combine (if there are more than two). In linear algebra they can be combined via addition or multiplication. In Boolean algebra they are combined via logical ANDs and ORs. It should be obvious that there are other ways one could combine a given number of independent variables (e.g., game theory, the topic of chapter 6).

For the rest of this chapter I focus on the set-theoretic approach to interaction terms. Many of the conclusions apply to the multiplicative interaction term in statistical models, but I shall not explore those much.

Case Selection: X_1 AND $X_2 \to Y$ Model

One might propose that the case selection and multimethod methodology for an interaction term X_1 AND X_2 is not fundamentally different from for a single variable, for convenience denoted I (defined as X_1 AND X_2 or $X_1 * X_2$ for statistical models). Hence, one need but apply the methodology developed in chapter 3. So while the theory might discuss the role played by X_1 and X_2 in producing Y, for methodological purposes one just uses the combined variable I. In practice this is what most people do in multimethod work. The case studies are $(1, 1)$ cases, where X is now the combined term I. However, this completely ignores the hypotheses embedded in the interaction term and as such is not adequate for a thorough examination of the causal mechanism.

Instead of the 2×2 tables of chapters 3 and 4 we now have eight cells (see table 5.4), where each cell is a different configuration of X_1, X_2, and Y. With the X_1 AND $X_2 \to Y$ model we have minimally three core hypotheses, two where X_i is necessary for Y and one where X_1 and X_2 together are sufficient for Y.

Not surprisingly, the $(1, 1, 1)$ cell is the focus of attention. It corresponds to the causal mechanism for sufficient conditions. In practice, when scholars do only one case study this is where they will go. The logic of this cell forms the default for most applied research, which treats X_1 AND X_2 as a single variable I.

Embedded in the X_1 AND $X_2 \to Y$ model are two necessary condition hypotheses. Hence, the principles discussed in the preceding chapter apply. The causal mechanism cases for

TABLE 5.4
Case selection possibilities: X_1 AND $X_2 \rightarrow Y$ model

X_1	X_2	Y
1	1	1
1	0	1
0	1	1
0	0	1
1	1	0
1	0	0
0	1	0
0	0	0

the necessary conditions are the $(1, 0, 0)$ and $(0, 1, 0)$ cells. The $(1, 0, 0)$ cell is the causal mechanism for the hypothesis that X_2 is necessary for Y. The $(0, 1, 0)$ is the causal mechanism cell for the "X_1 is necessary" hypothesis. Necessary conditions are most clearly investigated in cases of failure, i.e., $Y = 0$. Following the Avoid Overdetermination Guideline for necessary conditions means that any other necessary conditions should have value 1.

In short, the causal mechanism cells are $(1, 1, 1)$, $(1, 0, 0)$, and $(0, 1, 0)$.

As with the 2×2 tables we have falsifying cells. For necessary conditions, these are cells $(1, 0, 1)$ and $(0, 1, 1)$. In these situations Y occurs without X_i.

The falsifying cell for sufficiency is $(1, 1, 0)$. Here both causal variables are present and the outcome does not occur.

The clearest case for exploring equifinality lies in the $(0, 0, 1)$ cell. Here the outcome occurs when none of the causal factors are present. There must then be at least one other path to Y.

The other $Y = 0$ cells are ambiguous and do not directly address the three core hypotheses. For example, the $(1, 0, 0)$ cell means that X_1 is not sufficient for Y, but that was not the original hypothesis to begin with. The same logic applies to the $(0, 1, 0)$ cell.

Not surprisingly, the $(0, 0, 0)$ cell is of little use. It is not useful for sufficiency and is overdetermined for the necessary conditions X_1 and X_2.

In summary, for the X_1 AND $X_2 \rightarrow Y$ model, one applies the basic principles of case selection for sufficient conditions and necessary conditions.

Using Within-Case Variation to Analyze Interactive Models

A common reflex in comparative case studies is to contrast cases on the key variable of interest. With an interactive theory, i.e., X_1 AND $X_2 \rightarrow Y$ and all the implied hypotheses, this makes doing everything cross-case more complicated.

A very attractive option is to leverage over-time variation within cases. Aktürk (2011) provides a very nice example of this. His basic model is X_1 AND X_2 AND $X_3 \rightarrow Y$ and he is very explicit that it is a set-theoretic model:

> I argue that if $[X_1]$ "counterelites" representing constituencies with ethnically specific grievances come to power $[X_2]$ equipped with a "new discourse" on ethnicity and nationality and $[X_3]$ garner a "hegemonic majority," they can change state policies on ethnicity. These three factors are separately necessary and jointly sufficient for change. (Aktürk 2011, 117)

> Whenever these three factors were aligned, the ethnicity regime was changed. If any one of these factors was missing, change did not occur, and we witnessed continuity. (Aktürk 2011, 134)

He chooses three cases—USSR-Russia, Germany, and Turkey—and tracks the changes in these three variables over time. The basic logic is very clear: only when the three variables are present at the same time does change occur. His case studies argue that this happened in these three countries.

Absolutely critical to the analysis of the X_1 AND $X_2 \rightarrow Y$ model is what happens in the $(1, 0)$ or $(0, 1)$ cases. Because Aktürk is tracking variables over time, much of the analysis deals with what is not happening when some necessary condition factor is absent.

Central in the set-theoretic approach is the sufficiency effect of the individual factors. Conversely, this means reacting to claims that a given variable is trivial or relatively unimportant. Aktürk uses his process tracing analysis to explore this kind of objection. With a social constructivist variable like "new discourse on ethnicity," some might claim that this factor is doing little work, while the realist variable "hegemonic majority" is doing all the heavy lifting (see Goertz and Levy 2007 for many examples of this debate within a case study setting):

> I suggest that "being in power" (that is, being in government) and wanting to change state policies on ethnicity are not enough to change them. This is demonstrated more than once in different case studies. The SPD-FDP coalition government that ruled Germany for thirteen years (1969–82) had every reason to change the citizenship law or at least rapidly naturalize immigrants but was successfully prevented from doing so by the CDU-CSU opposition and the then-dominant discourse. (Aktürk 2011, 136–37)

So while the power variable was equal to 1 for long periods, the discourse variable was 0. The discourse factor is important since it prevented change from occurring for many years.

While Aktürk does three case studies, all of the causal arguments work via within-case causal inference. The three case studies are there to pile up some evidence that the causal mechanism works in a variety of situations. None of the causal inference rests on cross-case comparisons.

Longitudinal tracking is a natural way to go. John Kingdon did the same thing in his extremely influential book *Agendas, alternatives, and public policies*. He made the argument that there were three streams (X variables) and that when they intersected, an item got onto the agenda. He tracked over-time variation in various policy domains, such as health and education, to make this claim. So while it remains completely possible to do a cross-case comparison for the empirical analysis of the X_1 AND $X_2 \to Y$ model, process tracing within-case variation over time often makes more sense.

The Relative Importance of X_1 versus X_2

Since the researcher does not consider X_1 and X_2 as a unified variable in the X_1 AND $X_2 \to Y$ model, that means that X_1 and

X_2 are separate and important enough to be taken into account individually. If the final model is generated by QCA software, there is usually no sense in which X_1 or X_2 is more important. However, if one starts from the theoretical direction, it is quite likely that the theorist does not treat them as equal. In fact, the opposite is more commonly the case: scholars treat one variable as more important than the other.

Mansfield and Snyder (2005; see chapter 7 for more discussion) provide a nice example of this. In the statistical analysis they have an interaction term between "weak institutions" and "democratization." There is no doubt that democratization is what interests them the most. In a similar fashion, most people focused on Skocpol's state breakdown factor at the expense of the peasant revolt necessary condition.

There are two senses in which X_1 and X_2 can vary in relative causal strength in the X_1 AND $X_2 \rightarrow Y$ model: one is cross case while the other is within case. The basic cross-case rule is that the factor that occurs *least* frequently is more important (see Mahoney and Goertz 2004, as well as Goertz and Levy 2007 for extensive discussions). For example, Mahoney and I conclude that for Skocpol it is in fact the peasant revolt variable that is empirically more important.

Table 5.5 gives a hypothetical scenario where X_2 is significantly more important in the cross-case sense than X_1. These data are quite close to Mahoney and my analysis of Skocpol's *States and social revolutions* (see table 5.6). There are three positive outcomes and seven negative ones. Here, while both are necessary (the data fit perfectly the X_1 AND $X_2 \rightarrow Y$ model), X_2 is clearly more important than X_1 because $X_2 = 1$ occurs less frequently than $X_1 = 1$.

Table 5.5 is cross-case evidence for the relative importance of X_2 over X_1. When conducting *within*-case causal analysis, this hypothesis needs to be directly addressed: Does the within-case analysis support the cross-case evidence?

There is a *within-case* sense of relative importance that has not received the attention it deserves in the case study or multimethod literature. One need but think about what is more important in determining the final value for Y in the necessary condition model X_1 AND $X_2 \rightarrow Y$. The rule is to take the

TABLE 5.5
Relative importance of X_1 versus X_2, X_1 AND $X_2 \rightarrow Y$ model, hypothetical data

X_1	X_2	Y
1	1	1
1	1	1
1	1	1
1	0	0
1	0	0
1	0	0
1	0	0
1	0	0
0	1	0
0	0	0

Source: Each row is a case.

minimum of X_1 and X_2. This means that in each individual case it is the smallest value that is most important.

One can immediately contrast this with the contributing factor model, where it is the largest value that has the most importance.[2] This can be seen for the standard rule for aggregating the logical OR, which is the maximum.

Necessary conditions are most useful in explaining the nonoccurrence of Y. This matches the fact that the minimum is used when there are multiple necessary conditions (e.g., with fuzzy logic variables). A low value on just one X_i means that Y should take on a low value, and at the extreme when an $X_i = 0$ then Y must also be 0.

Figure 5.1 illustrates this with the standard fuzzy logic scatterplot. While in principle one should do this in three dimensions, two work quite well, particularly since everything is on the same [0, 1] scale. The different values of a_i and c_i produce different pairs of X_1 and X_2 variables, e.g., (a_1, a_3), or (a_1, c_4).

One can see the relative importance in action when contrasting a_1 with a_4 in the (a_1, a_4) observation. For the X_1 AND $X_2 \rightarrow Y$

---

[2] There might be complications due to overdetermination, but that does not fundamentally change things.

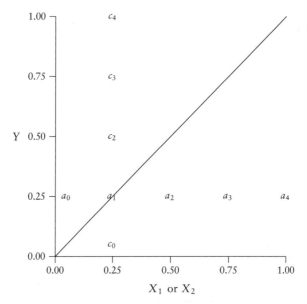

Figure 5.1: Choosing cases: X_1 AND $X_2 \rightarrow Y$ model.

model, $a_1 < a_4$, so $Y = a_1$. For this case, a_1 is the most important factor.

As we saw in the previous chapter, if one is focusing on necessary condition X_1 then one should choose a high value, if possible, for X_2. In terms of figure 5.1, the pair (a_1, a_4) is a better choice than (a_1, a_2). This is also better from a counterfactual point of view. The within-case analysis should explicitly pose the counterfactual hypothesis implied by the model: if X_1 were a_4 instead of a_1, the outcome would have been very different.

The most important case selection rule is to choose $(1, 1)$ cases to explore causal mechanisms. A $(1, 1, 1)$ case in the context of X_1 AND $X_2 \rightarrow Y$ has two separate considerations. The X_1 AND $X_2 \rightarrow Y$ is really three hypotheses, two about necessary conditions and one about joint sufficiency. One reason to prefer cases near $(1, 1, 1)$ for the model X_1 AND $X_2 \rightarrow Y$ is that one can do within-case counterfactual analysis for the necessary conditions. As such, if one is trying to get all three hypotheses with one case then the causal mechanism cell is the obvious choice. The cases near $(1, 1, 1)$ are essential for assessing the sufficiency effect of X_1 and X_2. Core to the within-case analysis will be the role—and relative role—of each in producing Y.

However, one needs to look closely at the necessary condition hypotheses embedded in X_1 AND $X_2 \to Y$, as well as the relative importance of X_1 versus X_2. One of the conclusions of the previous chapter was that for investigating necessary conditions one should choose cases that are favorable on other key causal conditions. Here this becomes a clear guideline when one does three or more case studies. One should use additional cases to specifically explore the necessary condition hypotheses. Choose one case with a high value of X_1 and a low value of X_2, hence a low value of Y, and choose one with a low value of X_1 and a high value of X_2, hence a low value of Y. These two are causal mechanism cases that are located near $Y = 0$. These allow the researcher to see the necessary conditions in real cases, as opposed to the counterfactual ones generated by the $(1, 1, 1)$ cell.

The same issue arises for the within-case use of the minimum. The fuzzy logic use of the minimum determines relative importance. There is, however, no guarantee, once one gets into the details, that causal process tracing supports this conclusion.

In summary, the within-case analysis of X_1 AND $X_2 \to Y$ should always cover the following points:

1. How X_1 AND X_2 together produce Y, their joint sufficiency.
2. The sufficiency effects of X_1 and X_2, and in particular their relative importance in sufficiency.
3. Why the absence of X_1 or X_2 prevents Y from happening or reduces the level of Y.

These issues need to be addressed in all the case studies, though obviously some case studies are more relevant than others for individual questions. In particular, one needs to always keep in mind the within-case counterfactuals. Much of the multimethod and comparative-case-study literature underplays the critical importance of within-case counterfactual analysis. Hoop tests are about necessary conditions and smoking gun tests are related to sufficiency. Hence the within-case analysis needs to use these kinds of tests explicitly.

Falsifying Cases

Falsifying cases play a large role in the methodology developed in chapters 3 and 4. Those chapters used only dichotomous variables, i.e., 2×2 tables. This section explores falsification in the fuzzy logic, i.e., continuous factor, context. Figure 5.2 lays out the basic issues for fuzzy set necessary conditions.

In the fuzzy logic context, falsification becomes a continuous concept. In OLS the basic idea is that the degree of falsification increases with distance from the OLS line, i.e., the size of the residual is the measure of degree of falsification. The function used for this measure of falsification is squared distance to the line, as in the name "ordinary least *squares*." It would be possible, and even desirable, to use other functions, like the absolute distance to the line, which generates the median line through the data.

The fuzzy logic falsification concept works from basically the same idea. In fuzzy set theory the line is always the diagonal, as in figure 5.2. The falsification concept for necessary conditions rests on the distance of the falsifying cases to the line. All cases on or below the diagonal are consistent with the necessary condition hypothesis. Only observations above the diagonal are potential falsifying cases (see Ragin 2008 or Schneider and Wagemann 2012 for a discussion).

Falsification increases with distance from the diagonal. So, for example, in figure 5.1 points c_2, c_3, c_4 falsify a necessary condition hypothesis. The fuzzy falsification concept question is, how does the linear distance between falsifying points and the diagonal relate to the concept of "falsification"? Fuzzy logic concepts usually involve a transformation or calibration of some raw data, e.g., GDP/capita, into a fuzzy logic concept, e.g., poverty: How does the concept "poverty" relate to GDP/capita data (Ragin 2008)?

The default fuzzy logic calibration function—or what Goertz and Mahoney (2012) call the semantic transformation—is the S-curve (see Ragin 2008 for an extensive discussion). The S-curve starts with the basic idea that points just above the diagonal do not really falsify at all (what Goertz and Mahoney 2012 call the principle of unimportant variation), so in figure 5.2 there

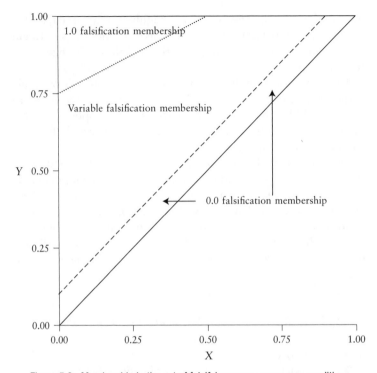

Figure 5.2: Membership in the set of falsifying cases: necessary conditions.

is a dashed line 0.10 above the diagonal. In this region, the fuzzy logic falsification concept has membership value 0.0, i.e., these observations do not falsify at all. Hence they constitute, in practice, consistent cases for necessary conditions.

At the other end, points near $(X = 0, Y = 1)$, such as c_4 in figure 5.1, are strongly falsifying cases; they have membership 1.0 in the set of cases that falsify a necessary condition hypothesis. For the purposes of illustration, if the observation is above the dotted line it is a 1.0 falsifying case. The dotted line in figure 5.2 establishes the strong falsification zone.

Between the zones of no falsification and complete falsification, the simplest thing to do is to consider that falsification increases linearly with distance, i.e., linear between the dotted and dashed lines. This gives a roughly S-shaped curve (or Z-shaped if you like). One could make it smooth (see Ragin 2008) but that would change relatively little in the figure 5.2 formulation.

The same logic applies to sufficient conditions. Fuzzy logic sufficient conditions are defined as $Y \geq X$, i.e., all the observations should lie on or above the diagonal. One applies the same basic falsification function to the cases that potentially falsify a sufficient condition hypothesis.

Because it includes both necessary and sufficient conditions, the X_1 AND $X_2 \rightarrow Y$ model makes extremely strong demands and claims on the data: they must lie on the diagonal. These are the only cases that satisfy the requirements for necessary conditions, i.e., $Y \leq X$, and those for sufficient conditions, i.e., $Y \geq X$. The OLS analogue would be to require that the R^2 for the model be near 1.00 (something that is extremely rare in practice).

The X_1 AND $X_2 \rightarrow Y$ Model: *States and Social Revolutions*

It is useful to explore an empirical example of the X_1 AND $X_2 \rightarrow Y$ model. A natural choice is Skocpol's famous analysis in *States and social revolutions*. I focus on the core part of the model of the form X_1 AND $X_2 \rightarrow Y$, but the complete model is significantly more complex (for a more complete analysis see Goertz and Mahoney 2005). We coded three fuzzy logic variables according to our reading of Skocpol's analysis, which are given in table 5.6. They can certainly be debated; notably, when social revolution did not occur, the degrees of nonoccurrence are more problematic. For purposes of methodological discussion I use these data.

The fuzzy X_1 AND $X_2 \rightarrow Y$ model puts quite strong demands on the data: to pass both necessity and sufficiency tests the data must lie on the 45-degree diagonal. Deviations from the diagonal result in some degree of falsification for a necessary condition or sufficient condition hypothesis.

Consider first the hypothesis, i.e., X_1 AND X_2 is sufficient for social revolution. This means comparing the "state breakdown

TABLE 5.6
The X_1 AND $X_2 \rightarrow Y$ model: *States and social revolutions*

Country	State breakdown	Peasant revolt	State breakdown AND peasant revolt	Social revolution
France	1.00	1.00	1.00	1.00
Russia 1917	1.00	1.00	1.00	1.00
China	1.00	0.75	0.75	1.00
England	1.00	0.00	0.00	0.42
Russia 1905	0.50	1.00	0.50	0.33
Germany	0.25	0.50	0.25	0.17
Prussia	0.75	0.50	0.50	0.25
Japan	0.75	0.00	0.00	0.42

AND peasant revolt" column with the "social revolution" column.

Skocpol's model works perfectly for the sufficiency hypothesis for all of her three positive cases: France, Russia 1917, and China satisfy the requirement that social revolution is greater than or equal to state breakdown AND peasant revolt. For her nonoccurrence cases—social revolution is less than 0.50—the requirements for sufficiency are met by England and Japan, but not by Russia 1905, Germany, and Prussia.

For sufficiency, Y must be greater than X, but in the case of Russia 1905 it is not, i.e., 0.33 (social revolution) is less than 0.50. In terms of figure 5.2 this means that Russia is a modestly falsifying case, as is Germany with 0.17 versus 0.25. Prussia is somewhat more falsifying with 0.25 for social revolution and 0.50 for X_1 AND X_2. In summary, all the falsifying cases for the sufficiency hypothesis are either modest or weak falsifying cases according to the logic of figure 5.2.

Turning to the necessary conditions hypotheses, the requirement is that X be greater than or equal to Y. This is true for state breakdown in all nine cases.

In the case of peasant revolt, there are falsifying cases. For example, England and Japan have 0.00 on peasant revolt but 0.42 on social revolution. The case of England illustrates the logic of the constraint model and its falsification. According to the theory, the complete absence of peasant revolt should have a very large constraining effect on the occurrence of social revolution. In the English case it did not have the predicted constraining effect (the same is true for Japan).

In terms of figure 5.2, England and Japan are significant falsifying cases for peasant revolt. By definition, X should be greater than Y, but social revolution has value 0.42 for both, while peasant revolt has value 0.00. These are probably the strongest falsifying examples in the whole model.

Probably more important is that China is a partially falsifying case for peasant revolt where social revolution occurred:

> Analysts have previously raised concerns about Skocpol's (1979) treatment of peasant revolt in China, suggesting that it is not fully consistent with her theory. For her part, Skocpol argues that the Chinese Communist Party created a high level of peasant autonomy and solidarity once the revolution was under way. If these organizational activities are taken into consideration, the Chinese case might be seen as having a 1.00 for the peasant revolt variable. (Goertz and Mahoney 2005, 529)

What are the good cases for the causal mechanism analysis of the sufficiency hypothesis? Clearly France and Russia 1917 are where the sufficiency hypothesis works the best; they are $(1, 1, 1)$ cases.

What are the best causal mechanism cases for the necessary conditions? The basic rule (see figure 5.2) is that cases where (1) X_1 is near 0 and (2) X_2 is near 1 and (3) Y is near 0 are the best causal mechanism cases for X_1.

So England is not too bad as a causal mechanism case for the peasant revolt necessary condition. The outcome variable is a relatively high level of nonoccurrence (i.e., 0.42). Ideally this should be closer to 0, but the strong contrast of peasant revolt at 0.50 with state breakdown, which is 1.0, makes it a stronger test (and better than the similar case of Japan). It is an ambiguous case because the constraint is not as strong as theory predicts (making it also a falsifying case).

The other cases of peasant revolt have values of 0.50 or 1.0. Germany is bad on the Avoid Overdetermination Guideline because it has a low value on state breakdown, 0.25. Prussia is a better case because of the 0.75 value of state breakdown. Both have relatively low values of the social revolution outcome, though lower than one would expect based on the theory.

The state breakdown variable illustrates how the two criteria for necessary condition case selection can be in conflict. The first is that good cases have low values of X_1. The second is that X_2 should have high values. Germany has the lowest value of state breakdown, 0.25, but not a very high value of peasant revolt (0.50). An alternative case is Russia 1905, which is not so low (0.50) but has a peasant revolt value of 1.0. An argument to be made for Russia 1905 is the magnitude of its constraining effect, since it reduces the effect of peasant revolt from 1.0 to 0.50, while for Germany the constraining effect is from 0.50 to 0.25. So applying the Avoid Overdetermination Guideline we would choose Russia 1905, and if we choose the strongest constraining effect we would also go with Russia 1905.

Ideally, for the state breakdown factor we would like cases of high membership in peasant revolt and low membership in state breakdown, i.e., 0 for state breakdown and 1 for peasant revolt. In our analysis of Skocpol's theory, we introduced other cases that are negative cases (i.e., no social revolution) that fit within her scope conditions (Mahoney and Goertz 2004, table 3, 667). We did not give fuzzy logic codings, but one can look for the cases with peasant revolt without state breakdown. For example, we noted that Spain in the mid- to late seventeenth century had major peasant revolts, but no state breakdown, hence this might constitute a good case for the state breakdown factor.

Which cases might be best if one were to choose only a few causal mechanism cases for Skocpol's theory? The clearest (1, 1, 1) cases are Russia 1917 or France. The best case for the peasant revolt variable necessary condition is probably England. For the state breakdown necessary condition, among her cases Russia 1905 is probably the best, but seventeenth-century Spain might be a better.

Given these considerations one might go back to the measurement of individual cases, particularly problematic ones. Obviously, if one changes the values for critical variables and cases then case selection decisions can also change. Notably, the

0.42 coding for social revolution for England and Japan might be revisited given that this produced some of the strongest falsifying evidence.

It is always very important to keep the possibility of tracking cases over time as a core option. My analysis of Skocpol has been completely cross-sectional. However, Russia appears twice in the table, the big difference being that in 1905 state breakdown is 0.50, while in 1917 it is 1.0, although in both cases peasant revolt is 1.0. This would be a natural choice for exploring the impact of state breakdown.

In summary, it is the peasant revolt variable that has the most problems in Skocpol's model. It is perhaps fair to say that she and her readers focused more attention on the state breakdown variable. Hence it is not surprising that the peasant revolt variable is more problematic. A sign of this is the absence of any case where state breakdown is 0, which is critical for the causal mechanism analyzing peasant revolt.

Interaction terms and multiple hypotheses mean that case selection can be quite complicated. Thus it is all the more important to have clearly in mind what kinds of cases are good for causal mechanism analysis. The cases that are most useful might not be the most obvious ones, e.g., seventeenth-century Spain. The X_1 AND $X_2 \to Y$ model, particularly the fuzzy logic version, makes very precise predictions that all the observations must lie on the $X = Y$ diagonal (the dichotomous version of the data fits the model perfectly). Given such high standards, the Skocpol model and data do remarkably well.

Constraint Causal Mechanisms Revisited

Constraint causal mechanisms often involve interactions between constraint and motivation factors. There are occasions when it makes sense to treat the motivation as given either in terms of a scope condition or for case selection, but that inevitably skews one's view, particularly if there is significant variation on motivation.

The social movement literature provides a natural and important setting to discuss "bringing motivation back in." The extremely influential political opportunity structure theory in all its variants is a constraint model. McAdam and Boudet's (2012) study illustrates what it means to bring motivation into the analysis. They explore the extent to which social movements arose or not in response to proposed risky environmental projects from 2000 to 2006.

As they stress, most of the social movement literature selects on existing social movements: little is known about where, when, and why social movements arise. To constitute the universe of cases they use motivation:

> At least three aspects of the project set it apart from the methodological conventions of most social movement research. First, as noted in the preceding text, we choose to study communities at risk for mobilization rather than movements per se.

> Because all large, potentially controversial, infrastructure projects are required to file an EIS [Environmental Impact Statement], these records provide a population of communities at risk for mobilization. (McAdam and Boudet 2012, 25, 36)

A community enters their population of cases where there is reason to believe that the proposed project involves serious environmental risk and hence motivation for environmental groups and individuals to mobilize.

McAdam and Boudet find support for classic social movement variables including political opportunity structure (see their figure 3.1). However, they find more support for what they call "community context." These factors include motivation. A key factor in their analysis is whether there are existing similar projects or industry in the community. For example, Louisiana is full of oil and gas projects. If the community already has such projects there might be much less motivation to protest a new one:

> Residents are also acutely aware of the positive economic impact these facilities bring to the area. Several interviewees explained how the oil and gas industry is a major contributor to the Louisiana economy. Many described the industry as part of the "culture" of Louisiana, along with hunting and fishing. For example, one interviewee grew up with a gas plant in his backyard. At the

time of the proposal, Cameron Parish was already home to nine pipeline processors, and nearby Calcasieu Parish housed twenty-three petrochemical facilities, which provided six thousand jobs. (McAdam and Boudet 2012, 86)

They stress that the classic political opportunity structure theory assumes that underlying motivation is present, e.g., the civil rights movement in the 1960s:

Although we have emphasized the continuity between our findings and the initial formulation of the political process model, we are nonetheless struck by an essential difference between "rights struggles" such as the civil rights movement—from which political process theory was derived—and the very different kind of conflicts that we are interrogating here. The difference concerns the causal salience of "threat" versus "opportunity" in the two types of struggles. The concept of political opportunity has been seen as critically important to the emergence of the kind of rights struggles that have been the focus of so much movement scholarship. Given the nature of these rights movements, the emphasis on perceived opportunities makes a great deal of sense to us. Normally, in such cases, the nature of the central issue group-based discrimination and disadvantage—is clear as is the underlying motivation to remedy it. It is only the long-standing power imbalance between the aggrieved population and its opponents that forestalls mobilization in such cases, movement emergence ordinarily does require some kind of rupture or crack in the system—an opportunity of some kind—as a catalyst to action. (McAdam and Boudet 2012, 96–97)

Motivation matters not only for understanding social movements but also is core to the oil and gas industry's actions and strategies. If you want to have a model of what projects were finally built, one needs to understand motivation on the gas company side. For example, McAdam and Boudet discuss how a company might propose multiple projects in a given region. The motivation of the company for any given project depends critically on *substitutes*. They find that when company motivation is lower for a given project—i.e., it has substitutes available—social movements are much more likely to be successful.

The configuration that did a good job explaining which projects were finally built was low environmental movement mobilization AND little regional saturation AND few or no substitutes (McAdam and Boudet 2012, 185). This can be seen as a variation on the opportunity and willingness framework popular in international conflict research. From the company's point of view, high environmental movement mobilization is a constraint (i.e., cost) to pursuing the project. The lack of substitute projects and no regional saturation means that the company is highly motivated for the project in question and hence likely to build.

. . .

Constraint versus motivation issues arise in the literature on women's representation in parliaments. Much early research, particularly statistical, focused on the role of proportional representation (PR) in encouraging women's representation. PR systems offer more opportunities—i.e., fewer constraints—for electing women representatives. Institutions are often constraints on behavior. Here the constraint–opportunity is the nature of the electoral system.

But there needs to be some motor in society pushing for the incorporation of women. Krook (2010) discusses three possible motivators: (1) women's status in society, (2) autonomous women's movement, and (3) strong left party (in particular strong new left parties).

Her QCA analysis of western democracies produced three paths to high representation.[3] The first path is women's status, which alone is sufficient for high levels of representation. This might be considered the Scandinavian route. In the context of this section it means that high women's status is strong enough to overcome the constraints of the electoral system.

This path demands within-case counterfactual and causal analysis. The Scandinavian countries are also proportional representation regimes. In fact, all the high women's status countries are also proportional representation states. The key

---

[3] I exclude a path generated by one complicated case, Luxembourg.

counterfactual question is, would these states have had high levels of representation with a majoritarian system?

The second path is women's movement AND proportional representation systems. Here we have the classic favorable constraint, i.e., PR, along with a clear motivation in the form of a women's movement.

The third path involves a gender quota AND strong left parties. Again we have a favorable electoral institution, i.e., gender quotas, along with political parties willing to take advantage of such opportunities.

Many QCA analyses can be interpreted as various combinations of constraint and motivation variables. QCA's stress on interaction terms makes it a natural way to look at causal combinations that include constraint variables. For QCA studies that explicitly use the opportunity–willingness version of constraint–motivation see Samford (2010) and Bara (2014). Samford, in his analysis of the paths to rapid trade liberalization in Latin America, uses this framework:

> These enabling conditions may be grouped into either "willingness" or "opportunity" conditions, or conditions that create "the will to act" or the "real-world situation that somehow permits action to occur," respectively. An authoritarian executive may be able (i.e., opportunity) to make rapid policy changes, for example, but without motive to do so (i.e., willingness), such a change is unlikely; the same is true when willingness (e.g., inflationary crisis) exists but opportunity does not. In this view, what becomes analytically important are not simply the individual conditions that enable an outcome but the combinations of conditions that are sufficient for an outcome to occur. (Samford 2010, 378; see his table 1)

It is thus not surprising that the social movement literature—along with the policy literature associated with Kingdon, and the punctuated equilibrium approach more generally—is full of interaction-term models. Many theories and explanations can be seen as variants of the motivation–constraint framework. In many empirical and theoretical contexts it is critical that motivation not remain exogenous in the research design and case selection.

Causal Mechanism Case Selection for X_1 OR $X_2 \rightarrow Y$: The Contributing Factor Model

The contributing factor model looks like the classic INUS model but without the usual causal complexity (i.e., AND) for each pathway. While the contributing factor model has not been used in QCA practice, experience from concepts and measurement would suggest that the typical model will have more than two, and more like four or five, contributing variables, i.e.,

$$(X_1 \text{ OR } X_2 \text{ OR } X_3) \longrightarrow Y. \qquad (5.6)$$

Typically equation (5.6) would be interpreted as meaning that each X_i is sufficient for Y. The contributing factor model is that the factors together are a sufficient condition, but the individual factors are not. That is why the model is called "contributing": each X_i contributes to sufficiency but is not sufficient alone. I have signaled this by putting parentheses around the X_i factors.

It is better to be more explicit about what the interpretation of $\rightarrow$ and OR is. QCA users typically define OR as the maximum. That is the standard default; however, some variation using addition is another possible implementation of OR in fuzzy logic. A simple family resemblance–style model is

$$\text{if } (X_1 + X_2 + X_3) \geq 2 \text{ then } Y, \quad X_i \in [0, 1]. \qquad (5.7)$$

This has the advantage of more clearly specifying when Y occurs and makes sufficiency more explicit. Clearly, now no X_i is sufficient for Y.

The simplest way to begin to think about this model is with a dichotomous outcome variable. Figure 5.2 illustrates how this works for two fuzzy logic independent variables and a sufficiency bar of 1.75. The outcome occurs in the upper-right corner of the figure. Everywhere outside this causal mechanism zone is the zone of nonoccurrence of Y because the sum is less than or equal to 1.75.

In terms of case selection—as usual—the causal mechanism cases are in the upper north-east corner near $(1, 1, 1)$. So these cases remain core to multimethod research.

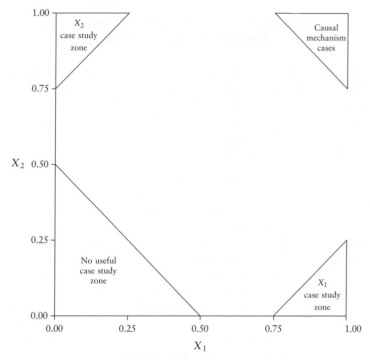

Figure 5.3: Case study selection: contributing factor model.

Because the contributing factor model is a sufficiency one, almost all the considerations discussed in chapter 3 apply. Instead of Z being an additional causal factor *outside* the causal mechanism, it is now X_2 within the mechanism. This changes the basic methodology relatively little.

Assessing the relative importance of X_i is straightforward, unlike necessary conditions where those without training in logic might find the idea that necessary condition X_1 is more important than necessary condition X_2 to be counterintuitive. This is in large part due to the contributing factor model's use of addition. Relative importance is simply the relative contribution of each X_i to the final sufficiency score.

Figure 5.3 illustrates the kinds of cases that are good for exploring the sufficiency contributions of X_1 and X_2, with

"X_1 case study" and "X_2 case study" zones marked. This is essentially the Avoid Overdetermination Guideline for sufficient conditions (Schneider and Rohlfing 2013). The logic is clearest in the overdetermination setting, where all X_i are very high and hence the outcome is overdetermined. Overdetermination is quite possible in situations with many X_i with large values.

The zone near the origin—where X_1 and X_2 are near zero—is pretty worthless for case studies. The region near $(0, 0)$ is the "no useful case study" zone in figure 5.2. The $(0, 0)$ cases were of little use for the sufficiency model outlined in chapter 3 and not surprisingly that does not change for the contributing factor model.

The logic of falsifying cases is straightforward. Falsification occurs when Y occurs but when $(X_1 + X_2)$ is near zero. In terms of figure 5.3, this means that the greater the distance from the causal mechanism cases in the upper right, the more the (X_1, X_2) case has membership in the falsification set. So the extreme falsification case is $(0, 0)$ and where the outcome occurs.

The fuzzy logic X_1 OR $X_2 \rightarrow Y$ model seems odd from the statistical point of view because there are no βs. There is nothing in fuzzy logic that prevents the researcher from claiming that X_1 has a larger or smaller sufficiency effect. One interesting way that this can happen is via adjectives that then change the membership function for X_i within specific conceptual sets. For example, one might argue that "moderate" wealth has important impact on Y in contrast to "very" wealthy. These adjectives change the membership functions (i.e., the concept is now "moderate wealth" or "very wealthy") and thus the sufficiency effect.

It would certainly be possible to use fuzzy logic computer algorithms to optimize the membership functions for X_1 and X_2 for a given data set (just like statistical algorithms such as maximum likelihood calculate βs). That is well beyond the scope of this book, but assessing relative importance should be a part of the case study analysis. In addition, the contribution of X_i to the occurrence of Y needs to be confirmed via process tracing and within-case analysis.

In short, the causal mechanism and multimethod logic of the contributing factor model follows that for sufficient conditions analyzed in chapter 3, which is as it should be. The main feature of the contributing model from the QCA point of view is that there are no necessary conditions in general, and no INUS conditions within paths.

Temporal Interaction Models and Sequencing

Another form of causal complexity involves bringing temporal relationships into the interaction term. Most statistical and QCA models have no real temporal specification. It is beyond the scope of this chapter and book to delve into these issues in any detail, but they are worth signaling.

While this chapter has treated $(X_1 * X_2)$ or $(X_1 \text{ AND } X_2)$ in purely cross-sectional terms, in some instances there is some temporal ordering between the two: X_1 comes before X_2. This is quite common when one X is an institution. For example, proportional representation exists as a constant in Krook's model, but other X_i variables are changing:

A central example is the electoral system, which most work identifies as one of the—if not the most—important factors explaining cross-national variations. Yet, before 1970, women's representation was roughly the same in PR and majoritarian systems, with differences emerging only after women inside parties began mobilizing for change. (Krook 2010, 888)

To put interaction terms in a causal chain of the standard $X_1 \rightarrow X_2 \rightarrow Y$ form is to assert, implicitly, a causal relationship between X_1 and X_2 that is not present in the interaction-term formulation. So one needs to be clear about the causal–temporal ordering of X_1 and X_2 versus temporal ordering without a causal relationship (see Beach and Rohlfing 2015 for various ways a three-way interaction term can be converted into a causal mechanism chain, e.g., their figure 5).

Another issue in the set-theoretic context is the interpretation of the causal arrow "$\rightarrow$." In a set-theoretic context these arrows could be sufficiency or necessity. Implicitly the interpretation is sufficiency, but that should be made explicit. For example, Mahoney, Kimball, and Koivu (2009) have explored in detail various kinds of causal chains like $X_1 \to X_2 \to Y$, where the arrows can be necessary or sufficient causal relationships. In statistical models, the causal arrow does not have this kind of interpretive ambiguity, it means significant causal effect. However, in both cases one needs to specify the nature of the causal arrow, given that constraint causal mechanisms look quite different from chains of sufficiency. Similarly, intervening variable statistical models should include "+" or "−" to indicate the nature of the causal relationships.

Soifer discusses a, probably common, temporal ordering of factors. One starts with permissive conditions, which are essentially necessary conditions, followed by the productive conditions that are sufficient for the outcome:

> Case selection to test a critical juncture argument should proceed in two stages. First, scholars should test for the permissive condition. Since this always takes the form of a necessary but insufficient condition, it should be tested by selecting cases where the outcome of interest is present and ensuring that the permissive conditions were present in each. Second, scholars should test the productive condition. The form of this test depends on the logical form of the productive condition. In all cases, however, the test of the productive condition should be conducted only in cases where the permissive condition is present. Since the relationship between the productive condition and the outcome is bound by the scope conditions of the permissive condition, cases where the permissive condition is absent are not relevant for testing. (Soifer 2012, 1590)

In constraint terms, this means looking at the constraints first and then within the constraints at what factors generate the outcome.

Goodwin's analysis of the revolutions in Eastern Europe (2001) illustrates nicely how permissive causes often are located at the beginning of a causal chain. In his figure 8.1, the process starts with Gorbachev's rejection of the Brezhnev doctrine and the decision not to use military force to maintain Communist governments in power: "And it is difficult to imagine that the revolutionary events of 1989 in Eastern Europe would or could have occurred had Soviet force been energetically deployed to stop them" (Goodwin 2001, 292). What happened once this permissive cause was present depended on the different kinds of domestic politics in the various countries, producing different trajectories of revolutionary change.

If temporal ordering matters, there is also the possibility for sequencing hypotheses (Pierson 2004, chapter 2). For example, a sequence hypothesis would be "if X_1 before X_2 then Y occurs." However, if X_2 occurs first and then X_1, then Y does not occur. The sequencing approach to temporal relationships has been explored in the QCA literature (Caren and Panofsky 2005; Ragin and Strand 2008; Schneider and Wagemann 2006).

Falleti (2005) in her study of decentralization, explores and contrasts sequences such as $(P \rightarrow A \rightarrow F)$, $(A \rightarrow P \rightarrow F)$, and $(P \rightarrow F \rightarrow A)$ (A=administrative decentralization, F=fiscal decentralization, P=political decentralization). In her analysis, temporal ordering is critical.

Bringing temporal ordering and various potential causal and noncausal relationships into the discussion means bringing interaction terms closer to causal mechanisms that often have a strong temporal character to them. Much more needs to be done to connect the atemporal interaction term with causal processes over time within individual cases.

Research Practice

Research practice varies significantly in how it deals with multimethod or multiple case study research involving interaction terms. In statistical research it was quite common for researchers to make methodological errors in interpreting interaction terms. It was not until some prominent publications (Brambor, Clark, and Golder 2006; Braumoeller 2004) pointed out how widespread these errors were that practice significantly improved. Given the lack of discussion in the case study and multimethod literature, it is not surprising that research practice varies quite a bit.

One can treat the interaction term $X_1 * X_2$ as a single variable I. This is a very common practice. If a researcher is doing just one case study then this is the obvious choice because it is a causal mechanism case. The case study can explore how and why X_1 and X_2 together produce Y.

For example, Rommetvedt et al. (2013) and Diez (2013) are both examples of the repeated selection of cases in the $(1, 1, 1)$ quadrant. Rommetvedt et al. (2013) argue that eroding corporatist channels and the rising importance of legislative power vis-à-vis the executive, reshape public–private relations by increasing informal lobbying of elected officials (and decreasing formal participation in policymaking with civil servants). They use two cases (Denmark and Norway) where that dynamic has been observed. Similarly, Diez (2013) uses a three-part inter-action to explain the adoption of same-sex unions in Mexico City and Buenos Aires: (1) well organized social organizations with (2) effective/resonant frames for their argument under (3) auspicious conditions of political opening. His case studies are both examples of where a three-part interaction term is present and the outcome occurs.

QCA multimethod work (e.g., Schneider and Rolfing 2013) recommends selecting cases according to paths (e.g., the Avoid Overdetermination Guideline) but have little to say about a more in-depth analysis of individual paths. Given that there are typically three to four paths, if one does one case study per path there is little space left—in an article context at least—for a more extensive exploration of the causal mechanism of a given path.

For example, Samford (2010) finds via QCA basically three paths to rapid trade reform. He then conducts case studies of Mexico, Peru, and Uruguay, one for each path. Particularly within an article context, three causal mechanism case studies are all that can be expected. It is quite clear in the QCA methods literature that good case studies for each of the paths (or main paths) constitutes multimethod QCA.

Problems arise with the single variable I route when thinking about the zero cases. Does the negative case mean that both terms of the interaction are absent or just one?

For negative cases, one possibility is when the negative cases are the absence of all the interaction-term variables, i.e., $X_1 = 0$ and $X_2 = 0$. Walsh (2012) takes this approach in her two-case study of the politics of women's rights in newly democratizing countries. She argues that two related conditions must be present for the progression of women's rights in democratizing countries: (1) conditions in society allowing for open debate about the role of women, and (2) the evolution of that debate such that policymakers are pressured under democratizing conditions to pass legal protections for women. She uses the common paired comparison—South Africa, which is a $(1, 1, 1)$ case, and Chile, which is a $(0, 0, 0)$ case.

Another scenario is when there is an interaction term, but the theoretical emphasis is mostly on one variable. Case selection is on one of the interaction terms and not the joint interaction term. For example, Mansfield and Snyder (2005) produce a statistical finding that recent democratization (X_1) and weak domestic institutions (X_2) together generate incentives for leaders to initiate bellicose behaviors in order to shore up domestic political support. They then provide numerous case studies that demonstrate the mechanism in operation. However, if one looks at case selection for their 8–10 case studies, it is exclusively on the democratization variable. The value of X_2—weak institutions—is not discussed, but obviously is critical to the final value of the interaction term in the statistical model. Selecting only on X_1 suggests implicitly that the value of X_2 does not matter, in contradiction to the statistical model. Looking at the case studies alone, one would not have known that the statistical model involves an interaction term.

Colgan illustrates the practice of choosing more cases on X_1 than on X_2 of the interaction term. The interaction of oil and domestic revolutionary regimes on international war is a central hypothesis: "H2: The difference between revolutionary and nonrevolutionary governments, in terms of their propensity to instigate international conflict, will be greater in petrostates than in non-petrostates" (Colgan 2013, 35). When he gets to the case studies in later chapters, all the states chosen—Libya, Iraq, Iran, Saudi Arabia, and Venezuela—are petrostates. Some of these cases, e.g., Libya, were not petrostates early on, but the case selection is very heavily weighted toward the petrostates. In contrast there is much more variation on the revolutionary government variable. While Colgan's statistical analysis includes many non-petrostates, in the case studies, petrostate acts much more like a constant scope condition. In summary, the number of cases where one X variable is zero is quite unbalanced, i.e., almost no cases of non-petrostates.

Rudra (2011) includes an interactive effect in her argument that the level of inequality mitigates the influence of openness of international trade on potable water availability. While trade openness has the effect of lowering access to potable water because of water use for export agriculture and manufacturing, at lower levels of inequality the relatively poor are able to resist the erosion of water quality and availability by pressuring the government to develop water infrastructure. Where inequality is high, the poor lack the organizational and institutional capacity to mitigate the effects of open trade. In her cases, India represents high inequality and trade openness, while Vietnam is relative equality and openness. So she does not include cases of non–trade openness.

In summary, multimethod practice with interaction-term theories varies quite significantly. With two independent variables there are eight possible case study configurations. I have never seen, in the applied or methodological literature, these eight possibilities explicitly analyzed. This is not surprising. The often-cited literature on multimethod or case studies work does not address the interaction-term situation. QCA multimethod work gives good advice about case selection at the path level, but has little to say about within-path causal mechanism analysis and case studies. So while interactive hypotheses and theories are quite common, much more needs to be done to connect the theories with causal mechanism case studies in a systematic way.

Conclusion

This chapter looked at case selection and multimethod work with more complex models involving interaction terms. In previous chapters I examined only sufficient conditions or only necessary conditions. This chapter explored three more complex models: (1) X_1 AND $X_2 \rightarrow Y$, (2) $(X_1$ OR X_2 OR $X_3) \rightarrow Y$, the contributing factor model, and (3) $(X_1$ OR $X_2)$ AND $X_3 \rightarrow Y$, SUIN or two-level theories. Much of the logic for these models rests on what one would expect based on the consideration of the logic of necessary or sufficient conditions.

While it remains outside the scope of this volume, there remains much to be done for those who have interactive hypotheses and want to do multimethod research. The statistical multimethod literature has had little to say about interactive hypotheses and theories, which are nevertheless not uncommon. Interaction terms pose significant methodological hurdles in statistical estimation and interpretation. It should not be surprising that multimethod work is going to involve similar difficulties.

A key fact for case study and multimethod work is that all of these models—statistical and QCA—contain *multiple* hypotheses about causal mechanisms. Therefore scholars need to take into account these multiple causal hypotheses in selecting cases and they must explicitly explore the hypotheses in the case studies themselves.

It is clear that multimethod work is among the major research agendas for QCA scholars (e.g., Schneider and Rohfling 2013; see the special issue of *Sociological Methods and Research* 2016 edited by Beach and Rohlfing). Ragin has always stressed the importance of case knowledge and case analysis for QCA. One of the key lines of QCA research is bringing more closely together the cross-case QCA analysis and the within-case analysis of causal mechanisms.

Once a researcher has an interaction term, temporal relationships and sequencing should be questioned. Case studies and causal mechanisms almost always have a temporal component. The research triad means bringing the cross-case analysis of interaction terms closer to the within-case, process tracing analyses of individual cases.

CHAPTER 6

Multimethod Game Theory

Introduction

Multimethod research can take many possible forms, although in practice scholars commonly utilize few. This chapter focuses on the mixture of game theory and case studies, where game theory refers to a mathematical model and calculations of equilibria.[1] Hence "multimethod game theory" means combining some serious case studies with a mathematical game-theoretic model. Most of the discussion applies to differential calculus models, which are the main other kind of formal model in political science; see, for example, Iversen (2005) or Ansell (2010).

There are reasons to think that the pairing of case studies and formal models should be a natural marriage. Game-theoretic models contain core elements such as beliefs, preferences, and uncertainty, which are difficult to establish empirically in a single case, but significantly more problematic in large-N cross-case settings. Game-theoretic models are complex and this complexity is quite hard to deal with using statistical methods. Because case studies can more easily handle this complexity, they are a natural partner for game-theoretic models in multimethod research.

Game-theoretic models constitute causal mechanisms. They describe strategic interactions that depend on the interaction of preferences, beliefs, information, etc.: "Formal models ... force clarity about assumptions and concepts; they ensure logical consistency, and they describe the underlying mechanisms,

---

[1] I exclude soft rational choice studies from consideration. Also excluded from consideration is the use of game theory to explain a given historical event (e.g., Bates et al. 1998; Nalepa 2010). The focus here is on a game-theoretic model and its empirical relevance.

typically behavioral, that lead to outcomes.... Absent mathematical modeling, the discipline lacks a basic tool to help identify causal mechanisms" (Granato et al. 2010, 783, 84).

Large-N testing makes quite heroic assumptions about the mechanism across cases. For example, the statistical variables might be quite distant from the causal mechanism. In the audience costs literature, often democracy versus authoritarianism is the statistical variable representing the audience costs mechanism. The idea is that audience costs in democracies should be higher or the mechanism more frequent. However, it is possible that other features of democracy are driving the statistical results and not the audience costs mechanism. Hence, statistical tests based on democracy are weak tests of audience costs hypotheses. Experiments can explore pieces of the causal mechanism but not the complex logic of the mechanism. For example, experimental tests of the audience costs causal mechanism (e.g., Tomz 2007; Levy et al. 2015) look only at one core assumption of the model. Case studies provide a valuable methodology for exploring the empirical relevance of the audience costs causal mechanism, its multiple assumptions, and the logic of the interaction among them.

While the marriage of game theory and case studies might seem natural, the nature of the relationship between the two is not clear in practice. There is little methodological literature on connecting case studies to game-theoretic models (though see Lorentzen, Fravel, and Paine 2016; Goemans and Spaniel 2016; Pahre 2005).

Citing the qualitative methods literature is somewhat rare for statistical multimethod work (see appendix A); it is virtually absent for game theory studies. So this chapter is also an exploration of multimethod game theory practice and its underlying implicit methodology. Fortunately, Peter Lorentzen and his colleagues have systematically surveyed articles using game-theoretic models. This forms the basis of my discussion of practice. How do game theorists choose cases? How many case studies do they choose? The core questions of previous—and future—chapters all apply to game theory multimethod work.

The analysis of the relationship between formal models and case studies continues in the next chapter. A number of very prominent game-theoretic models—e.g., Fearon on audience costs (1994) and Acemoglu and Robinson (2006)—have been the target of extensive case study analysis. Formal modelers might be somewhat hesitant to include case studies in their articles; their critics have not been shy on this count.

There is no doubt that most game-theoretic articles make claims to empirical relevance. Fearon (1994) used at least 5–8 historical cases as illustrations of his audience costs theory. There exists a potential tension between the claim that formal models are empirically relevant and the shallowness of much case study analysis.

The Research Triad

Chapter 1 argues that taking a causal mechanism view of research is bound together with the importance of doing case studies and within-case causal inference (see figure 1.1). The causal mechanism philosophy poses an alternative to the popular (at least among political scientists) covering-law view of science. If the researcher views game theory in terms of a covering-law model then it is (1) unlikely they will adopt a causal mechanism view of research and (2) they will have little use for case studies.

As Clarke and Primo (2012) discuss at some length, the covering-law philosophy remains the "standard" (to use Johnson's 2013 term) by which game theorists view the connection between models and empirical analysis. It is the standard view because it is widely taught in graduate classes and endorsed by large numbers of game theorists.

The Empirical Implications of Theoretical Models (EITM) project in general, and Morton (1999) in particular, take this view of the relationship between game theory and empirical testing. De Marchi illustrates the standard view:

> Normally the ideal paper for the mathematical modeling crowd is a well specified game that reaches some equilibrium outcome, which is then instantiated and tested in an appropriate statistical model. (De Marchi 2005, 2)

Within this framework the model itself is not empirically tested. Morton says that

> Empirical evaluation of formal models may be organized as follows: (1) evaluation of assumptions, (2) evaluation of predictions.[2] (1999, 101)

As with classic physics, the model generates *predictions* that can be empirically tested. Testing is almost always via statistical analyses in Morton's book and in EITM courses.

As Johnson notes,

> These examples [e.g., Morton 1999] should suffice to warrant my depiction of "the standard rationale" for using formal models. Not every political scientist subscribes to this rationale. And those who endorse it likely do not do so exclusively or consistently. However, especially in general assessments of formal models in political science, advocates and critics of the enterprise alike rely on criteria of predictive capacity and empirical performance. (Johnson 2013, 556)

Morton only briefly talks about case studies and has little good to say about them except in the context of theory building; for example, she says that they "do not constitute an in-depth empirical evaluation of the theory" (1999, 134). Tsebelis says that "case studies ... may provide very important insights, but it is not clear whether the conclusions are general or hold exclusively in the set of cases they study. Also, the explanations proposed may be correct, but it is not clear how the same variables would be measured in different cases" (2002, 273).

Conversely those who see value in case studies think in causal mechanism terms: "Formal models and process tracing, in particular, share an under-recognized affinity: a focus on causal mechanisms. Therefore, qualitative evidence strongly supporting or contradicting a model's causal processes can help to either uphold or invalidate the model's empirical applicability" (Lorentzen, Fravel, and Paine 2016, 2).

Bueno de Mesquita's research program and agenda provide an example where case studies are embraced as integral to the whole

---

[2] Morton includes a third "evaluation of alternative models" that is not discussed here.

research project. Bueno de Mesquita clearly argues that his models explain individual cases. This comes through in various ways in his research. He uses his models for prediction of individual events such as the future of Hong Kong (Bueno de Mesquita et al. 1985), the prospects for peace in Northern Ireland (Bueno de Mesquita, McDermott, and Cope 2001), or China's economic and political future (Bueno de Mesquita and Feng 1997). In fact he has a whole book entitled *The predictioneer's game* (2009). Here "prediction" really means predicting the future, not "empirical predictions" that are usually large-N ones using data sets of historical events. If his prediction is correct the claim is that the causal mechanism in the model generating the prediction explains why that event occurred.

Bueno de Mesquita also includes extensive case studies in his books (e.g., Bueno de Mesquita 1981; Bueno de Mesquita and Lalman 1992; Bueno de Mesquita et al. 2003; Bueno de Mesquita and Smith 2011). The use of case studies in books is quite common. What is less so are articles where a game-theoretic model is used to explain or understand a specific historical case. Bueno de Mesquita's work includes such research, for example, explaining King Leopold II's behavior vis-à-vis the Congo (2007), the origins of German hegemony (1990), or the Concordat of Worms and the origins of sovereignty (2000).

Hence it is quite possible to make case studies core to the agenda of formal models. Bueno de Mesquita does extensive statistical testing of his theories as well. He sees the case studies and statistical analyses as complements. The research triad in general stresses the interconnection of causal mechanism analyses of cases along with cross-case analysis. Case studies can be quite useful in evaluating some aspects of the model that are not easily amenable to statistical analysis.

The Empirical Analysis of Game-Theoretic Models

To see how case studies might be used to empirically explore a game-theoretic model, it is necessary to have an overview of how the modeling process works. Figure 6.1 gives such an overview

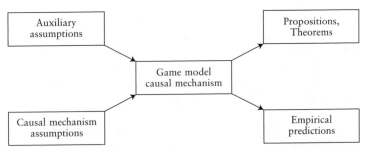

Figure 6.1: Game theory modeling and empirical evaluation: an overview.

that allows us to see at what points empirical evaluation can be made. According to the standard view (e.g., Morton 1999), testing comes at the beginning in evaluating assumptions or at the end in evaluating predictions.

In figure 6.1 there is a box of "causal mechanism assumptions" and another box of "auxiliary assumptions." All formal models use multiple assumptions. For example, the simple and ground-breaking Nash (1950) bargaining model has four assumptions. Many models have more than that. Each assumption plays some role in generating the theorems and predictions at the end of the modeling process. Typically they are jointly sufficient for the conclusions expressed in the theorems: "A model can be a precise and economical statement of a set of relationships that are sufficient to produce the phenomenon in question" (Schelling 1978, 87). Usually they are necessary within the model as well, since otherwise scholars would not include them.

Auxiliary assumptions are often necessary to produce mathematical results. For example, if the model has a utility function then assumptions about its form are often necessary. In spatial models of preferences, some measure of distance is usually required (e.g., Euclidean). These are not the assumptions that form the causal mechanism core of the model. The causal mechanism assumptions are what make the model substantively interesting and worthy of attention and publication. As Granato et al. note, *"A more general point is the EITM framework's focus on parameters separates variables that aid in fundamental prediction from other variables considered 'causal' but are of minor predictive importance"* (2010, 794; emphasis in the original).

This classification of assumptions is not a mathematical one. All the assumptions are needed for mathematical purposes. But the amount of attention given to each assumption will vary dramatically, which is a pretty reliable indicator of how important the assumption is for the causal mechanism. In addition, the line between causal mechanism assumptions and model is a blurry one.

The causal mechanism assumptions become clear if there are experiments designed to test the game-theoretic model. In an experiment, one can include only a limited number of treatments. Those assumptions chosen as treatments are causal mechanism ones. For example, audience costs models have been subjected to a variety of experimental analyses (e.g., Tomz 2007; Levy et al. 2015). Virtually all of these experiments test the assumption of the model that domestic publics care about consistency in the foreign policy behavior of elites. So when the authors say that they are "testing the audience costs model," what they are almost always doing is testing one assumption—a core one to be sure—of the model: "Throughout this article, I use the term audience costs as shorthand for the surge in disapproval that would occur if a leader made commitments and did not follow through" (Tomz 2007, 823).

As Levy et al. note in their conclusions, there are other assumptions of the model that merit experimental or empirical testing:

> Another significant step forward in audience costs theory would be to examine the beliefs of political leaders and external adversaries, whose behavior is central to audience costs theory. When deciding to issue a deterrent threat, do leaders consider the public's likely reaction—both to the initial threat and to subsequent actions, depending on the adversary's response? Do leaders (and adversaries) take their opponent's potential for domestic audience costs into account when making or responding to threats? (2015, 1000)

In figure 6.1 there are two outputs of the model: (1) theorems and propositions and (2) empirical predictions. Carrubba and

Gabel's model of international courts illustrates nicely this distinction. They prove a number of propositions that arise from their formal model, for example,

> Proposition 1: Governments defect from the regulatory regime's rules *if and only if* the cost of compliance is sufficiently large ($c_i > c_i^*$). (2014, 41; emphasis is mine)

> Proposition 6: Governments obey adverse rulings *if and only if* they have not exerted enough effort to persuade the other governments to permit them to ignore the court ruling and the judgment the court imposes is not too large. (2014, 43; emphasis is mine)

The empirical testing is done on two core predictions:

> Prediction 1 (the Political Sensitivity Hypothesis): The court is more likely to rule against a defendant government the more briefs filed against the government and the fewer briefs filed in support of it. (Carrubba and Gabel 2014, 47)

> Prediction 2 (the Conditional Effectiveness Hypothesis): Court rulings against defendant governments are more likely to change government behavior the more briefs filed in support of the ruling and the fewer filed against it. (Carrubba and Gabel 2014, 47)

They devote a chapter of statistical evaluation to each of these hypotheses. All the predictions are formulated in statistical terms about the probability of Y increasing with X.

Empirical testing primarily occurs with predictions within the EITM framework. This is consistent with the covering-law model where the model produces predictions that can be empirically tested. Classical Newtonian physics is a canonical example: the laws of gravity produce predictions about the movement of planets.

It is not clear why propositions and theorems cannot also be empirically investigated. Some of Carrubba and Gabel's propositions, such as Proposition 6, could be empirically investigated in individual cases. There seems to be no real reason why propositions cannot receive empirical investigation in individual cases or even in a large-N setting. For example, the previous chapter explored in some detail a model of the form Y *if and only if* X_1 AND X_2. Skocpol's model argues "social revolution if and only if peasant revolt and state breakdown." Testing her model required coding the core variables and evaluating how well the data supported, or not, the model.

Chapter 4 discusses the testing of necessary condition hypotheses in general. Testing of necessary conditions in some ways is easier than statistical testing because one can select on the $Y = 1$ cases. Dion (1998) has shown, using Bayes theorem with a uniform prior, that one needs only about 6–8 cases to become quite confident (e.g., 90–95 percent) in the hypothesis.

The propositions and theorems that formal models produce escape the testing philosophy of EITM. It is quite common to produce necessary and sufficient condition propositions and theorems; the propositions above from Carrubba and Gabel are examples since they explicitly make "if and only if" claims. Another nice example comes from Kydd's work:

> I examine the conditions under which mediators can facilitate cooperation by building trust between two parties. Assuming mediators have no intrinsic commitment to honesty, they can be credible trust builders in one-round interactions *only if* they care about the issue at stake, [*and*] have a moderate ideal point, *and* do not find conflict to be too costly. (Kydd 2006, 449, abstract; emphasis is mine)

I have emphasized the necessary condition—only if—character of the model's propositions. In addition, the multiple necessary conditions produce an interactive model (see chapter 5 for an extensive discussion). While not all formal models produce propositions of this sort, it is very common.

One reason perhaps for the separation between the two—theorems and predictions—is that predictions usually have a probabilistic character, e.g., "is more likely." Propositions and theorems on the other hand make extensive use of mathematical logic, e.g., necessary and sufficient conditions. That makes the propositions "deterministic." However, it is clear that many laws of physics are deterministic (e.g., differential equations) and yet have been subject to extensive empirical tests.

Favretto's study of major power intervention in militarized conflicts illustrates how a formal sufficient condition theorem becomes a probabilistic hypothesis:

Result 2. [If] When $s > s^*$ [s is the degree to which major power T prefers A], [then] A and B [the two disputants] settle because they are certain T [major power mediator that favors A] is resolved to fight B. (Favretto 2009, 253)

Hypothesis 2(i) When highly biased major powers intervene in a crisis, a peaceful settlement is more likely because bargainers are certain the intervener is resolved to enforce a settlement by military means. (Favretto 2009, 254)

In summary, in many instances there seems to be no reason why propositions and theorems cannot be the object of empirical investigation and evaluation.

Figure 6.1 shows the "model" to be linking assumptions to theorems and predictions. The model includes other elements needed for proving theorems (e.g., equilibrium concept) and puts all the assumptions to work: *the model is the causal mechanism.* It contains and uses the assumptions to produce theorems and predictions.

Game theory models as causal mechanisms is quite a different perspective. For example, Morton defines "formal model" as assumptions producing empirical predictions: "Formal Model—a set of precise abstract assumptions or axioms about the real world presented in symbolic terms that are solved to derive predictions about the real world" (1999, 61). She focuses on the ends of figure 6.1 while ignoring the middle.

If one adopts the research triad, the model qua causal mechanism becomes a focus of empirical research. In an individual case study, one can explore all the core causal mechanism assumptions and their linkages. For example, in a case study of audience costs, the researcher could answer Levy et al.'s set of questions regarding other aspects of the audience costs causal mechanism.

The research triad comes into play because cross-case evidence—particularly of the statistical type—cannot explore all—or even close to all—the core assumptions or predictions of the game-theoretic model. The motivation for case studies is the exploration of causal mechanisms. Cross-case statistical or experimental methods can explore parts of the model, but not all of the parts and usually not the interaction of the parts.

Part of the commitment to the research triad is that explaining individual cases has merit and value. The covering-law view of testing sees little value or need for the model to explain individual cases. For example, Clarke and Primo have little positive to say about individual case studies:

> Scholars disagree about whether models *ought* to be used for the purpose of studying lone events. It may seem that there is little to be gained from using models to understand a single event. After all, several different models may be written down that "fit the data."[3] (Clarke and Primo 2012, 92)

They constantly refer to case studies as "exploratory." When they talk about "testing" a game theory model, they mean statistical testing.

There is an inherent tension between the acceptance and encouragement of statistical empirical analyses and the downplaying of individual case studies. After all, data sets— conflict data sets for example—consist of individual events. The statistical analysis implies directly that some of those events are interpreted as supporting the hypothesis. Multimethod research comes into play in exploring whether those apparently supporting cases from the statistical analysis also contain the causal mechanism.

Primo and Clarke stress that models should be evaluated by their *usefulness*. Fearon suggests that his audience costs model is useful in explaining individual cases:

> In prototypical cases (e.g., the standoff leading to the 1991 Gulf War, the Cuban Missile Crisis, and July 1914), a leader who chooses to back down is (or would be) perceived as having suffered a greater "diplomatic humiliation" the more he had escalated the crisis.

---

[3] Of course, their criticism of case studies—that multiple models can fit the data—is true for statistical and formal models as well. More generally this is the famous Duhem–Quine problem in philosophy of science.

Conversely, our intuition is that the more a crisis escalates, the greater the perception of diplomatic triumph for a leader who "stands firm" until the other side backs down. (Fearon 1994, 580)

Fearon also includes the Seven Years War, the Britain–Spain crisis in Vancouver Island, and the Fashoda crisis between Britain and France in Africa. Hence there are minimally 5–10 cases where the audience costs model works.

This whole volume is motivated by the core philosophy that in order to be useful, game theory models—along with other hypotheses and theories of all sorts—need to help us understand individual cases. When economists and political scientists give policy advice, they are subscribing to the view that their theories work in individual cases. This is not to say that they need to work all the time, but that there is a set of cases where they do work (i.e., the (1, 1) cell cases).

In short, propositions and theorems are available for empirical testing via case studies. They have the advantage over "predictions" that they are more tightly connected to the model than the probabilistic (linear) predictions. The standard approach to game theory and empirical analysis excludes this rich source. In addition, game theory multimethod research opens the black box of the causal mechanism and game theory model to empirical analysis. The standard EITM approach looks only at two regions of figure 6.1—causal mechanism assumptions and predictions; using case studies opens up two other regions for empirical analysis.

Many see qualitative and quantitative research as complementary. Figure 6.1 expresses exactly this view. Some parts of the model, such as comparative static predictions, are amenable to statistical analysis; other parts, such as the causal mechanism and theorems/propositions, can be empirically explored via case studies.

How Extensive Is Game Theory Multimethod Research?

How often do game theorists use empirical data in the form of case studies to evaluate the empirical relevance of their

Table 6.1
Multimethod game theory: research practice

Type of case study	Number of articles	Percentage
Comparison only	8	21
Case study only	8	21
Evidence for assumptions only	14	36
Comparison and evidence for assumptions	0	0
Case study and evidence for assumptions	3	8
Comparison and case study	4	10
All three types	2	5
Total	39	100

Source: based on Lorentzen, Fravel, and Paine (2016).

models? The Lorentzen, Fravel, and Paine survey allows me to explore how often case studies are used in conjunction with formal models. Their survey covers all articles published with a formal model during 2006–13 in six major comparative politics and international relations journals.[4] Their definition of formal model is similar to that adopted here: "Papers were classified as having formal models and therefore included in our survey if they included analytical propositions and specified an equilibrium concept" (Lorentzen, Fravel, and Paine 2016, 40).

They found a total of 108 articles meeting their criteria for being formal theory. Table 6.1 gives a breakdown of those that included case studies.

So is game theory multimethod work common? Of course, it depends on one's view of "common," but about one-third (i.e., $39/108 = 0.36$) of articles with formal models contain some case study analysis. More specifically, 29 percent of the articles provided evidence that the game-theoretic mechanisms apply to real-world cases. Sometimes—about 16 percent—this took the form of extended multiple-page case studies. So one cannot say that game theory multimethod is common, but at the same time it is not rare.

---

[4] They also coded American politics game-theoretic articles, which are included in their data set, but which are not discussed in their paper.

If one had similar data on the frequency of statistical multi-method work—statistical analyses with case studies—36 percent might seem a high rate.[5] From my years of reading the large-N statistical conflict literature, it is clear that case studies are not likely to appear. Examples are given often—say in the introduction—but they are rarely more than a paragraph or two long. Analogously, one could explore the rate of statistical analysis within the universe of game theory articles, the EITM model. Finally, there can be all three—case studies, game theory model, and statistical analysis—such as Schultz (2001).

One conclusion is obvious: including some case study evidence is not a requirement of publication for formal models since about two-thirds of articles have little or no such analysis (e.g., Kurizaki and Whang 2015 on audience costs).

Case Studies as Empirical Existence Proofs

At their most skeptical, critics of game-theoretic models find them of little empirical relevance. This will be evident in the next chapter where Marc Tratchenberg could find *no* cases in his survey where the audience costs mechanism was in action: "The basic finding is quite simple. There is little evidence that the audience costs mechanism played a 'crucial' role in any of them. Indeed, it is hard to identify any case in which that mechanism played much of a role at all" (Trachtenberg 2012, 32).

One or two case studies can show that the model has some empirical relevance. If a model is to be empirically valid then it needs to provide insight into the events of history. A way to begin is by giving at least one or two serious case studies. Using an analogy from mathematics, I call such case studies "empirical existence proofs": they demonstrate the empirical relevance of the model by showing it helps to explain at least one historical case.

---

[5] One possibility would be to evaluate the extent of statistical multimethod research in a given substantive area, e.g., Lyall's (2014) survey of the civil war literature.

Some might deny that it is possible or desirable to do empirical existence proofs:

> Our empirical expectations are of the following sort: "on average, the likelihood of a ruling for the government defendant should increase with … " We cannot evaluate that sort of expectation with a single ruling or a small set of rulings. *Our empirical expectations apply to the aggregate and thus show up only in the aggregate.* (Carrubba and Gabel 2014, 19; emphasis is mine)

Despite this claim, Carrubba and Gabel have an extensive eight-page discussion of one European Court of Justice ruling (Schmidberger versus Republic of Austria). They analyze it as an example of how their model can help understand individual cases. This is typical of the tension that runs through much game-theoretic work and its relationship to individual cases.

"Testing" game-theoretic models often means "statistical testing." Within the EITM framework, the empirical predictions of figure 6.1 are taken to mean statistical or probabilistic ones. One often hears that one cannot test theories with a couple of case studies.

An empirical-existence-proof case study is, however, a test. To pass the test one must find and do a serious case study where the game-theoretic mechanism is at work. What it is *not* is a test of how general the causal mechanism is. Case studies and the generalizability of causal mechanisms are topics in chapters 7 and 8.

Within the research triad, there are multiple testing and empirical evaluations strategies. Statistical analyses and tests lie in the cross-case box while case studies are within-case tests. They are usually testing different parts of the game-theoretic model. As illustrated in figure 6.1, the statistical tests focus on different parts of the model from the within-case causal mechanism tests.

While the empirical existence proof might seem like a pretty low bar—find one historical case with the causal mechanism—it is nontrivial. I have reviewed articles for major journals using game-theoretic models and on several occasions I have not been able to think of a case where the causal mechanism worked as advertised. Haggard et al. illustrate this in their discussion of Acemoglu and Robinson's (2006) book:

> These credible commitment problems can generate a counterintuitive result. It might seem that transitions would be more likely when lower class groups are well-organized. Yet A&R argue that this is not necessarily the case "because with a frequent revolutionary threat, future redistribution becomes credible." As an historical example, they cite the fact that Germany—the country with the most developed socialist movement—created novel welfare institutions without extending the franchise while political elites in Britain and France were forced to extend the franchise as a result of pressures from below. We are hard pressed, however, to think of contemporary examples in which a high capacity for collective action on the part of the poor was responsible for stable, redistributive authoritarian rule. (Haggard et al. 2013, 4–5)

Ideally, such existence-proof case studies are cases considered substantively important by the subfield. If the best the author can do is an obscure event then that breeds little confidence in the usefulness of the model. For example, Lake (2010) argues for the usefulness of the bargaining model of war by saying it is helpful even in such unlikely places as the 2003 Iraq War.

It is not necessarily fair or justified to demand that the existence-proof case study be a historically or politically important case. However, as a pragmatic matter, audiences will not be impressed if the main example is a historically obscure case. Many will assume—rightly or wrongly—that the author could not come up with a historically or politically important example, and hence chose an obscure one.

Choosing a historically–politically important case is good from a methodological point of view, because these constitute harder tests. By definition, well-known cases are those that people know about; hence the probability that someone will contest the case study is much higher. This makes it a stronger existence-proof test.

In short, there is a basic rule for game-theoretic multimethod work:

Game-theoretic multimethod work must give at least one serious account of how the model helps explain or understand a good—usually substantively important—case of the phenomenon.

Johns (2007) provides a nice example of what a model plus existence proof looks like. It is a multiple principle–agent model intended to apply in particular to international organizations that have multiple principals in the form of member states:

International bureaucrats must often serve multiple principals who collectively choose policy. How does this affect bureaucrats' incentives to truthfully reveal their private information? I construct a cheap talk model in which a bureaucrat possesses private information about how policies translate into outcomes. The bureaucrat can communicate publicly observable messages about this information to two policymakers, who must then bargain over a set of policy choices. (Johns 2007, 245, abstract)

As is virtually universal in game-theoretic articles, she starts with an empirical example that will become the existence-proof case study. The international organization is the UN nuclear weapons committee (UNSCOM) charged with investigating Iraq's nuclear facilities. The multiple principals are the key UN Security Council members. In the course of developing her model she proves five propositions plus five "claims."

She sees the causal mechanism assumptions as basically scope conditions for the model (see below for more). If the basic assumptions are not met then it is not clear what the usefulness of the case study is. The assumptions do not need to match perfectly the historical situation, but they need to be relatively close:

Criteria for Evaluating the Model

When evaluating the model, it is important to begin by examining whether the assumptions of the model are consistent with the strategic situations of interest. This includes asking whether an international bureaucrat has preferences over the policies that result from her report; whether the potential for a multilateral agreement exists; and whether the choice of the NBS is appropriate for the institution under consideration. If these key assumptions hold, one can then proceed to examining whether the model's observable implications accord with reality. (Johns 2007, 263)

Then she carefully connects features of the Iraq case to the core parameters of the model, for example,

One can loosely think of the application of the fundamentals of the model to this case in the following manner. The unknown state variable, v, represents the extent to which Iraq was complying with Resolution 687 and the policy parameter, y, reflects the rewards and/or punishments imposed by the Security Council in response to Iraqi actions. Each permanent member of the Security Council had different preferences regarding how the level of compliance by Iraq should translate into UN policies. These preferences manifest themselves in the bias parameter, b_i. The disagreement payoff, d_i, reflects the utility that the UN Security Council members derived from the absence of any response to the actions of Iraq, including the end of both weapons inspections and sanctions. While policymakers may have differed regarding the relative desirability of this outcome, all believed that some form of multilateral response was preferable to doing nothing. Finally, the value of the outside option, f_i, represents the utility that each of the permanent Security Council members derived from abandoning the multilateral policymaking process. (Johns 2007, 263)

Often scholars fail to link the case study to the causal mechanism and formal model as well as Johns has. The above quote illustrates how she attaches central model parameters to features of the case.

She then goes on to spend seven pages exploring the relationship between the case study and the formal model. This is quite an extensive discussion in an article context. Few other articles in the Lorentzen, Fravel, and Paine survey do such a long and careful case study.

In the audience costs literature, the Fashoda crisis plays the role of the empirical existence proof. Fearon (1992) made that crisis the subject of an extended analysis in his dissertation, and others have followed him in using that example (e.g., Schultz 2001). This example is also one of historical importance because it seemed that Britain and France might go to war.[6]

Model Assumptions and Scope

Critical in case selection is establishing the scope of the causal mechanism. This is a crucial feature in the medium-N multimethod design developed in chapter 8. It is similarly important in the discussion of large-N qualitative methods in chapter 7 because scholars claim to examine *all relevant* cases. In the context of game theory multimethod work, there is an additional factor that complicates matters: the role of model assumptions in scope, and hence case selection.

My survey of practice regarding scope—see chapter 8—concludes that empirical or theoretical scope is rarely specified. Qualitative scholars are more likely to specify and construct scope (see Ragin 2000, chapter 2 for a forceful discussion); statistical scholars typically define scope limits implicitly by the limits of the data.

It is common for game theorists to argue that model assumptions determine the scope and applicability of the model. For example, Shepsle uses the conditions in the theorem to define the empirical scope of a model: "Duncan Black's famous theorem asserts: if alternatives are unidimensional, if preferences over them are single-peaked, and if decisions are made by majority rule, then the median alternative will be chosen. A rational choice theorist would claim that this assertion holds in all circumstances that satisfy the well-defined conditions appearing in the statement of the theorem" (Shepsle 2005, 20).

Sugden describes the same thing: "In many modeling exercises, it makes sense to describe the relationship between $A_1 \dots A_n$

---

[6] Trachtenberg (personal communication) suggests that the Cuban Missile Crisis would be a better existence proof, but still not a good one (see his discussion in Trachtenberg 2012). The Cuban Missile Crisis is the example Bueno de Mesquita (2013) uses in his textbook to illustrate the audience costs model.

[assumptions] and R [result] as a mechanism by which $A_1 \ldots A_n$ interact to bring about R. Then we can say that this mechanism operates in the model world, and that if $A_1 \ldots A_n$ were properties of the real world, then it would operate in the real world too" (Sugden 2009, 5).

One can use model assumptions as a way of bounding the scope of the model. Opinions about the importance of the match between empirical facts and model assumptions vary significantly. Some claim that for the model to be relevant, the facts of the case must satisfy model assumptions. The EITM project, and others such as Morton (1999), see assumptions as one part of the model that is subject to empirical testing. Others—notably Friedman (1953)—downplay the importance of accurate matching. In their survey, Lorentzen, Fravel, and Paine (2016) find about 20 percent of the articles offered some qualitative evidence to empirically justify model assumptions. So independent of various positions about the relative importance of assumptions, some scholars do think that they should justify assumptions as realistic and use individual cases to make that justification.

Johns illustrates the position that assumptions must have some empirical relevance: "The theoretical model above is not a representation of a particular international court. It is an abstract account of a court that creates governance from anarchy. Nonetheless, in order for this model to be meaningful its assumptions and mechanisms should be plausible for some areas of international politics" (2012, 270).

Almost by definition game-theoretic models assume rational actors. The bargaining model of war is an explanation of why rational actors might fight. Fearon's well-known article starts by noting that "the central puzzle about war, and also the main reason we study it, is that wars are costly but nonetheless wars recur. . . . one can argue that even *rational leaders* who consider the risks and costs of war may end up fighting nonetheless. This article focuses on arguments . . . which I will call rationalist explanations" (Fearon 1995, 379; emphasis is mine). The question is whether or to what extent the model applies when the assumption of rational decision making appears to be violated in important ways.

Lake (2010) finds in his analysis of the 2003 Iraq War that the bargaining theory of war does not work completely because of rationality issues (i.e., the missing cheer from the title's "Two cheers for bargaining theory: assessing rationalist explanations of the Iraq War"). To argue that leaders were "boundedly rational" means that some of the standard rational choice assumptions are not met. While Lake clearly finds that the Iraq War falls within the scope of the bargaining model, one could claim that it is does not, because both Bush and Hussein failed to meet the assumptions of rationality.[7]

Acemoglu and Robinson (2006) assume authoritarian governments set taxes and redistribution policy based on the interests of economic elites. The model's assumptions then have implications for mobilization that explain democratic breakdown. Slater et al. (2014), in their critique of Acemoglu and Robinson, focus on these assumptions when they argue mobilizations against democracy, e.g., military coups, do not fit the Acemoglu and Robinson model.

Those who critique—just like those who defend—can focus on one or both of these things—i.e., basic assumptions of rationality or model assumptions. Typically they tend to flow together as in Lake's analysis of the 2003 Iraq War.

Sometimes the assumption is critical and if it is empirically false then the whole model collapses. For example, Snyder and Borghard (2011) challenge a basic assumption of the audience costs model by saying that publics do not really care that much about consistency of leaders. To reject that basic assumption is to reject the whole audience costs model, which critically rests on it (see Lorentzen, Fravel, and Paine 2016 for a longer discussion of this debate).

Chapter 3 argued that a core use of case studies is to look at cases where the causal mechanism should work but does not. The (1, 0) cell of the 2×2 table is the scope cell exactly for this reason. Within a game theory context these cases could fail on

[7] What constitutes a "rational" actor is itself a nontrivial issue and there exist major debates about the line between rational and nonrational. The huge literature on behavioral decision making is typically about violations of core rationality principles, e.g., preference reversals, prospect theory, Allais paradox.

assumption grounds. If the case fails on assumptions then one possible conclusion is that it lies outside the scope of the model. For example, Fearon might make no claims about the utility of his model for irrational, or boundedly rational, leaders.

Determining the scope for any theory, model, or hypothesis is a nontrivial exercise. Assumptions constitute in large part the breadth and scope of the game-theoretic model. This becomes central when case studies are explicitly about exploring the boundaries of causal mechanisms—the paradigm of chapter 8.

Case Selection: Research Practice

It will not be a surprise after previous chapters and their discussions of research practice to see that when game-theoretic articles include case studies they are overwhelmingly chosen from the $(1, 1)$ cell. Looking systematically at the articles from the Lorentzen, Fravel, and Paine (2016) study with a single relatively substantial case study, almost all lie in the $(1, 1)$ cell. This would very likely remain true for the short examples (one paragraph) common in formal model articles.

There is a significant minority of articles in the Lorentzen, Fravel, and Paine survey that include two or more case studies, rarely more than three. While one might expect some examples of $(0, 0)$–$(1, 1)$ paired comparisons, these are extremely rare in practice. In fact, even when two or more case studies are included they are all $(1, 1)$ cases. This arises because, not uncommonly, the model predicts quite different equilibria depending on the values of crucial parameters. This leads to a case study for each of the different equilibria. As such these are still $(1, 1)$ case studies because they follow the model when it has different parameter values.

Confounders are rarely discussed in the context of case selection. So while authors discuss alternative explanations of the individual events or alternative formal models, this plays no role in case selection.

Very rare is a discussion of *which* of the $(1, 1)$ cases to select. The implicit methodology is almost certainly to choose prominent, historically important cases. The second criterion is probably "good" cases where the causal mechanism works well and clearly.

In short, game theory multimethod research chooses $(1, 1)$ cases. Other options, like disconfirming, scope, or equifinality case studies, do not appear. The main exception—discussed at length in the next chapter—lies with those who choose cases with the goal of critiquing a model rather than confirming it.

Conclusions

A central theme running throughout this book is the role of within-case causal inference in multimethod research. The central *raison d'être* for case studies is the investigation of causal mechanisms and making causal inferences in individual cases.

Within the context of this chapter, to what extent are game theory articles making within-case causal claims? Thanks to Lorentzen, Fravel, and Paine, we can get a sense of the extent to which game theory models make the counterfactual regarding the causal mechanism: if core features of the model are absent then the outcome does not occur.

In general, few game-theoretic scholars are bold enough to make such strong counterfactuals and the accompanying within-case causal inference. More common is a high degree of modesty regarding the case study. As with statistical multimethod case studies, scholars often present them as "illustrations."

For game-theoretic multimethod research to become a reality, it must move from illustrations to real case studies containing within-case causal inference. To say that a case study is an illustration is often a bit of a tease: the author suggests that the model applies to the case, but then pulls back from making within-case causal inferences. Researchers use the term "illustration" in exactly those situations where they are not really doing multimethod work. In contrast, Kydd (2007) has three model chapters, each followed by a case study chapter showing how the model explains a major Cold War or end-of-Cold War event.

This feature of game theory multimethod practice may be a combination of training and inclination. To engage in within-case causal analysis means taking on historians and experts on individual cases. One might suspect that this is less comfortable terrain for many formal modelers who are more used to talking about statistical inference than within-case causal inference.

In broad brush strokes, one can say that most game-theoretic articles claim that the model is applicable to real-world events and can help us understand the behavior of actors. Authors utilize numerous short historical examples implying or suggesting that the model is relevant. At the same time, these scholars hesitate to make serious causal inferences about any of these cases individually.

As an immodest proposal, it might be of worth for fields to demand an empirical existence proof for modelers who make empirical relevance claims about their models. One might minimally require a serious case study where the model explains *one* case at least. Sudgen argues for the importance of such empirical existence proofs:

> If there is to be a genuine demonstration of the potential usefulness of a theoretical tool, we have to be shown that it works. Continuing with the analogy, think of the old-style vacuum-cleaner salesman who scatters dirt on the carpet and then shows how successfully his product can clean up the mess. If this demonstration is to be at all convincing, the would-be buyer has to believe that the dirt is real dirt and the cleaning is real cleaning. Similarly, if the theorist is offering a tool that is intended to be used in explaining real-world phenomena, a convincing demonstration must display the tool explaining something. Just as the salesman's dirt is a contrived cleaning problem, chosen to engage the attention of the would-be buyer, so the theorist might choose as the focus of her demonstration some phenomenon that will attract the attention of her readers.... But the theorist still has to produce a real explanation of the phenomenon.... I have suggested that one should be skeptical whenever a theorist claims to have discovered a significant social mechanism, but is unable to give a concrete example of how that mechanism can be part of an explanation of some real-world phenomenon; and I stand by that. (Sugden 2009, 25)

Journal editors and audiences might well require that the case study stand up to expert review. Do those familiar with the case find the argument plausible? Most interesting historical events are the source of debates about causes. As we shall see in the next chapter, some have found no evidence for prominent game-theoretic models in some population of cases. In other instances, the models have received empirical support in the sense that some percentage of the population of cases contain elements of the causal mechanism.

It is safe to say that the standards for argument for within-case causal inference in political science and sociology are much lower than statistical causal inference. There is an extensive literature on process tracing, counterfactuals, etc. that is directly relevant to game theory multimethod research, but that is rarely cited in game theory multimethod articles.

By definition, multimethod research means being familiar with multiple methods. There exists a chasm between game theory and within-case causal methodologies. The research triad means instituting a dialogue between within-case causal inference and game theory models.

CHAPTER 7

Large-N Qualitative Testing: A New Methodology?

Introduction

In recent years a notable trend has developed for doing—and publishing in top journals—what I call "large-N qualitative testing." This expression is intentionally somewhat ironic and oxymoronic. "Large-N" usually implies statistical testing, while "qualitative testing" is almost by definition small-N and nonstatistical.

A common feature of large-N statistical tests is that the crucial variable in the statistical analysis is only indirectly related to the causal mechanisms in the theory, e.g., GDP/capita in studies of civil war. Hence strong statistical results only modestly support the causal mechanisms embedded in the theory.

Large-N qualitative testing examines a large percentage—ideally *all*—of the "relevant" cases for concrete, empirical evidence of the causal mechanisms in the hypothesis. Instead of indirect statistical tests, one has direct qualitative tests. The ideal scenario—i.e., publishable in the *American Political Science Review*, *American Sociological Review*, *International Organization*, or other top-ranked journals—is that the researcher, usually the critic, finds no cases where the causal mechanism can be found in the case studies done one by one. Hence, while the theory might be supported by statistical measures and analysis, the large-N qualitative tests falsify the hypothesis via process tracing and causal mechanism analysis.

This methodology rests not on cross-case comparisons and statistics, but rather within-case causal inference. The previous chapter argued for the use of empirical existence proofs as part of testing game-theoretic models. Such tests do not address how widespread or general the causal mechanism is. Large-N qualitative testing directly addresses the "how general?" question about causal mechanisms and theories. In the examples discussed here the answer typically is "not general at all."

This chapter explores examples of large-N qualitative testing. One set includes key works in the literature on the economic determinants of democracy. A second set comes from the realm of conflict studies. I shall use "critic" to refer to those authors and articles conducting the large-N qualitative testing, and "target authors" for those whose hypotheses and/or empirical findings are under examination.

Target authors: Acemoglu, D., and J. Robinson. 2006. *Economic origins of dictatorship and democracy.* Cambridge: Cambridge University Press.

Boix, C. 2003. *Democracy and redistribution.* New York: Cambridge University Press.

Critics: Haggard, S. and Kaufman, R. 2012. Inequality and regime change: democratic transitions and the stability of democratic rule. *American Political Science Review* 106:1–22. (See also Haggard and Kaufman 2016).

Target authors: Cusack, T., T. Iversen, and D. Soskice. 2007. Economic interests and the origins of electoral systems. *American Political Science Review* 101:373–91.

Critic: Kreuzer, M. 2010. Historical knowledge and quantitative analysis: the case of the origins of proportional representation. *American Political Science Review* 104:369–92.

Target authors: Mansfield, E., and J. Snyder. 2005. *Electing to fight: why emerging democracies go to war.* Cambridge: MIT Press.

Critics: Narang, V. and R. Nelson. 2009. Who are these belligerent democratizers? Reassessing the impact of democratization on war. *International Organization* 63:357–79.

Target author: Fearon, J. 1994. Domestic political audiences and the escalation of international disputes. *American Political Science Review* 88:577–92.

Critics: Snyder, J. and E. Borghard. 2011. The cost of empty threats: a penny, not a pound. *American Political Science Review* 105: 437–55.

Trachtenberg, M. 2012. Audience costs: an historical analysis. *Security Studies* 21:3–42.

Target author: Toft, M. 2010. *Securing the peace: the durable settlement of civil wars*. Princeton: Princeton University Press.

Toft, M. 2010. Ending civil wars: A case for rebel victory? *International Security* 34:7–36.

Critic: Wallensteen, P. 2015. *Quality peace: peacebuilding, victory and world order*. Oxford: Oxford University Press.

The work of the target authors has been very influential and there is usually an extensive literature surrounding the target author's research. Often there is extensive empirical evidence—statistical in nature—that supports the theory or hypothesis in question.

These examples involve prominent scholars but certainly one can find others (e.g., Ross 2004). My selection criteria are basically (1) prominence of theory or statistical results, (2) publication by critics in major journals, and (3) examples from international relations and comparative politics.

The purpose of this chapter is to lay out the implicit methodology of large-N qualitative testing underlying the critics' work and to raise some fundamental issues of case selection and testing philosophy. For example, the large-N qualitative tests do not include all—and typically nowhere close to all—the observations that appear in a statistical analysis. At the same time, there is usually a sense in which the critics attempt to examine all the relevant cases.

Statistics has well-developed procedures for rejecting hypotheses, e.g., p-values. It is not clear what the standards are or should be for large-N qualitative testing. Things are pretty clear if no cases can be found where the causal mechanism is present, but more likely there will be some support found. This is the "half-empty, half-full" problem, where from one perspective the support is weak, but from another it is significant. Also, cross-case statistical analyses can find no causal effect, but the within-case large-N qualitative testing does find "significant" support for the causal mechanism.

The Basic Setup

The debates listed above do not constitute the universe of large-N qualitative testing. Clearly selection effects are massive since almost all have appeared in top journals. But it does mean that editors and reviewers have found this methodology persuasive.

The list of target authors contains some prominent hypotheses, often backed by significant statistical results. Sometimes targets are game-theoretic models that are probed for their empirical relevance. Acemoglu and Robinson's book has been very influential, even though it contains almost no empirical analysis. Similarly, Fearon's audience costs formal model has generated a large literature, theoretical and empirical. In short, large-N qualitative testing chooses a prominent theoretical statement that has been given influential empirical (i.e., statistical) support or for which there is an influential game-theoretic model.

Haggard and Kaufman's *American Political Science Review* article illustrates clearly most of the features of the large-N qualitative testing setup. They make this quite clear in the abstract to their article:

> Recent work by Carles Boix and Daron Acemoglu and James Robinson has focused on the role of inequality and distributive conflict in transitions to and from democratic rule. We assess these claims through causal process observation, using an original qualitative dataset on democratic transitions and reversions during the "third wave" from 1980 to 2000. We show that distributive conflict, a key causal mechanism in these theories, is present in just over half of all transition cases. Against theoretical expectations, a substantial number of these transitions occur in countries with high levels of inequality. Less than a third of all reversions are driven by distributive conflicts between elites and masses. We suggest a variety of alternative

causal pathways to both transitions and reversions. (Haggard and Kaufman 2012, 1; complete abstract)

The basic setup in broad outline contains the following elements:

1. The target authors are quite clearly identified.
2. The target works are statistical or game theoretic.
3. The methodology of testing is within-case causal inference, looking for the causal mechanism via process tracing in individual cases.
4. Each case is coded as having the causal mechanism or not, i.e., within-case causal inference.
5. Critics look at "all" cases.
6. The critics base their conclusions on the percentage of case studies where the causal mechanism is present. Typically the percentage of cases where the causal mechanism is present is low, and ideally close to zero.

This basic procedure seems to be relatively unproblematic in that journal editors and reviewers have been convinced by it. In addition, even the target authors and their allies seem to accept the basic framework. However, as the next two sections explore, there are major issues of case selection and testing methodology that need to be made explicit and discussed.

Case Selection

In general, it is quite rare for all the cases in the statistical analysis to be examined in the qualitative testing. However, it might be that the statistical analysis itself has relatively few cases. This is the situation in Kreuzer's analysis of the Cusack, Iversen, and Soskice data, which has only 18 cases (basically pre-1920 developed democracies). In this situation it is then in fact possible to look at all the cases.

Even here case selection is an issue:

Sampling. CIS [Cusack, Iversen, and Soskice] use a very small sample of 12 to 18 pre-1920 electoral system choices. This historically restricted sample makes sense because it increases the equivalence of cases and indirectly controls for possible period effects. This benefit, however, is offset by a sampling bias, evident in their selection of 18 of the 32 available cases of electoral systems chosen in Europe prior to 1920, and the lack of any explanation for the exclusion of the other 14. CIS clearly oversample West European cases, leaving out the ten East European democracies that emerged after 1918. They also undersample failed democracies, including only Germany, Italy, and Austria, but excluding Portugal, Spain, Greece, and all East European democracies except Czechoslovakia. (Kreuzer 2010, 373)

In all large-N qualitative testing, the universe or population of cases is up for dispute. Taking an existing study like Cusack, Iversen, and Soskice makes things easier, but there will almost certainly be boundary disputes, e.g., including all failed democracies or not.

One factor that makes large-N qualitative testing possible is that the number of "cases" might be significantly smaller than the number of observations in the statistical data set. For the within-case causal mechanism analysis, basically each country is a case for Kreuzer, hence only 15–30 potential cases. Statistical analysis becomes possible when the observation in the data set is dyad–year, easily several hundred observations.

While it is hard to determine based on few examples, the upper limit for large-N qualitative testing is probably around 50 cases. In almost all the examples the issue of scope is very central, because that influences the selection of case studies, and hence potential selection bias. In many situations, critics think long and hard about the scope limits to their analyses; the main exception is when they use exactly the same data set as the target authors. In part this is because the methodology of large-N qualitative testing is unclear and because rarely will all the cases in the statistical analysis be examined.

· · ·

Core to large-N qualitative testing is evaluating how general or generalizable the hypothesis is. One might be able to find one or two examples, e.g., empirical existence proofs, but how widespread is the causal mechanism? Narang and Nelson's critique (2009) of the hypothesis that democratization leads to an increased likelihood of international war illustrates the role of scope and generalization in large-N qualitative testing.

In a series of influential articles and a book, Mansfield and Snyder (2005) challenged the democratic peace literature that implied that democratization was good because it would lead to less war. Their core hypothesis is that incomplete transitions to democracy AND weak institutions produce war. It is not just democratization but democratization AND weak institutions. While an interaction-term argument, for the purposes of this chapter, I treat the interaction term as one variable.

They have significant statistical results: "Using regression analysis, Mansfield and Snyder show that this specific class of states is roughly eight to ten times more likely to be involved in war than a stable state undergoing no transition" (Narang and Nelson 2009, 357). Hence we have the standard setup where a provocative hypothesis is supported by statistical analysis. Large-N qualitative testing proposes to look at the cases themselves.

The core of large-N qualitative testing lies in the analysis of cases in the (1, 1) cell. As such it forms the centerpiece of the Narang and Nelson critique. The number of wars is relatively large at 111, but the relevant wars are those produced by the proposed causal mechanism, which in this instance is only 6 cases; see table 7.1.[1] Six is definitely not too many cases to look at individually.

One dramatic finding is that "there are no instances of an incomplete democratizer with [AND] weak institutions participating in, let alone initiating, an external war since World War I" (Narang and Nelson 2009, 365). In other words there are no (1, 1) cases after World War I.

As discussed in the previous chapter, scholars are sensitive to the importance and relevance of the cases in multimethod research. For many, it is quite damaging that the scope of the results appears limited to the pre–World War I period. Had all the cases been good post-1989 ones then the hypothesis would have been more relevant.

---

[1] Thanks to Vilpin Narang for help in constructing table 7.1.

TABLE 7.1

Case selection: democratization, weak institutions, and international war

	$X = 0$	$X = 1$
$Y = 1$	111	6
$Y = 0$	2271	142

$X = 1$: weak institutions AND democratization.
$Y = 1$: international war.

In short, Narang and Nelson thus find (1) very few cases in the $(1, 1)$ cell and (2) they all occurred before World War I. So the Mansfield and Snyder causal mechanism has limited scope and is not very general, at least empirically.

If the $(1, 1)$ cell draws the majority of attention in large-N qualitative testing then conversely the $(0, 0)$ cell receives almost none. As table 7.1 indicates, there are a couple of thousand cases there. Clearly, Narang and Nelson, in addition to having no interest in this cell, would not be able to do case studies on this many cases. In many situations there are a large number of cases in the $(0, 0)$ cell. These observations are obviously used in statistical analyses, but rarely appear in large-N qualitative testing. Other cells of the 2×2 table play roles in large-N qualitative testing, but the $(0, 0)$ cell receives almost no attention from anyone (a conclusion also from chapter 3).

What makes large-N qualitative testing possible is relatively few cases in the $(1, 1)$ cell. If this cell has 50 or fewer cases then the statistical findings can be examined via large-N qualitative testing. For example, the large literature on nuclear weapons proliferation has less than 20 positive, i.e., $Y = 1$, cases. Hence almost any statistical finding in this literature could be subject to large-N qualitative testing. So while the total N of cases in the statistical analysis could easily be in the thousands or higher, the number in the $(1, 1)$ cell is what drives whether large-N qualitative testing is possible or not. In contrast, the number of cases in the $(0, 0)$ cell is almost completely irrelevant.

Narang and Nelson differ from most of the other examples in that they do not directly look at the 6 cases for evidence of the Mansfield and Snyder causal mechanism. The fact that there are only 6, and none in the last 100 years, suffices to suggest that at best the mechanism is not very general and may only have a pre–World War I scope. A key methodological point is that the large-N methodology directly addresses the question of generalization and generalizability of causal mechanisms.

• • •

If one is looking for the causal mechanism that produces Y, i.e., $Y = 1$, then attention is naturally focused on the set of cases where Y is present. I call this the Y-centric approach to large-N qualitative testing. Haggard and Kaufman are quite explicit about the Y-centeredness of their analysis: "Selecting on the dependent variable is a central feature of this approach, which is designed to test a particular theory and thus rests on identification of the causal mechanism leading to regime change. In contrast to the more common practice of purposeful or random selection of cases for more intensive analysis, our approach is to select all transition and reversion cases in the relevant sample period (1980–2000)" (Haggard and Kaufman 2012, 4). Such an approach is quite possible, particularly when the number of $Y = 1$ cases is relatively manageable.

To focus on the $Y = 1$ row means to have data on the causal mechanism cell as well as the equifinality cell (i.e., the $(0, 1)$ cell). For example, in table 7.1, out of 111 wars only 6 have been produced, maybe, by the Mansfield and Snyder causal mechanism. The $Y = 1$ row is the center of attention if the research question involves the relative importance of different causal mechanisms. This is exactly one of Haggard and Kaufman's main questions: How important is the Acemoglu and Robinson causal mechanism vis-à-vis others in transitions to and from democracy? To answer this involves comparing the two $Y = 1$ cells.

In the Narang and Nelson critique, how do we know that 6 is a small number? Implicitly, the reader is comparing that to the population of wars. However, if the scope were post-1989, 6 would be a significant percentage of the total.

For Haggard and Kaufman, the Y-centric strategy is critical because they have alternative mechanisms that they think are more common, and hence have greater explanatory value, than the Acemoglu and Robinson one.[2]

There are two general kinds of case selection. The first looks at all the $Y = 1$ cases, as illustrated by Haggard and Kaufman who examine all transitions to and from democracy in the post-1980 period. The second focuses on those $Y = 1$ cases that could have been produced by X (as coded in the statistical analysis), i.e., those in the $(1, 1)$ cell as illustrated by Narang and Nelson. The difference between the two approaches depends on the importance of equifinality in the analysis of the critics.

. . .

Another possible strategy is what I call the X-centered approach. Here one looks at all the $X = 1$ cases to see how often the causal mechanism produces Y. In the Y-centered approach it could be that all the cases in the $(1, 1)$ cell are in fact produced by the hypothesized causal mechanism. However, choosing only $Y = 1$ cases overlooks instances in which X does not function as advertised and fails to produce Y; it might be that there are quite a few cases where the causal mechanism does not work, i.e., $(1, 0)$ cases.

Trachtenberg's empirical analysis of audience costs theory is a nice example of the X-centered approach. He looks for cases where the causal mechanism might be present based on the theory's scope and the causal mechanism variables. Most of the literature on audience costs focuses on democracies, the regime type where audience costs mechanisms are most likely to be present:

> I will be looking at a set of crises—episodes in which there was a significant perceived risk of war—involving great powers, at least one of which was a democracy, and that were settled without war. These criteria were chosen for the following reasons. The cases are all crises because the Fearon theory explicitly deals with crises, but I will be looking only at great power crises for essentially practical reasons. . . .

---

[2] Haggard and Kaufman do not only pursue a Y-centric approach, but others as well, e.g., statistical analysis.

The focus here, moreover, is on crises in which at least one of the contending parties is a democracy, since much of the debate on this issue has to do with whether the audience costs mechanism gives democracies an advantage over not-democratic regimes. This means that the crises to be examined all took place after 1867.... Finally, only those crises that did not terminate in war will be examined here.... That set of criteria generates a list of about a dozen crises. (Trachtenberg 2012, 5–6)

Trachtenberg thus uses an X-centric strategy by looking at cases of $X = 1$ and seeing whether the audience costs causal mechanism is present. He is not concerned with the $X = 0$ cases at all. This is also the basic idea behind Snyder and Borghard's case selection: "In choosing cases for more detailed research, we looked in particular for cases that should be easy for domestic audience costs theory to explain" (Snyder and Borghard 2011, 444). Cases that should be easy for audience costs theory is a variant on the X-centered case selection strategy.

Trachtenberg uses the basic principle "choose the cases for intensive analysis where the causal mechanism is most likely to work or be present," i.e., major power democracies in not-war crises. If we cannot find evidence of the causal mechanism in these cases then that is very damaging for the theory because our priors would suggest that the causal mechanism would be even less likely in other kinds of cases. So while the scope is quite narrow, it contains very good $X = 1$ cases. As discussed in chapter 3, causal mechanism case selection always places a high priority on good $X = 1$ cases.

He also follows the principle of selecting politically important cases, i.e., involving democratic major powers. Most would argue, usually implicitly, that the mechanism should work for any democracy in all crises (e.g., Kurizaki and Whang 2015). So there are some important scope limits to his analysis (see below for more). However, if audience costs theory were to fail here, but were to work for minor power democracies, something would seem quite wrong with the theory, which could require some, probably major, changes. Core to testing in this setting is politically important events. This is certainly a motivation behind Haggard and Kaufman's decision to look at post-1980 transitions as opposed to, say, pre–World War II ones.

In line with the goal of critics using large-N qualitative testing strategy he finds,

> So what conclusion is to be drawn from the discussion in this whole section of the great power crises won by democratic states [(1, 1) cases]? The basic finding is quite simple. There is little evidence that the audience costs mechanism played a "crucial" role in any of them. Indeed, it is hard to identify any case in which that mechanism played much of a role at all. There are all kinds of ways in which new information is generated in the course of a crisis, and that new information, for the reasons Fearon outlined, plays a fundamental role in determining how that crisis runs its course. Audience costs, however, were not a major factor in any of the crises examined here.[3] (Trachtenberg 2012, 32)

RESPONSES TO CRITICS

In most debates listed in the introduction, the target authors or their allies have had a chance to respond to the large-N qualitative testing. It is useful to see what kinds of strategies they have used. No one has really challenged the underlying testing logic, but rather the responses have more to do with interpreting the results of the testing or how it was carried out. Perhaps most useful in this regard is the *Security Studies* symposium around audience costs, since people from a variety of perspectives contributed to it.

One strategy is to contest the causal interpretation of cases themselves, making the argument that, say, audience costs were in fact present. For example, Cusack, Iversen, and Soskice have

---

[3] As noted in the previous chapter, the Cuban Missile Crisis might be the best empirical-existence-proof case. Trachtenberg himself notes that "for the Kennedy period [Cuban Missile Crisis], however, things were not that simple, and a case can be made that the audience costs mechanism did play a certain role at that time" (Trachtenberg 2012, 30). However, he concludes that in even this case the theory does not work, because Khrushchev did not take US audience costs into account when making his decisions: "The American political situation was not taken into account in any serious way" (Trachtenberg 2012, 30).

vigorously contested Kruezer's interpretation of many cases in an online appendix. However, in my international relations examples this approach has not been taken.

Another strategy is to contest the choice of cases. One variant of this is to say that important cases were ignored. This came up in the responses to Trachtenberg. Both Levy and Schultz mentioned that audience costs theory could play a large role in the decision to initiate a crisis, whereas Trachtenberg looked only at audience costs once a crisis had occurred:

> This implies that the best place to look for audience costs is in prior state decisions whether or not to initiate a threat or stand firm in response to a threat. Audience costs theory would be supported by evidence that leaders refrained from making a threat or issuing a counterthreat because of the fear that they might subsequently have to renege on their threat and incur domestic costs in doing so.... Admittedly, identifying the population of cases where leaders decided whether or not to initiate threats poses a difficult problem. (Levy 2012, 384–85)

Another variant is that the critic included irrelevant cases. Slantchev implicitly uses this strategy by requiring a severe selection criteria for a valid test:

> *If* (1) backing down in a crisis makes an actor suffer costs in addition to those arising from conceding the stakes, (2) these costs increase as the crisis escalates, (3) these costs can become so large that war becomes preferable to a concession, (4) no other mechanism for coercing the opponent exists, and (5) attempting to coerce the opponent does not increase his costs of conceding, *then* escalation can commit an actor to fighting, and the resulting risk of war discourages bluffing, which makes escalation informative and gives it a coercive role. (Slantchev 2012, 377)

These are five pretty important conditions that must all be satisfied. This implies narrow scope and relatively few cases. However, this strategy has the obvious negative consequence of seriously reducing the scope of audience costs theory.

Another strategy—which is common among game theorists—is to argue that the theory is useful and generates important questions, orients research, etc. Not surprisingly, supporters of Fearon, such as Schultz, adopted this tactic: "Our ideas are ultimately accountable to the empirical world, but theories can be valuable for other reasons as well, such as identifying puzzles, offering tentative solutions, and provoking new avenues of research" (Schultz 2012, 374–75).

SUMMARY

This section argued that large-N qualitative testing does not look at all cases, representative cases, or random cases. The focus is on the $(1, 1)$ causal mechanism observations. These are cases where the causal mechanism should be present, at least as coded on the X and Y variables in the statistical analysis or core factors in the game-theoretic model. In general, the causal mechanism cell forms the centerpiece of large-N qualitative testing. This is where the predictions of the theory or causal mechanism are looked at directly. These are the cases where the supposed causal mechanism should be present and if it is not then the statistical findings or game-theoretic model are directly called into question.

Conversely, the $(0, 0)$ cell is almost of no interest whatsoever. It is probably safe to assume that selecting cases from this cell never crossed the mind of the critics.

In all of the examples cited above, the number of cases in the $(1, 1)$ cell is much smaller than the N of the statistical analysis. The small number of cases in the $(1, 1)$ cell makes it possible to do relatively intensive case studies.

Chapter 3 concluded that most of the interest lies in the $X = 1$ column. The Trachtenberg selection process illustrates that nicely. For the Y-centric strategy, one brings into play the $(0, 1)$ equifinality cell. A large part of the Haggard and Kaufman project is to suggest that other causal mechanisms are much more important than those defended by the target authors. Hence there should be quite a few cases in the $(0, 1)$ equifinality cell. This cell is the focus of attention when exploring other causal mechanisms. In short, the X-centric and Y-centric strategies map nicely onto the basic logic of case selection outlined in chapter 3.

Scope and generalization play a core role in large-N qualitative testing. Scope and theory considerations played a key role in Trachtenberg's constitution of his universe of cases. Narang and Nelson's finding that all the Mansfield and Snyder cases were pre–World War I seriously limited the empirical scope of their theory. Haggard and Kaufman have quite a broad scope by including all transitions to and from democracy since 1980. Similarly, Kreuzer looks at all cases pre-1920 using the scope limitations of his target article. Large-N qualitative testing means doing systematic case study analyses to evaluate the empirical scope and validity of theories.

Absolute versus Relative Criteria for Testing

To think about the half-empty, half-full problem, we can use methodologies developed in the context of cross-case analysis, e.g., statistics and QCA. Hence this section abandons the idea that judgments are made based on within-case causal inference. However, we can use cross-case ideas to develop ideas about standards for evaluating results based on within-case analyses.

Trachtenberg uses what one might call an "absolute" criterion for judging whether there is support for the audience costs model. He looks at the proportion of $(1, 1)$ cases in the $X = 1$ column. If that proportion is near 1.0 then support is strong, if that proportion is near 0.0 it is weak. For reasons that will become clear, this can be called the iron law version of Trachtenberg's audience costs hypothesis. But there will inevitably be some half-full or half-empty situations. How should one draw the line or decide whether the hypothesis receives "significant" support in the middle region between 1.0 and 0.0?

Table 7.2 illustrates the half–half situation. Levy and Thompson test one of the most influential theories in the history of international relations: balance of power. A core version of the balance of power hypothesis involves balancing against hegemons: if there is a hegemon then other states will form an alliance to balance the hegemon. Levy and Thompson look at this systematically among great land powers in Europe,

TABLE 7.2
Relative importance criterion: balance of power theory

	Nonhegemon	Hegemon
No balancing	0.70	0.45
Balancing	0.30	0.55

χ^2=28, $p = 0.000$, N = 445.

Source: based on Levy and Thompson (2005, table 2).

1495–1999. They define hegemon as at least 33 percent of the system capability, and define balancing as an alliance agreement against the hegemon. The short version of the hypothesis is "if hegemon then balancing."

As they note in another article, "The proposition that near-hegemonic concentrations of power in the system nearly always trigger a counter-balancing coalition of the other great powers has long been regarded as an 'iron law' by balance of power theorists" (Levy and Thompson 2010). An iron law could be interpreted as a probability near 1.0. One could formulate the "Trachtenberg iron law": the odds of seeing audience costs in crises with democratic states are 0.0.

If we apply the Trachtenberg strategy, we look at the $X = 1$ (i.e., hegemon) column to see how often there is balancing. Table 7.2 shows balancing 55 percent of the time. Obviously, this does not support the iron law view of balance of power.

Yet, they do conclude that there is a significant tendency to balance: "Nevertheless, our principal hypotheses, which emphasize balancing against leading states that pose a hegemonic threat based on a high concentration of land-based military power, which we operationalize as 33 percent or more of the total capability in the system, find ample support from the data" (Levy and Thompson 2005, 30). How do they come to that conclusion?

The Trachtenberg strategy looks only at the $X = 1$ column. The Levy and Thompson strategy is a *relative*, comparative one. They use the information in the nonhegemon, $X = 0$ column. In table 7.2, $\chi^2 = 28$, which is very significant. This high χ^2 value comes in part from the fact that in the nonhegemon column there is an alliance response only 30 percent of the time. That 30 percent is significantly lower than 55 percent.

Because of the relative nature of the test conclusions, a 55 percent success rate varies in sign and significance depending on the numbers in the $X = 0$ column. If the percentage in that column were 70 percent then one would conclude that countries significantly *do not balance*.

If Trachtenberg had found, say, 20 percent of the cases with audience costs, that could easily be compatible with a conclusion that there is significant support for audience costs if the percentage in the $X = 0$ column were close to zero.

The absolute and relative criteria for judging large-N tests do not have to agree. It is quite possible to have a high absolute score and still conclude that the evidence is weak. Conversely, the absolute test might be weak but the relative test quite strong.

Those interested in necessary conditions or QCA have thought about standards for absolute tests. This is clearest in the literature on testing necessary conditions (Dion 1998; Ragin 2000; Braumoeller and Goertz 2000). These analyses take the iron law versions where the hypothesis is that X is necessary for Y. Using an example from this chapter, this would be the hypothesis that the Acemoglu and Robinson mechanism finds support in all cases of democratic transition.

The same logic holds for sufficient conditions. The balance of power hypothesis as posed by Levy and Thompson is a sufficient condition one: if hegemon then balancing. Within QCA there are some common standards for saying that there is significant support for the hypothesis. These tend to have a minimum bar of around 75–80 percent (often higher for necessary conditions; see Schneider and Wagemann 2012). Within QCA this constitutes the criterion for passing the sufficient condition test. Since the balancing hypothesis is a sufficient condition one, percentages above this bar constitute passing the test. One can certainly raise the bar, for example, Braumoeller and Goertz use 90–95 percent as a necessary condition test criterion.

Trachtenberg's analysis illustrates how this works. His finding is that 0.0 percent of the 12 cases have audience costs. This would certainly and easily pass the QCA bar. In fact, Dion shows, using Bayes' theorem, that one would be very confident, well over 95 percent, in the hypothesis that one would never find an audience costs example. While counterintuitive at first glance, he shows that you already become quite confident with only five or six case studies.[4] The intuition comes from coin tossing: If you had tossed a coin 12 times and it always came up heads, what would you conclude about future tosses?

The QCA procedures do use information from the other column (e.g., nonhegemon). However, it is *not* used in a comparison with the $X = 1$ column but rather in order to assess how trivial or important the necessary or sufficient condition is (i.e., coverage in QCA). For example, the democratic peace in 1820 is a trivial sufficient condition. While the democratic peace does hold, there are almost no democracies in that period, so it holds in a trivial manner. However, by 2010 the democratic peace is definitely not trivial because about half the countries in the world are democracies. In QCA, the $X = 0$ column would be used evaluate whether Trachtenberg's result is a trivial one.

As Braumoeller and Goertz (2000) show, in most instances passing the nontrivialness test is not problematic. One can see this in table 7.2: if the $X = 1$ column were 80 percent then it is very likely that the percentage in the $X = 0$ column would be significantly less, hence a nontrivial sufficient condition. Remember that Levy and Thompson already got statistically significant results with 55 percent.

Going back to Levy and Thompson, to answer the absolute criterion question about balancing requires a clear null hypothesis. QCA standards require percentages greater than 75–80. Another obvious candidate for the balancing hypothesis would be 50 as a null hypothesis: the percentage in the $X = 1$ column must be significantly greater than 50 using simple binomial tests. The Levy and Thompson result of 55 probably would not pass this 50 null hypothesis.[5] As noted above, they use an implicit null hypothesis of 30, which comes from the $X = 0$ column. So the 50 null hypothesis ups the bar significantly.

---

[4] Braumoeller and Goertz (2000) come to basically the same conclusion via a different statistical route using power analyses.

[5] This "probably" is because they use year as the unit of analysis in the 2×2 table, which produces a large N. If one used (non)balancing "episode," the N would be much smaller.

In short, one can use relative or absolute ways of thinking about the half-empty, half-full problem. Statistical analyses offer a relative criterion perspective; set theory and QCA offer an approach to the absolute criterion.

Large-N Qualitative Testing

One of the fascinating features of large-N qualitative testing is that no author has explicitly defended their causal inference strategy or compared it with statistical procedures. There are important differences in making causal inferences between large-N qualitative testing and statistical approaches.

If one goes to the basic 2×2 table, the $(0, 0)$ cell plays essentially no role in large-N qualitative testing. However, *all* cells of a 2×2 table are used in two-way measures of association, such as χ^2, e.g., table 7.2. In particular, the potential outcomes approach relies on the counterfactual, which determines whether there is a causal effect: if X—treatment—had been zero then the outcome counterfactually would have been zero, i.e., the $(0, 0)$ cell.

Conversely, most of the attention in large-N qualitative testing focuses on the $(1, 1)$ cell. This radical difference in importance between the $(0, 0)$ cell and the $(1, 1)$ cell is completely foreign to the logic of 2×2 statistical measures. Statistical significance, e.g., of χ^2, depends on the relationship between all of the cells.

A statistical approach focuses on *cross-case* comparisons, while large-N qualitative testing depends fundamentally on *within-case causal inference*. Large-N qualitative testing works by accumulating systematically within-case causal inferences. This is fundamentally different from cross-case comparisons, be they randomized experiments or observational data.

The basic procedure takes statistically significant or theoretically important hypotheses and submits them to within-case causal inference testing. The conclusion is sometimes that the within-case causal inference contradicts the significant statistical results. But what about the opposite direction, results that are not statistically significant from the cross-case statistical analysis, but are significant in the within-case causal inference testing?

TABLE 7.3
No statistical significance and large-N qualitative testing

	$X = 0$	$X = 1$
$Y = 1$	30	15
$Y = 0$	60	30

Table 7.3 gives some hypothetical data that show no relationship between row and column, indicated clearly by the row and column ratios being exactly the same for $Y = 0$ and $Y = 1$. In other words, the odds of getting Y are exactly the same for $X = 1$ and $X = 0$. The same would happen in table 7.2 if the $X = 0$ column had 55 percent.

Large-N qualitative testing focuses on the $(1, 1)$ cell. For the purposes of argument, assume that within-case causal inference of the 15 cases in cell $(1, 1)$ reveals that the hypothesized causal mechanism was present in all. What should we conclude?

If we take the Y-centered approach and look across the $Y = 1$ row, we see that quite a few cases of Y occur when causal mechanism X is not present. Should that invalidate or influence our conclusions? This row determines the relative importance of different causal mechanisms. For example, Haggard and Kaufman are very clear on this in their analysis of the question of the relative importance of causal mechanisms:

> However, we did find several alternative causal mechanisms. In several cases, incumbent democratic governments were overthrown not by socioeconomic elites seeking to block redistribution, but by authoritarian populist leaders promising more redistribution. Even more commonly, however, reversions were driven by conflicts that either cut across class lines or arose from purely intra-elite conflicts, particularly conflicts in which factions of the military staged coups against incumbent office holders. (Haggard and Kaufman 2012, 2)

They found some support—often for part but not all of the mechanism—for the causal mechanisms proposed by the target authors, usually in the range of 30 percent of the cases studied. However, this is overshadowed by the greater importance of other mechanisms.

This result leads to the conclusion that distributive theories receive some support in the data, but other causal mechanisms are more important, as illustrated by the hypothetical data in table 7.3. But as such, these alternative mechanism cases do not disconfirm or falsify that the distributive mechanism does work in some cases.

A much greater threat to the causal mechanism is posed by the $(1, 0)$ cases. These are the cases where we should see the causal mechanism in action. In the hypothetical data in table 7.3 we have some cases where the causal mechanism produces the outcome, i.e., $(1, 1)$ cases, and some where it does not, based on causal mechanism analysis, i.e., the $(1, 0)$ cases. A natural move is to ask in what percentage of cases does the causal mechanism work; in table 7.3 it is $15/45 = 0.33$.

From this brief discussion and example, one notices several important features of the implicit testing philosophy behind large-N qualitative testing. This assumes that the cases in the $(1, 1)$ cell have the causal mechanism, and the presence of the causal mechanism has been confirmed by within-case analysis:

1. Comparison across the $Y = 1$ row compares the causal mechanism X against other potential—and possibly unknown—causal mechanisms, but does not invalidate the causal mechanism per se.
2. Comparison down the $X = 1$ column potentially suggests that the causal mechanism does not work all the time. This is direct evidence against it.
3. Some empirical support for the causal mechanism does exist. In contrast, statistical measures suggest that there is no relationship at all between X and Y.

If one combines the X-centered and Y-centered approaches, then the $(0, 0)$ cell remains of little or no importance. Where the two approaches intersect is the $(1, 1)$ causal mechanism cell. The is the core of large-N qualitative testing.

Large-N qualitative testing can certainly contradict the conclusions of statistical analysis: the statistical analysis can find no relationship, while within-case analysis does produce support. The statistical logic is that the odds of success for $X = 0$ are exactly the same as for $X = 1$ in table 7.3, i.e., no evidence that the occurrence of X makes any difference.

In fact there are at least two different questions: (1) how important the causal mechanism X is vis-à-vis other causal mechanisms, which comes out in the Y-oriented approach, and (2) how often the causal mechanism actually works when the theory says we should expect to see it in action, which comes out in the X-oriented approach.

Critical is the assumption of placing cases on the basis of within-case causal analysis where the causal mechanism is shown to be present or not. Table 7.3 assumes that the (1, 1) cases were produced by the causal mechanism in question; the within-case shows cases in (1, 0) are produced by other mechanisms; based on within-case analysis the causal mechanism is not working in the (1, 0) cell. This is different from most of the multimethod examples discussed in this book where the statistical measures put cases in these cells.

In the hypothetical data in table 7.3, the causal inference is occurring *before* and *as* the table is being constructed. Cross-case statistical inference can really only begin when there are numbers in each cell to compare. Another way to think about this is that large-N qualitative testing does not need all four cells to work. The X-centric strategy, e.g., Trachtenberg and audience costs, proceeds nicely with only the $X = 1$ column, whereas 2×2 measures of association require data for all four cells.

Large-N Qualitative Testing: Final Example and Summary

Often, large-N qualitative testing adopts the X-centric approach. Given that it is a *test*, that means there is an existing X that the target author claims is a cause of Y. As a final example I use Wallensteen's (the critic) large-N qualitative test (2015) of Toft's (target author) provocative hypothesis and statistical analysis (2009; 2010), where she "makes a case for victory," claiming victory in civil war has a number of positive outcomes for the post-civil-war state, including (1) reduced likelihood of recurrence of civil war, (2) increased economic growth, and (3) democratization. I focus in particular on the impact of rebel victory on democratization. Wallensteen (2015) explores all three claimed positive features of victory in civil war in general. I limit myself to the claim that rebel victory leads to democratization.[6]

In short, Toft's work and argument present a classic scenario for large-N qualitative testing, prominent and provocative argument by a well-known scholar and based on statistical analyses.

Her analysis drew a lot of attention from conflict scholars and made it into the general foreign policy discourse, e.g., articles in *Foreign Affairs*,[7] *Newsweek*,[8] and the *Christian Science Monitor*;[9] this last one is by Toft herself. In Colombia, her research was presented to the Parliament. It made a strong argument against current international and UN policy preferring negotiated settlements in civil wars, and was seen by many realists as illustrating the utility of military force in producing positive outcomes.

Even more provocatively, Toft claims that *rebel victory* has particularly strong positive effects:

> Rebel victories paint a more positive picture. Put simply, following rebel victory, democratization increases. Within ten years, autocracy has decreased by more than one point, and by twenty years that amount has more than doubled. This trend on the whole is statistically significant compared to other termination types (though the slight increase in authoritarianism at the fifteen-year mark is not). Although still within the authoritarian range, these countries demonstrate that repression eases for a good portion of the citizenry following a rebel victory. In fact, states where rebel victories have taken place perform better on average than all of the other types on the democratization front when measured twenty years after the end of conflict—a finding that is statistically significant. (Toft 2009, 65–66)

---

[6] She argues that victory is better than negotiated settlement on these three dimensions. I do not address this aspect of her analysis. Wallensteen gives those claims close examination as well.

[7] https://www.foreignaffairs.com/articles/syria/2013-01-02/no-settlement-damascus

[8] http://www.newsweek.com/why-wars-no-longer-end-winners-and-losers-70865

[9] http://www.csmonitor.com/Commentary/Opinion/2011/0913/Why-a-rebel-victory-in-Libya-is-better-than-a-negotiated-settlement

Since rebel victory is relatively rare (not surprisingly most of the time if there is a victor it is the central government), this makes it quite easy to explore the causal mechanism cases. These are then rebel victories ($X = 1$) followed by democratization ($Y = 1$).

In her statistical analysis she looks at the level of democracy 20 years after the end of the war.[10] This is a relatively long period—and typically much longer than customary in conflict studies, which tend to use around 5 years, rarely 10, and very rarely 20 years or more. In practical terms, this means that *all* post–Cold War civil wars are excluded from her analysis.[11] The most recent rebel victory in Toft's data is that of Yoweri Museveni in Uganda, 1986.[12] In short, the post–Cold War outcomes are not covered.[13]

With the 20-year period for democratization, the N of causal mechanism cases (i.e., the $(1, 1)$ cell) has now become quite small in her analysis. Wallensteen notes that there are only three cases with significant increases in the Polity democracy score. He can now proceed to briefly explore whether rebel victory was responsible for the democracy level 20 years later:

> In fact, there are only three cases with dramatic increases in polity scores, and this alone explains a large degree of the variance. None of them, however, are reassuring for the thesis of the democratizing effects of rebel victory. Let us quickly review them. They include the

[10] "Democratization" typically means either (1) the state has passed the democracy threshold on the Polity scale, or (2) it is moving in the democracy direction. None of Toft's cases fit (1), so democratization for her means moving in the democratization direction; the country could still be quite undemocratic and even quite authoritarian.

[11] This is particularly problematic given that she is arguing against negotiated settlements, which became much more common after 1989, in fact more common than victory by either side; see Goertz, Diehl, and Balas (2016) and Fortna (2009) for a discussion of changing victory rates in civil war.

[12] Interestingly she includes Uganda as a case study. She notes that the *first* election in Uganda occurred in 2006, 20 years after the civil war was over, hardly a strong case for the positive impact of rebel victory on democratization.

[13] One could easily imagine an analysis that tracks the level of democracy (according to the Polity data set) for each year after the civil war, with a running tally of net democratization (negative would mean net move toward authoritarianism). This would have significant advantages over comparing democracy at victory with democracy 20 years later.

short but bloody coup against President Juan Peron in Argentina in 1955, the coming to power of the Khmer Rouge in Cambodia in 1975, and the Iranian revolution in 1979. However, the increased scores following these rebel victories are difficult to attribute to the rebel victory, if we follow the cases more closely.

After the coup that removed Peron in 1955, Argentina went through a period of considerable political instability and remarkably by the twenty-year cut-off point in 1975, Argentina again saw a Peron at the helm, but this time his wife and widow, Isabel Peron, as President. She was removed in another military coup the following year. Moving from one Peron to another, interspersed with military coups and political turbulence, hardly appears to be a major gain in democratization.

The second case refers to the events after 1975 in Cambodia. The victorious rebels of the Khmer Rouge led by Pol Pot were deposed by the Vietnamese invasion in 1979, which in turn was ended through international pressure and the Paris peace agreement in 1991. This gave space for elections in 1993. By that time the rebels, who were victorious in 1975, had been marginalized. Thus it is hard to attribute Cambodia's dramatic change in polity scores to this particular rebel victory.

As to the Iranian revolution, the increased score by 1999–2000 is harder to understand, but reflects the coding in Polity IV, where there is an increase recorded for Iran. For the period 1997–2003 a more open, "liberal" President, Ayatollah Mohammad Khatami, was at the helm of the Islamic Republic, although the real power remained with the clergy. It is hard to conclude, however, that there was a dramatic move toward democratization that can be attributed to the rebels-turned-government. (Wallensteen 2015, section 3.4)

In fact, according to Wallensteen, she fails to produce even an empirical existence proof. The Wallensteen analysis of Toft illustrates all the procedures and features of large-N qualitative testing. He pays particular attention to the (1, 1) causal mechanism ones.

• • •

Some version of large-N qualitative testing can easily become a part of multimethod research. Doing case studies on the

$(1, 1)$ cases can support the claims based on the statistical analyses. In this sense, large-N qualitative testing can be used—should be used—to verify statistical analyses. Proponents of causal mechanism philosophy work from a basic premise: no successful causal inference without a causal mechanism (see Goertz and Mahoney 2012 for a discussion). If one cannot produce convincing case studies showing the causal mechanism in action, it is hard to find the statistical analyses convincing at all.

The purpose of this chapter has been to explore the logic underlying large-N qualitative testing. A key theme is that the logic of large-N qualitative testing differs from that of the cross-case procedures used in statistics. This has played out in my analysis of how statistics looks at 2×2 tables versus how large-N qualitative testing uses or does not use the various cells of the 2×2 table for within-case causal analysis.

Any statistical analysis with an N of 50 or less in the $(1, 1)$ cell is a potential target for large-N qualitative analysis. Major areas of political science and sociology are thus open for exploration. The literature on nuclear weapons proliferation often involves statistical analyses with thousands of observations. For example, Gartzke and Jo (2009) use nuclear weapons as an independent variable in a statistical analysis with over a million observations. However, depending on the dependent variable, there are at best a couple of dozen cases of nuclear proliferation, and therefore even fewer cases in the $(1, 1)$ cell.

One can see the wide-ranging implications of large-N qualitative testing for the literature on the democratic peace. The causal mechanism cases are those dyads that are good democracies and that are clearly at peace (i.e., high-quality peace). If one limits the population to contiguous states, there are not really so many dyads in the $(1, 1)$ cell. For testing, one can limit oneself to, for example, high-quality democracies that are contiguous. For much of the nineteenth and twentieth centuries this is not a large set of case studies. Yet, none (that I know of at least) of the case study analyses of the democratic peace have focused on this set of relationships.

This chapter does not pretend to have covered all the issues involved in large-N qualitative testing. Rather, I hope that it stimulates methodological debate about the properties of this approach. As the examples discussed here illustrate, the potential payoff of large-N qualitative testing is considerable, as indicated by the journals and presses that have published my examples.

CHAPTER 8

Case Studies, Scope, and Generalization

Introduction

This chapter outlines a new research design, the "medium-N paradigm." This paradigm focuses on generalization based on within-case causal analyses. Large-N qualitative testing asks the generalization question. The goal of doing within-case causal inference in all relevant cases clearly means the scholar wants to assess how generalizable or how general the hypothesis or game-theoretic model is. The core question raised by the last chapter—how to use case studies to evaluate models—continues in this one, reformulated in terms of extrapolation, generalization, and scope.

There is a range within which there are relatively few research projects, starting with about 7–10 cases and extending to about 50 cases. The vast majority of books and articles examine fewer than 7–10 or more than 50. The in-between, medium-N range has not really been the subject of case study and multimethod discussions. Outside of Ragin and QCA, this research space is a virtual desert. Indeed, a primary justification for QCA has often been that the N is too small for statistical analysis and too large for comparative case studies. Medium-N multimethod research targets this range in particular.

Once one gets to 30–50 positive $(Y = 1)$ cases it is sometimes quite easy to do statistical analyses. This occurs for a couple of reasons. First, as illustrated by the comparative industrial countries literature, one can do time-series analyses, so 30 countries over 30 years becomes 900 observations. Similarly, 50 civil wars become thousands of observations when all not-war years for all countries are included in the data set, i.e., 150 nations times 50 years = 7500 observations. It is not uncommon in the statistical conflict literature to see analyses in the top journals with less than 1 percent of $Y = 1$ cases.[1]

If one uses the number of $Y = 1$ cases as the measure of N, the medium-N paradigm includes many quantitative studies in its range of application. Many of the examples discussed in the previous chapter illustrate that the medium-N paradigm can and should coexist with statistical analyses.

The medium-N range, while not very popular in absolute terms, is arguably a site where many of the most influential comparative politics works reside. If one looks at the classics, many of them fall in the medium-N range: Skocpol (1979), Downing (1992), Ertman (1997), Esping-Andersen (1990), and Rueschemeyer, Stephens, and Stephens (1992) lie in this range. Recent influential books also appear in this the medium-N range, such as Levitsky and Way (2010) and Mahoney (2010).

Cross-case approaches use a large N to generate many comparisons (e.g., $X = 1$ versus $X = 0$ as in matching). In contrast, the medium-N paradigm relies on within-case causal inference. Classic statistical multimethod typically works from a cross-case statistical analysis to a within-case causal mechanism case study. The medium-N paradigm starts from within-case causal inference and then asks how one can do more case studies to explore how generalizable the causal mechanism is.

Generalization is closely related to scope: wide scope implies wide generalization. Generalization is also related to extrapolation. If we can extrapolate successfully then the causal mechanism is more general.[2]

A central question for the medium-N paradigm is how case studies relate to generalization. The same question applies to experiments: How can we generalize based on an experiment

---

[1] This is obviously problematic from the statistical point of view.

[2] Yin uses the term "analytic generalization" to refer to the generalization of case studies: "An analytic generalization consists of a carefully posed theoretical statement, theory, or theoretical proposition. The generalization can take the form of a lesson learned, working hypothesis, or other principle that is believed to be applicable to other situations (not just other 'like cases')" (Yin 2012, epub 241).

run on only a few dozen or a few hundred people conducted in a limited locale, often with a very nonrepresentative group of subjects?

Generalization has not been an issue for those pursuing experiments in political science. Looking at major methodological works such as Dunning (2012), Druckman et al. (2011), and Morton and Williams (2010), the question of generalization or extrapolation receives little attention. In experimental economics this is less the case (Fréchette and Schotter 2015; Guala 2005). However, as the debate about the generalization of welfare reform experiments indicates, there are important policy and practical issues involved in large-scale policy changes based on a few randomized experiments.

In short, this chapter is in large part devoted to thinking about scope and generalization issues. Core to the medium-N paradigm is using additional cases and within-case causal inference—just like one could with additional experiments—to generalize.

Conceptualizing Scope and Constituting Populations

This book poses the rarely asked methodological question about how case studies intersect with causal generalization. This question is rare as well in methodological discussions of experiments. For example, in the policy world it is common practice to generalize from a few experiments and other quasi-randomized designs, e.g., if it works in Indonesia then we extrapolate and generalize to other developing countries.

One of the features of qualitative methods is that scope and generalization are very much key questions (Ragin 2000; Goertz and Mahoney 2012). Social science has this in common with drug testing: it is not at all clear what might happen outside the experimental test groups. For example, historically most drugs were tested on men and then generalized to women. This is the same problem as testing on rats and extrapolating to humans (see Steel 2008 for an extensive discussion of this kind of extrapolation).

To focus on scope and constituting populations leads to one of the most useful practical suggestions of this volume:

Guideline: when choosing case studies, one must list the population of possible cases to analyze.

I have used this guideline many times over the years, and it has almost inevitably provoked long and thoughtful discussions on the part of PhD students. By providing a list, the researcher is forced to be explicit about populations and scope limits. For example, cherry-picking—a major problem with traditional comparative case studies—becomes much more obvious.

The guideline to identify the possible population of cases actually has two different components. The first is the population of $Y = 1$ cases. All concepts should be conceptualized as continuous (e.g., Goertz 2005; Goertz and Mahoney 2012), which means unclear boundary lines. Suppose the dependent variable is civil war; the widely used Uppsala Conflict Data Program (UCDP) data set (Themner and Wallensteen 2013) has two thresholds: 25 battle deaths per year and 1000. Does the causal mechanism apply to low-level civil wars, high-level civil wars, or both? Many civil wars—conceptualized in dichotomous fashion—are in fact interrupted ones, i.e., about half of civil wars repeat.

The second component of the guideline is the population of $X = 1$ cases. As discussed in chapter 3, much of the case selection logic should be based on X. The same problems with $Y = 1$ appear for $X = 1$. There is almost always a gray zone where the treatment is weak. Many discussions of methods focus on experiments with dichotomous treatments and controls. However, the real world is one of continuous variables.[3]

Mahoney and I (Goertz and Mahoney 2012, chapter 16) used the example of oil monarchies as one where scope considerations intersect with causal mechanism issues. In looking at the relationship between GDP/capita and democracy, oil monarchies appear to be a special case. It might make life—and

---

[3] Similarly, drug research experiments have to include the amount of drug because drug prescriptions are continuous—i.e., how much—rather than dichotomous.

empirical analysis—much simpler to treat oil monarchies as a scope condition and exclude this class of countries.

Another core scope question for much research is temporal limits. This too needs to be made explicit. For example, international relations often start the international system with the Treaty of Westphalia in 1648. Many think international relations fundamentally changed with the end of the Cold War. For example, Boix and Stokes (2003) strongly criticize Przeworski et al. (2000) for starting in 1946. By starting there, Przeworski et al. miss important earlier cases of democratization. Boix and Stokes replicate Przeworski et al.'s analysis for 1950–90. They then contrast that with an analysis over a much longer time period starting in 1800, which produces quite different results. However, going for long periods risks the "subset" problem discussed below, and perhaps introduces significant heterogeneity into the data set. The question of temporal scope for theory as well as testing should always be on the list of considerations for research design.

Constructing scope means looking at cases where the causal mechanism works—i.e., (1, 1)—versus those where it should work but does not, i.e., (1, 0). This was the point of the oil monarchy scope condition; the relationship between economic wealth and democracy does not seem to work for this set of countries. Another classic example is Skocpol's exclusion in *States and social revolutions* of countries with a colonial history.

The back-and-forth between cases and causal mechanisms can lead to refinement of the concepts and basic causal mechanisms. Off-the-internet data sets may be conceptually heterogeneous in ways that lead to problems. For example, a significant minority of civil wars are in fact military coups. If the causal mechanism fits the usual government versus rebel scenario, then these military coups—i.e., intra-elite conflicts—can be removed for conceptual reasons related to causal mechanisms.

The goal of generalization often directly conflicts with the goal of few counterexamples. This trade-off needs to be open and transparent. Qualitative scholars in general—and QCA in particular—strive hard to have very few cases in the (1, 0) cell. The standards for sufficiency in QCA are typically quite high, usually around 70–80 percent success (Schneider and

Wagemann 2012). The pressure to remove counterexamples in this context is quite strong; the same can be said of much classic medium-N comparative historical research.

A key step in analyzing the generalizability of a causal mechanism is to define the population of cases that could be possible sites for within-case causal inference. Doing this means theorizing and exploring scope.

Varieties of Generalization and Scope

Considering a theory's scope and degree of generalization starts by questioning how general a given causal mechanism is. For example, using Trachtenberg's restrictions on the audience costs test population (discussed in the previous chapter), there are 12 major power, democratic (at least one power is a democracy) not-war crises. If audience costs had been found in all of them, then the theory is somewhat general in its empirical scope. However, can one extrapolate from the major power democracies to other democracies? Can one generalize to crisis initiation?

The first step is to see whether there are scope limitations, explicit or implicit, in the theory itself. For example, chapter 6 discussed the scope role of assumptions in game-theoretic models. These can often limit the scope to situations where the core causal mechanism assumptions are met.

Trachtenberg (2012) limits himself to not-war crises because they play a central role in Fearon's theory of audiences costs:

> Finally, only those crises that did not terminate in war will be examined here. The rationale has to do with the basic thrust of the Fearon theory. His argument, both in his audience costs paper and in his very important article "Rationalist Explanations for War," is that rational states in a sense should be able to reach a bargain that would enable them to avoid war but sometimes cannot do so because they suspect each other of bluffing. It follows that anything that would allow them to credibly reveal their actual preferences might point the way to a clear outcome and thus enable them to head off an armed conflict, and the audience costs mechanism, in Fearon's view,

provides an effective way for them to do so. What this means is that if this mechanism is as important as Fearon suggests, we are more likely to see it in operation in crises that end peacefully than in those that end in war. (Trachtenberg 2012, 6)

One can say that Trachtenberg's analysis is applying "testing scope." While the theory might well cover other situations, such as crisis initiation, his test looks at a core part of the theoretical scope.

Testing scope and extrapolation have been a central method in the case study literature. The basic intuition is that if a test fails in the core, a "most likely" case, then one assumes—extrapolates—that it is not likely to work in more peripheral areas. Social constructivists used this strategy in their early debates with realists. They argued (e.g., Katzenstein 1996) that if social constructivism worked for war and national security, then it was widely applicable. Hence they did not start with "easy cases" where values, ideology, and norms were more obviously relevant, but with situations where the odds were stacked against constructivism.

Thus the first kind of scope is theoretical scope. Are the assumptions of the game-theoretic model widely true? In what kinds of situations does the audience costs mechanism apply? Could it be extended to nonmilitarized interactions? Testing scope then is typically a subset of theoretical scope.

The next step involves defining the scope in the concrete terms of $X = 1$, when the causal mechanism is or should be present. If the phenomenon X is common then that implies wider scope. For example, as the world becomes more democratic, the empirical scope of the democratic peace increases. Extrapolating, if the world consisted only of democracies, there would no longer be international war.

Thus another kind of scope relies on the empirical frequency of occurrence of X: Is the causal mechanism a common phenomenon? This can be called the "empirical scope" of the research project.

Empirical scope leads to exploring how reliable the mechanism is in producing the outcome. More general mechanisms are more reliable, they generally work to produce the outcome.

This involves looking at the percentage of $(1, 1)$ cases in the $X = 1$ column. This can be called the reliability dimension of generalization.

Another way to think about generalization is via the $Y = 1$ cases. One might say that a completely general causal mechanism explains all the $Y = 1$ cases. Looking at the $Y = 1$ cases is thus an outcome-oriented approach to generalization. The causal mechanism might not be very general in the sense that it is rarely the mechanism by which Y is produced. Most of the Ys might be generated by other causal mechanisms. As discussed in the previous chapter, Haggard and Kaufman are very interested in how general are distributive causal mechanisms in transitions to and from democracy.

These kinds of scope and forms of generalization can vary independently. Sometimes the phenomenon is important but relatively rare, such as the possession of nuclear weapons. In addition, it is useful to be explicit about how the testing scope relates to the theoretical scope, in particular how big or small a subset the testing scope is, and how critical the testing scope is for the theory.

All this suggests that it is important and not easy to arrive at a list of possible case studies for multimethod research. Scope and generalization aspects of the research triad can then feedback on the cross-case or large-N statistical analyses. If there are some cases, $Y = 1$ or $X = 1$, that do not seem suitable for causal mechanism case studies then their usefulness in statistical analyses is called into question. For the research triad to work, there must be consistency between the various corners, theory, within-case, and cross-case analyses.

Generalization and Robustness

The concern for valid causal generalizations has led to a very strong emphasis in statistical research on robustness checks. This practice has become a common, standard part of quantitative articles, often accompanied by extensive web appendices. Questions of robustness and generalization, however, are not limited to statistical research.

In statistics, a core potential problem is that if one analyzes a given statistical model on subsets of the data, one can get quite different parameter estimates across those subsets. These can potentially go from positive to negative or from significant to not.

As such, there are really two issues confronting statistical multimethod research. The first is within-sample causal mechanism testing and analysis. When one does case studies within the sample used for the statistical analyses, does one find the causal mechanism at work? A second issue is that if one were to choose case studies in a different subset, the result of the case study might be different.

For example, in international relations scholarship, researchers sometimes estimate the statistical model for different historical periods, e.g., 1946–1988 and 1989–present. The intuition is that the post–Cold War period is a fundamentally different international system than the Cold War.[4] The same sort of thing would be possible in comparative politics when looking at different regions. Putting all periods and regions together produces the potential problem of "pooling disparate observations" (Bartels 1996).

Thus if the within-sample testing fails to reveal the causal mechanism, it might be because the case is within a subset with different causal relationships. Hence case studies in statistical multimethod work need to be aware of the subset sensitivity of the statistical analysis.

QCA is very different in this regard, a fact not often realized. The statistical problem as framed above was about *subsets* of the statistical data set. QCA is itself a set-theoretic methodology. It is all about set relationships.

Suppose that one finds via cross-case analysis that X is necessary for Y. What does that mean if we look at various possible subsets of the population P? By definition, if X is necessary for Y then when $Y = 1$ we know that $X = 1$; Y is a subset of X. So for *any* subset of P—e.g., any subset of the $Y = 1$ cases—it must be the case that $X = 1$.

---

[4] Also common is a dummy variable for period, but that just means a different intercept for each period and not a fundamentally different causal relationship.

If X is necessary for Y in the cross-case analysis of P, then X is necessary for Y in all subsets of P.[5]

Thus QCA makes robust within-P necessary condition generalizations. This contrasts notably with statistical methods that have weak within-P robustness. In other words, within-P robustness is contingent in statistics: it depends on the data and the statistical model. In QCA, within-P robustness is a feature of the methodology itself.

The same principle holds for sufficient conditions. By definition, if X is sufficient for Y then when $X = 1$ we know that $Y = 1$; X is a subset of Y. If we know in P that whenever X occurs then Y occurs, then this must be true in any subset of P.

QCA produces subsets with different causal mechanisms as a matter of course. So while necessary conditions imply homogeneity across the population P, the existence of multiple sufficiency paths means causal heterogeneity. Because these subsets can intersect, a given case can be on multiple paths.

In addition, there is an important subset of cases not explained. QCA implements the philosophy of narrower scope for better fit. QCA analysis can produce a subset of cases that are "do not know" cases in terms of sufficiency. The analysis produces no explanation of these cases.

In short, QCA assumes causal heterogeneity for sufficiency, i.e., multiple paths to Y. In contrast, statistical analysis focuses on the *average* treatment effect; the individual causal effects can vary significantly across subjects. While one can explore this heterogeneity (i.e., heterogeneous treatment effects), it is not a first-order agenda item.

Where QCA is not robust is in the number of paths leading to the outcome. Some paths might not exist in some subsets of P. So QCA is fragile in the sense of equifinality. What we do know is that equifinality in a subset of P *must* be a subset of the paths in P: in other words, we can only lose paths in subsets, we cannot find new ones.[6]

---

[5] I am ignoring, for the purposes of this discussion, situations where there are a few cases of $Y = 1$ where X is not present, which might be quite unevenly distributed across subsets.

[6] Again, this ignores counterexamples that might not be evenly distributed across subsets.

In statistical terms, QCA looks for "separation." Separation is a significant problem for statistical methods (see Goertz 2012 for an extended discussion). From a larger perspective, separation is good and desirable; it means strong causal effects. What is true of QCA is also true of separation in statistics: it holds for all subsets of P.

An important take-away point for statistical multimethod work is that if the case study does not work as expected, one should think about this as a subset or scope issue.

GENERALIZING FROM EXPERIMENTS

While it might seem odd to put case studies and experiments together in the same bed, in fact they do constitute bed fellows (Small 2009; Yin 2012). The core commonality is that they stress the importance of internal validity, usually at the expense of external validity. Both are vulnerable to the generalization query, how generalizable is the case study or experiment?

Generalization often appears under the umbrella rubric of external validity. External and internal validity as methodological issues were brought onto the agenda by the classic discussion of Campbell and Stanley (1963). In that account there is often a trade-off between the two, with experiments being the classic example: well-done experiments have high internal validity but external validity is potentially low:

> The term "external validity" was coined in the short landmark book on experimental design by Campbell and Stanley (1963). The book was originally published as a chapter in the *Handbook of Research on Teaching*. Stanley was an educational psychologist. His interest in external validity probably originated in thinking about educational experiments—for example, what teaching methods produce the best learning under highly specific ecological conditions. (Camerer 2015, 253–54)

Stanley was interested in the educational policy generalizability of experiments. Would one get the same successful results in other educational settings?

External validity contains a variety of methodological issues, the parallel of interest here with case studies is the generalizability of experiments.[7] How generalizable are the experiments themselves? If one repeats an experiment in a different setting or context, does one get the same result? Morton and Williams illustrate the common position:

> What sort of empirical analysis is involved in establishing external validity? Simply a researcher replicates the empirical results on new populations or using new variations on the experiment in terms of settings, materials, etc. (Morton and Williams 2010, 196)

Experiments may be more or less robust in this generalization sense, which is naturally a scope sense as well. One replicates the experiment on new populations to answer the generalization question.

Robustness has two senses. The first is that "minor" variations on the experiment produce the same result:

> However, a preliminary answer goes as follows: successful replications help in proving that an experimental phenomenon is robust to small or big changes in the experimental setup. In several respects, experimenters speak of robustness in the same way as theoretical scientists do—a theoretical result being "robust" when it does not depend on some detail of the situation or on the assumptions used to derive it. A good scientific result is always robust to some kind of variation or change, either in the concrete experimental setup or in the abstract initial conditions of a theoretical model. (Guala 2005, 15)

I shall ignore this sense of robust and focus on the second, generalization sense, of robustness.

Camerer notes that generalization has not been a principle concern of experimental economists: "The consensus among most experimental economists [is] that realism, generalizability,

---

[7] Discussions of external validity often focus more on how realistic the experiment is or conversely how artificial the experimental environment is. This leads to another generalization or extrapolation question: "A critical assumption underlying the interpretation of data from many laboratory experiments is that the insights gained in the lab can be extrapolated to the world beyond, a principle we denote as generalizability" (Levitt and List 2015, 208).

or external validity are not especially important" (Camerer 2015, 253). Guala finds the same for philosophers as well:

> To write on external validity is challenging. Philosophers of science, surprisingly, have very little to say about it. Experimental economists also tend to ignore or downplay the relevance of external validity; they typically say that it is not a particularly useful concept and, moreover, that worrying too much about it may turn attention away from more important issues of experimental design. (Guala 2005, 142)

The best known economic experiments, which are also often cognitive psychology experiments, focus on testing the predictions of rational choice or expected utility theory. The most famous are the Kahneman and Tversky experiments that won Kahneman the Nobel Prize in Economics, which he shared with Vernon Smith, a founder of experimental economics.

Chapter 6 discussed the relationship between case studies and game-theoretic models, often with the case studies not supporting game-theoretic models. The same thing happened with experimental tests of rational decision making: experiments did not support predictions of standard expected utility models. Classic examples were preference reversals and the importance of fairness–ethics in decision making (i.e., justice and fairness factors lead people to violate the predictions of money-maximizing economic models).

The initial experiments played the role of theory falsifying case studies. Given that experiments often use a limited set of people (e.g., students in psychology or economics classes), many asked the generalization question:

> In the early years, most economists viewed experiments with a mixture of skepticism and amused curiosity; whenever we presented our results to audiences of economists, we had to justify our methods. We were often asked whether it was valid to draw general conclusions from experiments carried out using demographically unrepresentative subject pools. (Most of our experiments recruited subjects from populations of British university students. These were clearly unrepresentative of the general British population with respect to

age, educational attainment, and social class). (Bardsley et al. 2010, Kindle location 2567–2570)

For political scientists who put particular emphasis on generalizability, the use of student participants often constitutes a critical, and according to some reviewers, fatal problem for experimental studies. (Druckman and Kam 2011, 41)

Sometimes experiments find that behavior differs significantly between students and more realistic subjects. For example, Mintz, Redd, and Vedlitz ran an experiment with both students and military officers about counterterrorism decision making. They found that students and military officers differed on various dimensions in their behavior. They conclude that "student samples are often inappropriate, as empirically they can lead to divergence in subject population results" (2006, 769). Similarly one might expect economics students to behave differently from others in rational choice experiments, given their specific training in the area.

As Bardsley et al. discuss, after 20 years some experiments have become classics in large part because they have been widely replicated, in different countries, at different levels of education, wealth, in different cultures and religions, etc.

In summary, experiments and case studies face similar problems of generalization. One does not know how robust the causal mechanism is when potentially relevant causal features vary. The only way to know is to conduct further experiments, varying potentially important factors. The only way to know the generalizability of a case study is to conduct further studies, varying potentially influential Z factors.

The Medium-N Paradigm: Case Studies and Generalization

The medium-N paradigm focuses on doing 10+ case studies. This is a fairly unpopular range in actual research. Yet, it is a good place to be. The medium-N design takes on directly the question almost always asked of qualitative case studies: How generalizable is the case study?

Often in comparative work the basic unit of analysis is the country or state. If the population of interest is post-Communist countries, one could conceivably do case studies of the universe of post-Communist countries, 20 or so states. For example, Mahoney (2010) limits himself to Spanish-colonized Latin America. He can thus conceivably do relatively serious case studies of all of these countries.

One approach then is to analyze all cases within some scope conditions. For example, Grzymała-Busse (see chapter 2) had democratic post-Communist states as her scope. Generalization questions arise because naturally the question is the extent to which the analysis works for other kinds of states. For Mahoney (2010), does the same logic apply to both Portuguese and English colonies?

Subset robustness is normally high in these medium-N analyses because each case is examined in detail. But generalization remains an open question. This is the classic trade-off: high quality within-case causal inference often goes along with generalization weakness. By covering a significant range of cases, e.g., Spanish Latin America or post-Communist democracies, the theories travel further than one or two case studies.

The medium-N paradigm consists of two parts: (1) in-depth causal mechanism case studies and (2) generalization case studies. The rationale, selection, and within-case analysis in the case studies differ according to their role in the overall research design.

So in contrast to many case study designs, not all cases are treated with the same depth of analysis. In much practice, multiple case study analysis treats each case study as relatively equal. The methodological literature, e.g., Gerring (2017), George and Bennett (2005), tacitly assumes each case study is about equal.

The medium-N design is about a fairly large number of not-too-deep case studies. In general, this means extensive use of secondary sources and weaker claims about within-case causal inference:

The medium-N design is a few intensive causal mechanism (1, 1) cases along with a relatively large number of other—generalization—case studies.

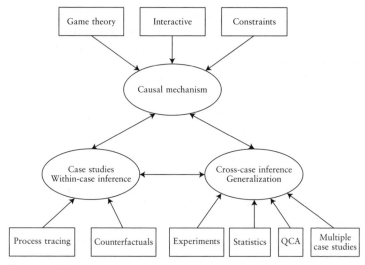

Figure 8.1: The research triad: causal mechanism, cross-case inference, and case studies.

The generalization case studies thus play some of the role of statistical analysis in statistical multimethod research. They provide cross-case analysis that speaks to generalization rather than within-case causal inference. They are similar also in that they are not deep analyses, but relatively shallow.

The research triad, reproduced here as figure 8.1, illustrates the different roles that case studies play in the medium-N paradigm. On the left side of the figure are the intensive causal mechanism case studies. On the right are typically the cross-case, usually statistical, analyses. However, on the right there are also "multiple case studies." They are there because they play a role different from the causal mechanism case studies on the left. They address how general the causal mechanism is. As such, the medium-N design is multimethod. Instead of cross-case inference via large-N statistical analysis, the cross-case analysis focuses specifically on the generalization question.

In terms of the research process, the causal mechanism cases usually come first. If the researcher cannot find good examples of the causal mechanism in action, then pursuing generalization makes little sense.

The question then is what would be the best choice—given limited resources—for these other cases? While this will of course depend on the specifics of the situation, some general principles can be stated.[8]

The $(1, 0)$ cell is often a good place to start after the causal mechanism case studies, since this is the scope cell. In the best-case scenario, there are relatively few cases in this cell. If this is true then these cases deserve to be included.

Often in medium-N research—defined as around 10+ case studies—there is a sense about cases that do not work so well. Mahoney (2010) explores the incredible stability over time of the relative economic development of Latin American countries. This stability is punctuated by a period of rapid change, where the core becomes the periphery and vice versa. Rich countries early in colonization, such as Peru and Bolivia, become the poor ones; the early poor ones, such as Argentina and Chile, become the rich ones. This pattern is quite general, but there are a couple of countries that do not fit this pattern so well. Mahoney finds that oil explains Venezuela's exceptional performance: "The only unambiguous exception is what oil did for Venezuela, lifting this country from a regionally intermediate level to a regionally high level of economic development" (Mahoney 2010, 227).

Cases may not fit well because of idiosyncratic factors. However, the concept of an idiosyncratic factor is related to generalization: if the causal factor appears often it is no longer idiosyncratic. So Mahoney has to make a judgment about whether oil is important enough to bring into the overall causal mechanism. "Oil exports" become less idiosyncratic if the causal mechanism becomes profitable export commodities: "Profitable export commodities rarely changed anything over the long run" (Mahoney 2010, 227).

Such an approach is very consistent with comparative historical practice. If the total population is relatively small, then the importance of potential counterexamples increases significantly.

---

[8] It is best to start assuming that the causal mechanism does not involve a necessary condition and does not involve some sort of interaction term (statistical or set theoretic), basically the situation presented in chapter 3.

One needs to determine whether these are indeed counterexamples or whether there is some kind of measurement error. Sometimes these counterexamples can be dealt with by modifying the causal mechanism. Often this means moving up in abstraction and noting substitutable factors. The basic causal mechanism is maintained but the details are modified to take into account some of the functionally equivalent mechanisms. Sometimes the counterexamples are best dealt with via scope conditions. Regardless, the $(1, 0)$ cases merit inclusion; the details will vary depending on the nature and number of cases in this cell.

In chapter 3, the Z variables had a significant scope role. Generalization means choosing cases that are significantly different on Z. This means implementing a most different system design. Therefore variation on Z is good.

What sort of factors make good generalization variables? In many statistical analyses, these Z variables are of little interest in and of themselves. They are fixed effects for countries; they are dummy variables for regions; they are statistical analyses for different historical periods. These Z variables are used in a most similar system or matching context. The goal—say in matching—is not generalization but controlling for other causal factors.

In the medium-N paradigm, generalization and scope variables—aka Z variables—should have theoretical relevance.

This becomes clear when the case studies show that in some circumstances the causal mechanism does not travel. Immediately one must ask why. If the generalization variables are nation names (e.g., fixed effects) one is forced to ask why, say, France is different. Long ago Przeworski and Teune (1970) argued against proper name variables for exactly this reason. If the generalization variables are theoretical ones then we can begin to understand where and when the causal mechanism works.

A core rule for selecting the few intensive causal mechanism case studies is *avoid overdetermination*. More specifically this means choosing cases where $Z = 0$. Once one moves to selecting 10+ cases, the realities of social science data impose themselves. In the QCA world this is known as limited diversity (Ragin

2008); in statistical analyses it is the problem of collinearity. This means that it becomes very likely that when exploring the $(1, 1)$ cases, there will be cases where $Z = 1$ on confounding causes.

Scholars are often interested in what one might call "theory contests." This means a situation where $X = 1$ and $Z = 1$. Two causal mechanisms seem to apply to a given case. While statistical methods cannot adjudicate, within-case causal inference might be able to evaluate the relative usefulness of these two theories (Beach and Pedersen 2016). One might think of this via the popular detective metaphor in process tracing. In a first look at the murder case, there are some clear potential suspects (X and Zs) for the murderer. But as one digs into the case, using hoop tests, smoking gun tests, and other process tracing tests, some of these suspects can be eliminated or moved up on the list.

A medium-N approach offers a unique perspective on paired comparison. As Tarrow notes (2010; see also Slater and Ziblatt 2013), pairwise comparisons are quite popular. This volume argues that the classic pairwise comparison—$(1, 1)$ paired with $(0, 0)$—does not make a lot of sense. Since the causal inference work is done by within-case process tracing and counterfactuals, the cross-case comparison of $(0, 0)$ to $(1, 1)$ no longer has any raison d'être.

The other popular paradigm—particularly in security studies—is the book with one theory chapter and five or six case studies. From the medium-N paradigm perspective, this is also not an optimal number of cases. Each case study is typically treated equally. Hence it is *neither* a very intensive case study of the causal mechanism *nor* very good on generalization. The two central features of the medium-N approach are high-quality causal mechanism analysis, along with generalization case studies, thus the five-or-six-case-study book is not the way to go.

My analysis suggests that the paired comparison and the five-or-six-equal-case-study designs are not optimal. The paired comparison mimics statistics, so it is better if possible to do a statistical analysis instead. Instead of five or six equal case studies, one should allocate research effort to detailed causal mechanism analysis and generalization and choose case studies for these different goals.

Thinking about case studies in terms of generalization also suggests a statistical multimethod variant whereby one does a number of less in-depth case studies exactly to explore the issues of subset robustness discussed above. The causal mechanism $(1, 1)$ cases are cherry picked to demonstrate how the causal mechanism works. Other considerations apply when the case studies serve a robustness and generalization function.

Generalization is a critical aspect of many famous experiments. For example, one of the most dramatic examples of generalization occurred in the famous Milgram (1974) experiment. Milgram set out to explain the compliance of ordinary Germans with Nazi extermination of the Jews. Milgram's experiment placed test subjects in a situation where they were asked by an authority figure to administer what they thought were real electric shocks to another individual. Prior to the experiment, every psychiatrist consulted predicted that only the worst, most rare psychopaths would administer the maximum amount of shock. Milgram (and later others such as the famous Stanford Experiment) found that ordinary people were quite capable of extreme behavior given the right environment.

Generalization and Extrapolation from (1, 1) Cases

Initial causal mechanism case studies focus on good case studies of the causal mechanism, i.e., those in the $(1, 1)$ corner. Causal mechanism extrapolation and generalization then is the extent to which the causal mechanism still works as one moves away from the $(1, 1)$ corner. Framed in this manner, one can talk about X-generalization and Y-generalization. Moving from $X = 1$ toward zero means the mechanism becomes more weakly present. Moving from $Y = 1$ toward zero means the outcome becomes less strong.

The democratic peace literature provides a nice illustration of how this can work in one important area of political science. I use the sufficient condition version of the democracy peace: joint democracy is sufficient for peace.[9]

---

[9] See chapter 4 for a discussion of the necessary condition version.

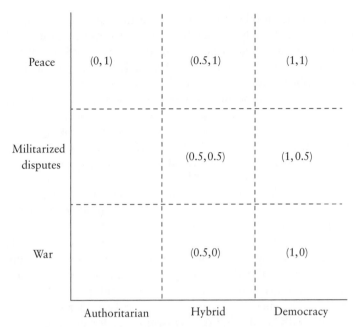

Figure 8.2: Generalization and extrapolation: the democratic peace.

As shown by figure 8.2, the zone near the $(1, 1)$ corner is that of high-quality democracy and clear, unambiguous peace. Case studies here would involve dyads clearly at peace, such as Western European states or USA–Canada.

A key form of generalization then is Y-generalization. This would be the $(1, 0.5)$ cell of figure 8.2. Lower levels of Y are less severe militarized disputes, which might involve serious threats of force or low-level use of force. If the democratic peace Y-generalizes then this cell should have few cases.

In fact, a large part of the statistical literature on the democratic peace has focused on this zone, using the Correlates of War militarized dispute data set. Most of these disputes are of low severity, e.g., last only a day or two, or involve no battle deaths. So the $(1, 0.5)$ zone constitutes one core part of the "generalization zone" for the democratic peace.

Generalization relates to subset robustness (see above). Standard statistical analyses include wars and not-war militarized disputes. If one were to do statistical analyses with just wars, separation in the data would be quite likely (see, e.g., table 4.1). Subset robustness in the generalization sense means looking at the $Y = 0.50$ zone of lower-level conflicts. Since almost all statistical studies include wars as well, it is not clear at all whether the democratic peace is Y-generalizable. Looking at the cases (i.e., no statistical analyses) suggests that it is. Most not-war militarized disputes between democracies are quite low level (see Mitchell and Prins 1999).[10]

Another less explicitly examined form of generalization involves looking at countries that are not very good democracies. In terms of figure 8.2, this is X-generalization because one is moving along the X-axis. If there are many cases in the $(0.5, 1)$ zone then that supports the democracy peace generalization. Cases in the $(0.5, 0.5)$ zone suggest that the democratic peace has some validity in that only less severe disputes occur between democracies. Finally, many cases in the $(0.5, 1)$ zone means that one really needs high-quality democracy for the democratic peace to function.

The debate launched by Mansfield and Snyder (2005; discussed in the previous chapter) about the war-proneness of democratizing regimes illustrates X-generalization. Most of these democratizing countries are not high-quality democracies and hence many are in the 0.5 hybrid zone. Their argument was that there should be many cases in the $(0.5, 0)$ cell. So while the $(1, 0)$ cell might have zero observations, once we try to X-generalize, the causal mechanism no longer works.

There are then three areas that constitute the main generalization zone for the democratic peace. This is the band of cells bordering the $(1, 1)$ cell. Exploring case studies in this area can

---

[10] Mitchell and Prins suggest another mode of analysis of the democratic peace, which is to add a temporal third dimension to figure 8.2. They find that "while less than 50 percent of democratic disputes in the 1950s involved no fatalities, over 80 percent of disputes in the 1980s and 100 percent of disputes in the 1990s saw no fatalities. The average duration of democratic disputes has generally decreased over time as well" (Mitchell and Prins 1999, 175).

help establish how generalizable the democratic peace is in the X and Y directions.

As discussed in chapter 3, the $(0, 1)$ zone is equifinality and not really relevant for the generalization of the democratic peace. Few contest that there are other potential pathways to peace.[11]

Figure 8.2 shows that generalization can mean extrapolating into nearby areas, either in terms of the causal mechanism X or the outcome Y. Existing statistical analyses do not tell us much specifically about what is going on in the generalization zone. Statistical analysis draws a line through the data of figure 8.2. Hence a standard statistical approach does not specifically explore the generalization zone.

The medium-N paradigm sheds some interesting light on democratic peace debates. It allows one to formulate more clearly what the generalization of the basic empirical finding consists of. It also permits an identification of possible case studies to explore in more detail the degree of generalizability of the democratic peace.

Research Practice

Including 10+ case studies is relatively rare in practice. At the same time, many of the classics of comparative historical and institutional research fall into this category. Because medium-N designs do not appear as a specific type on the methodological landscape, I have compiled a bibliography of studies that include about 10 or more case studies (available via this book's Princeton University Press web page). This is not a systematic bibliography but rather it grows as I discover more examples (and is updated online about once a year).

One distinctive feature of the medium-N design is its division into a couple of intensive case studies that explore causal mechanisms and a medium-N of more superficial case studies used to determine generalization. Special attention is frequently

---

[11] This depends on how one conceptualizes peace; see Goertz, Diehl, and Balas (2016) for an argument that democracy is a necessary condition for high-quality peace.

given to deviant cases but often it is not clear whether these are (1, 0) or (0, 1) cases. Another trend is to give less attention to the contrast or negative cases (sometimes called "shadow cases").

Medium-N research is a book or dissertation research design. Articles with medium-N case studies tend to be of the large-N qualitative testing variety. Typically the findings are negative; the case studies do not support a prominent theory or hypothesis. Chapter 3 gives examples where two or three case studies are used to present and explore a given causal mechanism. There were no articles in our systematic journal survey, 2006–2015, that used the medium-N paradigm.

Rosen has two in-depth case studies and 18 abbreviated case studies in her analysis of women's parliamentary representation. She argues, "These country comparisons allow me to evaluate differences across levels of development, and assess whether the institutional mechanisms highlighted by the statistical analyses operate as anticipated in light of contextual details and specific national histories. The qualitative component of my research design also suggests new hypotheses that can be tested more generally" (2013, 17).

Lange uses a similar sort of design: "Specifically, I use a three-tiered nested research design that includes a statistical analysis of thirty-nine former colonies, in-depth comparative-historical analysis of four former colonies, and abbreviated case studies of eleven former colonies. While the first step of the analysis provides insight into general causal processes, the second highlights particular causal mechanisms, and the third tests the generalizability of these mechanisms, thereby providing a systematic analysis of uneven development among former British colonies" (2009, Kindle location 167–169).

These two examples illustrate how the medium-N paradigm and statistical analyses can be part of a multimethod research project. In both instances, in-depth case studies analyze causal mechanisms and then statistical and medium-N case studies are there to explore generalization.

The discussion of large-N qualitative research in the previous chapter focused on its use in a testing mode. It can, however, be used in a more positive mode to deal with generalization issues.

For example, Copeland focuses on Y-generalization by selecting major power crises and wars: "By covering such a broad range of great power cases—including those cases that do not work well for my argument—the study can assess the overall explanatory power of trade expectations theory relative to its competitors while at the same time avoiding any selection bias that would call its value into question" (Copeland 2015, 2–3). With this Y-generalization setup he can assess the relative importance of various causal mechanisms, but is limited in what kind of X-generalizations he can make.

The outline of medium-N practice can found in the later chapters of books. To conclude and to address issues of generalization, the author does some fairly abbreviated case studies that complement the more intensive ones in earlier chapters. For example, using some research discussed in earlier chapters,

> I take a preliminary look as well at patterns of violence in ten randomly selected cases from the post–Cold War period using proxies for the character of rebel behavior. Large-N analysis of the type utilized here complements the theory-generation aspects of this study with a test of its cross-national (or cross-conflict) validity. Yet such approaches, in spite of their strengths, involve abstracting away from the individual and group-level processes and mechanisms given priority throughout the book. (Weinstein 2006, 305; core case studies are Uganda, Mozambique, and Peru)

Ziblatt generalizes from Italy and Germany to 17 contemporary European cases in his study of federalist origins, stating that this provides an opportunity to examine his causal logic in "a broader and more diverse set of cases" (Ziblatt 2006, 147).

Cammett, in her last substantive chapter, investigates the case of the BJP in India alongside her core case of Lebanese political parties, showing that "the broad logic of the arguments holds outside of the Middle East" (2014, 207). This most different system philosophy is quite common in books with a strong regional focus; some case studies from other regions are required to show generalizability.

The Research Network on Gender Politics and the State (RNGS) project[12] on women's policy issues provides an excellent example of a large-scale research project incorporating many case studies (often published in separate anthologies) along with cross-case analysis in the form of QCA (McBride and Mazur 2010).

The medium-N design suggests these generalization and extrapolation case studies are central to the whole research design. This design can easily coexist with statistical analyses, as well as being a multiple-case-study-only design.

Conclusions

This chapter has focused on the methodology of case studies and generalization or extrapolation. High-quality within-case causal inference has the same generalizability issues as experiments. In practical terms, however, the problems are more severe for qualitative case studies. Experimenters can easily ignore the generalizability question, case study researchers do not have that luxury.

My (nonsystematic) survey of books by major presses such as Princeton, Cambridge, and Cornell showed that case study scholars are clearly aware of the generalization issue and often address it using additional case studies. What is typically lacking is any methodological framework for thinking about and choosing these generalization case studies. This chapter is a step toward providing such a framework.

The first classic problem of case studies and most comparative case studies is generalizability: Does the case study generalize to some population? The second classic problem is the use of case studies for testing: To what extent does a case study constitute a test of some hypothesis or causal mechanism?

The medium-N paradigm provides one research design answer to these two questions. In contrast to existing paradigms, *there*

---

[12] https://pppa.wsu.edu/research-network-on-gender-politics-and-the-state

is no cross-case causal inference from the case studies. The medium-N paradigm has some notable features:

- It requires one to think seriously about the scope of the causal mechanism.
- Case studies serve different purposes: they (1) explore in detail the causal mechanism, (2) explore how general the mechanism is, and (3) explore scope via falsification cases.
- The core methodological skills required are those of within-case causal inference, such as process tracing, hoop tests, and counterfactuals.

The research triad means combining theory, causal mechanism analysis, and cross-case inference. Often the cross-case inference has a generalization or scope dimension. The point of statistical analyses of observational data is to suggest that X has causal effects systematically across a population. More needs to be done by both methodologists and scholars to make clear how they are addressing generalizability and the role of multiple case studies in that endeavor.

A Statistical Approach to Multimethod Research and Case Studies

Introduction

This appendix explores the statistical and potential outcomes approach to multimethod research. "Statistical" is not the same as "potential outcomes." The potential outcomes approach to statistics has come to dominate the causal inference literature in political science and sociology. However, the majority of multimethod research combines classical statistical methods such as OLS and logit with case studies. Some very influential articles (e.g., Lieberman 2005; 2015) explicitly frame multimethod research in the context of standard regression-type analyses. In spite of differences between classical general linear models and potential outcomes I shall refer to them globally as the "statistical approach" to multimethod and comparative-case-study research and highlight how they differ from the approach defended in this book.

Also considered are small-N comparative case studies. In recent years there have been a series of articles attacking the case selection problem for comparative case studies from the potential outcome approach (e.g., Glynn and Ichino 2015; Nielsen 2016; Herron and Quinn 2016; Lyall 2014); the second edition of Gerring's case study book (2017) has explicitly adopted the potential outcomes approach (the first edition was a general statistical approach).

A key question—little discussed—is whether there is a difference between doing small-N selection for comparative case studies alone versus case studies in conjunction with large-N statistical analyses or experiments. One thing is quite clear: those working in the statistical tradition argue that the same logic of causal inference should inform small-N case studies as well as large-N statistical analyses and experiments. This, of course, was the theme of King, Keohane, and Verba (1994) and influenced much of the qualitative literature on comparative case studies. Many in the qualitative methods literature have defined small-N methodology in terms of statistical methodology, for example,

> The comparative [case study] method can now be defined as the *method of testing hypothesized empirical relationships among variables on the basis of the same logic that guides the statistical method, but in which the cases are selected in such a way as to maximize the variance of the independent variables and to minimize the variance of the control variables.* (Lijphart 1975, 164; emphasis in original)

In short, I shall assume that the same logic applies to comparative case studies as well as multimethod research.

Highlighting potential differences between comparative-case-study and statistical multimethod research is a critical issue because my whole approach is based on multimethod research being defined as cross-case analyses along with within-case causal inference. The statistical approach to case selection in comparative case studies works from the notion that causal inference in case studies follows that of the statistical approach. *Case studies do causal inference in the same manner as large-N studies or experiments.* The fact that the methodology and research is often referred to as *comparative* case studies already suggests that causal inference is cross case. As such, within-case causal inference plays a very reduced role.

Earlier chapters almost always use the term "multiple case studies" exactly because the point is multiple within-case analyses. Causal inference does not come from comparing cases, but from within cases. This is perhaps the most fundamental reason why the research triad differs from the statistical approach.

Another reason for this essay is that I differ from those who advocate the statistical approach. This appendix outlines an alternative view on the statistical approach on its own terms. For example, below I provide an alternative pathway selection technique that is more faithful to the potential outcomes approach than Gerring's approach (2006; 2017). My technique is based on the fundamental counterfactual at the heart of the potential outcomes approach, while Gerring's is based on relative model estimations.

In short, this appendix examines case study and multimethod research from a statistical and potential outcomes perspective.

Framing Multimethod Research

While one can do case studies for various reasons—checking measurement, "as if" randomization, etc.—the core of the statistical analysis is estimating causal effects of the treatment or X. In the experimental context this is the average treatment effect (ATE); in the general linear models setting it is the estimate of parameters (β), usually with observational data.

In the various recent studies (cited above) of case selection in small-N comparative case studies this is always the goal. For example, Herron and Quinn state that "the specific research goal that we consider in this article is inference about the effects of causes. By inference, we mean the use of data from a fixed number of cases to make claims about a larger set of cases" (2016, 460). In a multimethod context, one then naturally links the average treatment effect or β to the case studies.

• • •

One widely held notion is that the case study should be *representative* of the population or causal effect. The case studies should explore a typical case of the causal effect, where "typical" is a synonym for "representative."

Gerring is explicit about the key importance of representativeness to case studies, since he makes it core to defining the goal of case studies:

> When selecting cases, one aims for cases that are representative of a larger population. This is a core ("omnibus") goal of case selection, as discussed in Chapter 3. If a chosen case, or cases, is representative of the population—in whatever ways are relevant for the hypothesis at hand—then one has jumped the first hurdle to external validity. (Gerring 2017, 220)

The goal is understanding a population. With that goal one chooses a case that is representative of that causal effect. Gerring (2017, table 3.1) has representativeness as an omnibus goal of case study research with the criterion "generalizability."[1]

Herron and Quinn (2016) use Gerring to define the "typical" or "representative" case study:

> Gerring (2007, 91, 94) writes: "In order for a focused case study to provide insight into a broader phenomenon, it must be representative of a broader set of cases. It is in this context that one may speak of a typical-case approach to case selection. The typical case exemplifies what is considered to be a typical set of values, given some general understanding of the phenomenon." And he goes on to state: "When a case falls close to the regression line, its typicality will be just below zero. When a case falls far from the regression line, its typicality will be far below zero. Typical cases have small residuals."

If one examines methodological works on multimethod or case studies that rely on a statistical logic, they frequently make representativeness a core criterion:

> Once again, though, we run into a problem of representativeness. If one is selecting a few cases from a larger set, why this one and not another? Why shouldn't the reader be suspicious about selection of "good cases" if no explanation is given for the choice? If an explanation is given and it amounts to convenience sampling, don't we still need to worry about representativeness? (Fearon and Laitin 2008, 762–63)

> From a purely statistical sampling perspective, focusing attention on cases that are not representative of the population as a whole will usually lead to a huge waste of resources. While such cases may be useful for exploratory analysis and/or theory construction, the amount of information they can provide about population-level

---

[1] In his core table 5.3 where Gerring (2007) lists the case selection techniques, each is evaluated on its degree of representativeness. As a rule, those techniques that are not representative can only be used in conjunction with other case studies. In the second edition (2017) Gerring has removed all reference to representativeness in his discussion of individual case study research designs.

average causal effects is, by definition, limited. (Herron and Quinn 2016, 488)

The second principle for gaining external validity is to capture *representative variation*. Such empirical works are most likely to generate. . . . externally valid findings when the *variation in the sample broadly mirrors variation in some broader and explicitly defined population of cases.* (Slater and Ziblatt 2013, 1311–12)

Wood [Elisabeth Wood's (2003) book, *Insurgent collective action and civil war in El Salvador*] selected her five field sites according to a fourfold criterion. . . . Taken together, it appears that these regions do offer representative examples of broader patterns of participation and violence in El Salvador's contested areas. (Lyall 2014, 190)

These methodological works make explicit a very common rationale (see also Weller and Barnes 2014, 80–81). If one examines the justifications for case selection, they often rely on the argument that the case is a representative one.

Representative or typical has two dimensions that need to be kept separate. The first is what representative means in a univariate sense, i.e., for X or Y alone. The second is the causal effect sense: a representative case of the causal effect of X on Y.

It turns out that to operationalize "representative" can be quite problematic. Kruskal and Mosteller (two of the most famous statisticians of their day) in a very readable series of articles (1979a,; 1979b; 1979c; 1980) give a wide-ranging analysis of what representative might mean and the meanings that have been given to it.

"Representative" or "typical" in the univariate sense is often interpreted as the mean or average observation, i.e., $\overline{X}$. From a statistical perspective it might be quite normal—pun intended—to assume normality, i.e., bell-shaped distribution of X as a default interpretation of representative in the univariate sense.

However, the mean does not always work well as the interpretation of representative. Democracy data illustrate a potential problem with using the mean. These data are very bimodal in distribution (see Goertz 2008 for a histogram and discussion). The vast majority of cases are either clearly democratic or clearly authoritarian. So in this case, the mean is not representative at all of the population. The hidden assumption behind the idea of the mean being typical or representative is that the data are relatively symmetric (i.e., not heavily skewed) and that they are unimodal. If these criteria hold then the mean is not a bad choice, but a large proportion of social science data do not fit these requirements.

Another popular option is the median—which is better with skewed data or data with a few big outliers. For dichotomous or nominal data the most popular choice is the mode (i.e., the most common value).[2]

Gerring (2017) supports this view of what constitutes representative or typical. He includes in his typology "descriptive" case studies, i.e., noncausal case studies. His approach illustrates how representative or typical in a univariate sense can be interpreted. His table 4.1 defines "typical" as the mean, median, or mode of variable D. He notes, "Descriptive cases aim directly and explicitly at representativeness ... A case chosen by virtue of representing features that are common within a larger population may be described as typical. The typical case is intended to represent the central tendency of a distribution" (Gerring 2017, 56).

The second sense of "representative" is representative of the causal effect of X on Y, aka β. Take a simple case, OLS: the causal effect, i.e., β, is constant for all cases. As such, *any* case on the line can be considered representative of the causal effect. Much of the multimethod literature makes the on-line versus off-line distinction. On-line cases are where the theory is working. So a representative case of the causal effect is an on-line case.

Combining the two senses of representative gives a guideline for case studies in the continuous X and Y case:

Explore a representative case of the causal effect by choosing a case of $(\overline{X}, \overline{Y})$.

[2] One needs to ask what kind of case $\overline{X}$ or $\overline{Y}$ is likely to be in terms of the concepts X and Y. By definition, mean or average cases are in the middle of the conceptual continuum; they lie in the gray zone (Goertz 2005). Often, representative cases are different from good cases, e.g., good students versus average students.

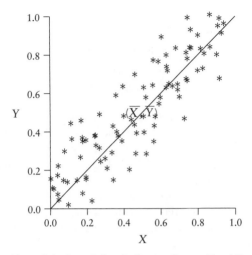

Figure A.1: Case study selection: continuous X and Y.

As illustrated in figure A.1, $(\overline{X}, \overline{Y})$ is representative in the causal effect sense, as well as in the univariate sense.[3] This matches with the experimental emphasis on *average* treatment effects.

It is useful when asking case selection questions to have a basic bivariate scatterplot in mind, i.e., figure A.1, as well as a corresponding 2×2 table, i.e., table A.1. One can then locate various case selection options in the figure or the table. The 2×2 table provides a convenient notation whereby $(1, 0)$ means choosing a case where $X = 1$ and $Y = 0$.

What would be the two kinds of representative cases in the 2×2 setting?

For dichotomous variables the most popular definition of representative is the mode. For example, in logit analyses (see below for more) dichotomous control variables are set to the mode while continuous variables are usually set to the mean.

If we follow the logic of figure A.1, we would be choosing between the on-line cells $(0, 0)$ and $(1, 1)$. Here we assume a positive relationship between X and Y, as in figure A.1. The

---

[3] Depending on the statistical model and estimation technique, $(\overline{X}, \overline{Y})$ may not fall on the estimated line.

TABLE A.1
X–Y configurations

	$X = 0$	$X = 1$
$Y = 1$	$(0, 1)$	$(1, 1)$
$Y = 0$	$(0, 0)$	$(1, 0)$

off-line cases are then to be found in the cells $(0, 1)$ and $(1, 0)$. In the context of 2×2 tables—table A.1—causal effect representative case studies would come from the $(1, 1)$ or $(0, 0)$ cells; Herron and Quinn (2016, 470) interpret "typical case" selection in this manner.

Another way to explore these issues is the fundamental counterfactual of the potential outcomes approach. The randomized experiment is the model and one asks about the causal effect of the treatment—aka X—on the outcome Y. Ideally, we would like to look at the effect of the treatment on individual i versus no treatment on individual i. The basic counterfactual is what *would have happened* to i had they not received the treatment. Following this logic we would compare an $X = 0$ with an $X = 1$ case. The question is then, what should the Y values be?

If X has a causal effect that the researcher is looking for, when $X = 1$ then $Y = 1$. Conversely one might expect to see $Y = 0$ when $X = 0$. This is the pair that would illustrate the causal effect of X on Y, leading as well to $(0, 0)$ and $(1, 1)$ cells as containing on-line cases.

The $(1, 1)$ and $(0, 0)$ cases are symmetric; there is no particular reason to prefer one cell over the other. In the continuous OLS case, all the on-line cases have the same causal effect. In short, the same point applies: all on-line cases satisfy the representative causal effect criterion.

Combining the univariate and causal effect meanings of representative would usually put the case study choice in the $(0, 0)$ cell. In most comparative politics and international relations settings, there are many more observations in the $(0, 0)$ cell than the $(1, 1)$ cell. The $(0, 0)$ cell becomes the dichotomous version of $(\overline{X}, \overline{Y})$ as representative for X and Y.

Following the statistical approach to multimethod research thus leads exactly in the opposite direction from that proposed in this book. The $(0, 0)$ cell is of little use when multimethod research means within-case causal inference about causal mechanisms.[4]

Variation on *X* and *Y*

Following the publication of King, Keohane, and Verba qualitative researchers became extremely conscious of the issue of selecting on the dependent variable. For many, variation on *Y* became a critical factor in choosing case studies. In the quote above (in the introduction to this appendix) Lijphart emphasizes the importance of variation on *X*. It is quite common in comparative case studies with 5+ case studies to see variation on *X* and *Y* as justification of case selection. For example, "In this article, we make the case for why small states matter in comparative politics. Our rationale is methodological; to meet the standard conventions of case selection—representativeness and variation (Gerring 2007)—we argue that comparative scholars need to pay closer attention to small states" (Veenendaal and Corbett 2015, 528). Weinstein makes the same argument in his study of civil wars: "Following John Stuart Mill's method of difference, the selected cases maximize variation in the behavior of rebel groups but are drawn from a sample of civil wars that exhibit similar general characteristics" (Weinstein 2006, 54). Kupchan, in his choice of about 20 cases, argues that "the successful and failed instances of a stable peace examined in this book thus represent a diverse subset of a broader universe of cases" (2010, 9).

Much of the debate about case selection for comparative-case-study and multimethod work is framed in terms of 2×2 tables like table A.1. If one follows the logic of statistical analyses of such tables then with 4+ case studies one should do a case study from each cell.

Each cell is critical to 2×2 measures of association such as χ^2. Choosing cases from all four cells naturally matches measures of association for 2×2 tables, which use information from all four cells.

---

[4] Except for necessary conditions, which would be a negative β in the context of this appendix.

The importance of choosing from each cell can be seen in debates about QCA. For example, Paine states, "Recognizing that all four cells matter raises crucial issues about how to combine information from the cells to make valid inferences" (2016, 794). Weiffen et al. (2011) provide an example of a 2×2 table with case studies from each cell (see their table 2); Lange (2009) chooses one case per cell of a 2×2 table.

Putting these considerations together we get a case selection rule when doing four or more case studies:

Choose at least one case from each cell of the 2×2 table.

By choosing cases from all four cells of table A.1, one is adding off-line cases to the project. In the context of figure A.1 these are cases with large residuals. Good applied statistical research always examines cases with large residuals. The goal is often to look for omitted variables. If all the large residual cases have some common feature then a new variable can be introduced into the statistical model and these off-line cases can become on-line ones.

As with the $(0, 0)$ and $(1, 1)$ on-line cells, the off-line cells $(1, 0)$ and $(0, 1)$ are also symmetric: there is no real difference between the two from a statistical perspective. Cases from these two cells are all falsifying cases or cases where the statistical model is not performing well.

The statistical approach sees off-line and on-line as symmetric, i.e., $(0, 0)$ and $(1, 1)$ are equally on-line cases while $(1, 0)$ and $(0, 1)$ are equally off-line. As previous chapters (notably chapter 3) have discussed in detail, my approach sees them as quite different and not symmetric. For example, $(1, 0)$ cases are falsifying–scope cases while $(0, 1)$ cases are equifinality cases. This is a major difference between the approach proposed by this volume and the statistical approach.

Potential Outcomes and Paired Comparisons

The potential outcomes approach, along with its associated counterfactual, leads to *comparative, paired comparisons*. The basis of the potential outcomes approach lies in the counterfactual of what would happen to the subject X_i if, instead of receiving the treatment, it had received the control. This means comparing what would have happened if $X = 1$ had been $X = 0$. If the treatment has a significant effect then this counterfactual would produce a $(0, 0)$ most of the time. Hence, it is not surprising—independent of the potential outcomes approach—that scholars have had a long-standing preference for paired comparisons involving $(0, 0)$ and $(1, 1)$ cases. These pairs illustrate what should be happening if the treatment is effective. Not surprisingly, the paired comparisons in published articles are typically cases that support the author's hypotheses.

The paired comparison lies at the core of the potential outcomes approach. The basic idea is to systematically compare $X = 1$ and $X = 0$ pairs. As Weller and Barnes note, "The most important difference [in our approach] is our emphasis on *comparison.* Specifically, to understand causal mechanisms requires selecting cases based on both the expected relationships and variations in case characteristics using information about the values of key variables and the relationship in individual cases" (2014, 67). Lyall makes the same point in his discussion of process tracing: "To be confident about one's inferences, within-case process tracing should thus be paired with cross-case process tracing in a control observation where the presumed relationship between treatment and outcomes is not present" (Lyall 2014, 92).

Matching: Confounding Factors and Most Similar Systems

Usually there is a long list of possible paired comparisons, i.e., all possible combinations of $X = 1$ and $X = 0$ observations. One needs some rationale for choosing among this long list of paired comparisons: Which pairs of $X = 1$ and $X = 0$ should scholars choose and why? Matching procedures provide a partial answer to that question: one chooses pairs that are very close on all the confounders Z (e.g., Weller and Barnes 2014, chapter 6; Nielsen 2016; Herron and Quinn 2016; Gerring 2017). Depending on how strict the criteria for matching are this will significantly reduce the size of the list of paired comparisons.

Matching fits quite naturally with the most similar systems logic. Gerring (2017) treats them as basically the same thing: matching is a more rigorous and well-defined specification of the most similar design that qualitative-case-study researchers have used for years. Among statistical methodologists, matching is certainly one of the hottest topics over the last 5–10 years. Taking the statistical approach to case studies makes a matching logic quite compelling for choosing pairs for comparison.

Whether one should choose $Z = 1$ or $Z = 0$ pairs is not an issue in the statistical matching literature. Thus it is not surprising that it does not arise much in the case study and multimethod literatures either (e.g., Weller and Barnes 2014). The matching logic has no real preference for the $Z = 1$ versus the $Z = 0$ matches. The key thing is that Z is the same for both cases.

Matching thus presents a different logic from the various overdetermination rules discussed in previous chapters. For overdetermination it matters a great deal what the value of Z is. For matching this is of no importance.

Matching reduces the population of possible case studies but often additional criteria are needed to get to a manageable number of paired comparisons. Are certain pairs of cases on the matching variable of more interest than others? Sticking with the simplest two pair setup, one has three options: (1) choose both pairs with $Z = 1$, (2) choose both pairs with $Z = 0$, and (3) choose one pair having $Z = 1$ and one pair with $Z = 0$.

Options (1) and (2) versus option (3) illustrate how matching can be about scope. Implicitly in options (1) and (2), we know nothing about the effect of the treatment for the other value of Z. Option (3) has differing values of Z so we can see whether the treatment has an effect in different contexts.

It is quite likely that $Z = 0$ is much more common than $Z = 1$. This is because much social science data is very skewed and highly collinear (limited diversity in the QCA world). So choosing $Z = 0$ might be more representative of the data set population (using the mode as the interpretation of representative).

TABLE A.2

Z variables: matching on $Z = 1$ or $Z = 0$

Pair	Country	X–treatment	Z–civil conflict
1	Cameroon	1	0
1	Gabon	0	0
2	Kenya	1	0
2	Cote d'Ivoire	0	0
3	Malawi	1	0
3	Zambia	0	0
4	Tanzania	1	0
4	Guinea-Bissau	0	0

Source: Source: based on Glynn and Ichino 2015.
Dependent variable is "opposition harassment."
Treatment is "plurality electoral rules."

Glynn and Ichino (2015) illustrate the scope issues of matching on Z in a comparative-case-study context. They have a total of eight cases (i.e., four pairs in table A.2). Their first matching variable is whether there was a civil conflict prior to the transition. This is a confounder since former combatants can be readily mobilized to harass opponents. Notice that in this particular data set, $Z = 0$ for all the matched pairs, i.e., they are all cases of no civil conflict; $Z = 0$ is the mode—no civil war is much more common than civil war—and thus more representative of the population.

In the Glynn and Ichino study, Z functions as a scope variable. Since all the pairs are "no civil conflict," we have no idea whether the treatment has an effect when there is civil conflict. It is completely possible that a parallel table where $Z = 1$—i.e., civil wars—would produce a different story.

Implementing option (3) above—one pair with $Z = 1$ and one pair with $Z = 0$—one produces a different system design. As Z takes on differing values for different pairs, we explore how far the treatment effect travels.

Under the statistical approach to multimethod research and case studies, Z variables naturally become matching variables. Typically the potential outcomes approach does not concern itself with the value of the matched variables. However, nothing in the potential outcomes approach prevents the use of Z as a scope variable as well, in a most different system design.

The Final Choice of Cases

The case selection suggestions found in Gerring, Lieberman, and Weller and Barnes only narrow down the list of possible case studies. For example, there might be many on-line cases. There might be quite a few matched pairs. So additional guidelines and procedures are needed to get to a final choice of cases.

Statistical logic naturally leads to the recommendation of random selection from the long short list of possible case studies or paired comparisons. Fearon and Laitin (2008) have made the strongest argument for random selection of case studies. Particularly, they argue that this hedges against "cherry-picking" cases favorable to the author.

One might also stress how random selection, on average, produces representative cases (Frankfort-Nachmias, Nachmias, and DeWaard 2014). Herron and Quinn (2016) find in their simulations that random selection of case studies does very well in capturing the average treatment effect and the mode is good for causal representativeness as well: "Finally, if one can only choose a very small number of cases, say fewer than three, for case analysis, then the very simple method of randomly choosing cases from the largest cell [mode] of the 2×2 (X,Y) table (largest cell case selection) is extremely competitive with other, more complicated, cases selection strategies" (Herron and Quinn 2016, 488).

In the statistical framework, random selection makes the final decision about which case studies to do. All of the considerations above, e.g., matching, produce a set of cases that are potentially numerous, so the researcher will almost always be confronted with getting to the final set of case studies. Random selection can always produce a final choice.[5]

[5] This ignores practical problems (e.g., no sources, language problems) in doing a given case study. The assumption throughout is that every observation is a possible case study.

Pathway Case Methodology

The pathway case study as defined by Gerring (2007; 2017) is the type most closely linked to the analysis of causal mechanisms. It is the kind of case study most often found in actual statistical multimethod research. It is, in fact, the type that Weller and Barnes (2014) devote a whole book to (there is no book-length or even article-length treatment of Gerring's other case study types).

Gerring defines the pathway case study design as follows:

A pathway case is one where the apparent impact of X on Y conforms to theoretical expectations and is strongest (in magnitude), while background conditions (Z) are held constant or exert a "conservative" bias. This might also be called a *conforming* or *typical* case, since it conforms to or typifies a causal relationship of interest. However, the ideal pathway case does more than simply conform to an expected pattern. . . . In a setting where the relationship between X and Y is well established—perhaps as a result of cross-case analysis (the researcher's or someone else's)—the pathway case is usually focused specifically on causal mechanisms (M). (Gerring and Cojocaru 2016, 405)

In short, the goal of pathway cases is to explore causal mechanisms.

Gerring (2007; 2017) provides a methodology for selecting pathway cases (which Weller and Barnes 2014 use):

1. Estimate a statistical model with all confounders Z.
2. Estimate a full statistical model with X and all confounders Z.
3. The pathway cases are those where the absolute difference between the confounder-only model residual for observation i and the full-model residual for i is large.

The logic is that "we want to find a case where the addition of X pushes the case towards the regression line, i.e., it helps to 'explain' that case, according to the terms of the theory that is being assessed" (Gerring 2017, 110).

This is the logic of the omitted variable and outlier case. If one looks *only* at the confounders then the theory or hypothesis implies that there is an omitted variable X. This omitted variable could explain some of the off-line, large residual cases. If we then include X and find that for observation i the residual is now quite small, then i is defined by Gerring as a pathway case. Essentially pathway cases are those where the inclusion of X makes an off-line case an on-line one.

I propose an alternative methodology for determining the pathway cases. The procedure relies directly on the potential outcomes logic at the individual case level. It also avoids the issues of estimating two models. Hence the procedure is (1) more faithful to the potential outcomes logic and (2) has fewer practical problems because only one model is estimated and not two, as in the Gerring procedure.[6]

The potential outcomes approach starts with an individual case counterfactual: What would have happened if observation i had not received the treatment? Much current methodological research is about either choosing an existing case that is very close to the treatment case on all confounders but not on the treatment, or creating a counterfactual comparison case: "In this design, comparison units are intended to reproduce the counterfactual of the case of interest in the absence of the event or intervention under scrutiny" (Abadie et al. 2015, 496). Abadie et al. want a counterfactual case in order to assess the effect of German unification on German economic growth. To do so, they formulate a statistical model and use data from countries "similar" to Germany, i.e., matching countries, but without the treatment of German unification.

My proposal is best illustrated with standard procedures for evaluating the effect of X on Y in nonlinear models such as logit. These procedures (see Goertz and Mahoney 2012, chapter 9 for more) rely on a generic counterfactual where X is moved, say, from its minimum to its maximum, while all confounders are

---

[6] Teorell criticizes Gerring's formula on grounds that should be familiar from chapter 3: "There is, instead, another criterion that needs to be added [to Gerring's criteria]: that the case in question actually experiences the outcome that should be explained. It makes little sense to trace the mechanisms causing democratization, for example, in a case that never democratized. Unfortunately, Gerring and Seawright forget this crucial aspect of how to select a good pathway case. Although alternative ways to incorporate this third consideration might be envisioned, I propose a slight modification of Gerring" (see Teorell 2010, 184–85 for details).

held at medians, means, or modes (depending on the nature of the specific confounder). The effect of X is then the change of the probability of Y occurring in this *generic* counterfactual. The basic idea is to convert this generic counterfactual into an individual observation counterfactual.

Given that we have estimated a model, we can take this basic logic and do *individual case* counterfactuals. The basic procedure is (assuming a positive causal effect of X)

1. for each observation i we make a counterfactual change from the actual value of X_i to the minimum of X;
2. all confounders are held at their actual values for observation i;
3. pathway cases are those i with the largest counterfactual change in the probability of Y_i based on the counterfactual change in X_i.

This procedure is very general. The basic requirement is that there be a mathematical model upon which to base the counterfactual.[7] The mathematic model generates counterfactuals by plugging in counterfactual values of X_i and contrasting them with what the model predicts for the real value of X for observation i.

Gerring's proposal requires estimating two models, with and without X. Given the nature of social science data (e.g., significant collinearity), it is quite likely that the parameter estimates of some of the Z variables will change once X is introduced. So the residual depends also on the new parameter estimates for the Z variables. This could be a reason for the reduction in the size of the residual as well. In my procedure there is just the full model, hence this problem does not exist.

In most instances it will be extreme, large values of X, i.e., values close to the maximum of X, that will generate the pathway cases. Given that the parameter estimates, βs, are the same for all i, the change in probability will be driven by the size of the counterfactual change in X_i. Large counterfactual changes will be in those X_i with values close to the maximum of X.[8]

---

[7] For example, one could use the same basic idea for game-theoretic models.

[8] Teorell with his modification of Gerring's procedure finds this: "Figure 3.1 also highlights some other features of my pathway criterion. The first is that most pathway cases are fairly extreme outliers in the sense that there is a large amount

262 • Appendix A

The counterfactual difference in the probability of Y depends of course on the parameters for Z variables along with the values of Z for observation i. One interesting scenario is when the Z variables by themselves predict that Y is quite likely, i.e., near 1.0. Since the probability is already near 1.0, counterfactual changes in X cannot increase the probability of Y by much. In earlier chapters this was the problem of overdetermination. While this remains to be explored, it seems like the pathway cases are likely to be very high on X and low on the Z variables.

In short, instead of comparing models and residuals (Gerring's approach), my procedure uses the basic counterfactual at the core of the potential outcomes approach to define pathway cases.

Interestingly enough, this pathway procedure produces an emphasis on extreme values of X that agrees with the analysis in chapter 3. In addition, pathway cases are likely to be those that agree with the Avoid Overdetermination Guideline. This pathway procedure agrees in important ways with the methodology developed in chapter 3.

Research Practice

It is always useful to connect methodological theory with actual practice. With statistical methods, there are textbooks and standards about citing as justification of practice. It is not uncommon in multimethod work for there to be no citing of the relevant methodological literature. Many statistical multimethod scholars have not had classes in qualitative methods or multimethod

---

of change in their level of democracy that is unaccounted for even considering their degree of economic crisis (i.e., they have large residuals). As argued in Appendix D, I see no reason why this should disqualify them as pathway cases for assessing the mechanisms responsible for this particular determinant. Second, by Gerring's (2006) account, most pathway cases experience little or no change in their level of democracy. The top-ranked pathway case according to their criterion, for example, is Gabon in 1975, positioned right on the regression line to the very left of the figure (not labeled). Gabon in 1975, however, experienced zero change on the democracy scale, and thus would provide very weak evidence of potential mechanisms linking economic performance to democratization" (Teorell 2010, 72).

research. Statistical multimethod research is rarely a part of statistical methods courses or sequences. It is a central topic at qualitative methods summer institutes—e.g., IQMR at Syracuse University—but rarely a topic at statistical ones, such as ICPSR (Inter-university Consortium for Political and Social Research).

The vast majority of multimethod research in journals and books is statistical multimethod, defined as statistical analyses plus case studies. Not surprisingly, in articles the case studies tend to be quite abbreviated. Conversely, in books they can be quite expansive. Books with one or two statistical chapters followed by five or six case studies have become quite common in recent years.

Experimental multimethod work is quite rare in political science and economics (as far as I can tell). Why this should be the case seems to be part of the norms and beliefs of research subcultures. Multimethod experimental work is frequent in psychology and sociology, which have a much longer tradition of experimental research. For example, it is often easy to debrief subjects once the experiment is over.

There is some evidence that economists, and political scientists following them, do not find this very useful. For example, Dunning (2012) has no discussion about debriefing or interviewing experimental subjects as central to experimental work. A group of prominent experimental economists (Bardsley et al. 2010) argue that self-reports by individuals of their decision-making process are not reliable. Certainly, like autobiographies, one must treat self-reports with skepticism. However, it is not clear that economists inferring from the outside and with their own (perhaps biased) beliefs is not without serious problems. In any case, from my reading, experimental multimethod work thrives in sociology, psychology, and education, but not in economics and political science.

My survey of journals and books revealed that the actual use of statistical models and results to choose cases is extremely rare, two articles in 10 years in our systematic survey of the major international relations and comparative politics journals, and equally rare in books. It is virtually obligatory in books with statistical analyses to have case studies, but it is very rare to use statistical analyses to choose the case studies.

This conclusion is confirmed by Rohlfing who looked at all journal articles that cited Lieberman (2005) on "nested analysis," an article that has been widely read, cited, and used in graduate courses, the focus of which is using estimated regression models to choose case studies. Rohlfing found that a very small number of articles actually used regression analyses to pick case studies. Gerring (2017) lists only a few cases of "algorithmic" case selection, which usually means using statistical models.

Here is a complete list of articles and books that I have found that directly use statistical analyses in their case selection:

Agrawal, A. and A. Chhatre. 2011. Strengthening causal inference through qualitative analysis of regression residuals: explaining forest governance in the Indian Himalaya. *Environment and Planning A* 43:328–46.

Back, H. and P. Dumont. 2007. Combining large-N and small-N strategies: the way forward in coalition research. *West European Politics* 30:467–501.

Back, H., H. Meier, and T. Persson. 2009. Party size and portfolio payoffs: the proportional allocation of ministerial posts in coalition governments. *Journal of Legislative Studies* 15:10–34.

Bush, S. 2011. International politics and the spread of quotas for women in legislatures. *International Organization* 65:103-37.

Dafoe, A. and N. Kelsey. 2014. Observing the capitalist peace: examining market-mediated signaling and other mechanisms. *Journal of Peace Research* 51:619–33.

Fearon, J. and D. Laitin. 2005. Civil war narratives. Manuscript. Stanford University.

Fink, S. 2008. Politics as usual or bringing religion back in? The influence of parities, institutions, economic interests, and religion on embryo research laws. *Comparative Political Studies* 41:1631–56.

Kim, D. 2013. International nongovernmental organizations and the global diffusion of national human rights institutions. *International Organization* 67:505–39.

Lange, M. 2009. *Lineages of despotism and development: British colonialism and state power.* Chicago: University of Chicago Press.

Luetgert, B. and T. Dannwolf. 2009. Mixing methods: a nested analysis of EU member state transposition patterns. *European Union Politics* 10:307–34.

Madrigal, R., et al. 2011. Determinants of performance of community-based drinking water organizations. *World Development* 39:1663–75.

McGuire, J. 2010. *Wealth, health, and democracy in East Asia and Latin America.* Cambridge: Cambridge University Press.

Pearce, L. 2002. Integrating survey and ethnographic methods for systematic anomalous case analysis. *Sociological Methodology* 32:103–32.

Rosen, J. 2013. Explaining women's parliamentary representation: political institutions, development thresholds, and gender equality in national politics. PhD Dissertation, Northwestern University.

Sambanis, N. 2004. Using case studies to expand economic models of civil war. *Perspectives on Politics* 2:259–80.

Teorell, J. 2010. *Determinants of democratization: explaining regime change in the world, 1972–2006.* Cambridge: Cambridge University Press.

Bush (2011) provides an example of multimethod study that combines quantitative models with the selection of a case study. Her study examines the causes of the adoption of gender quotas in legislatures worldwide (excluding developed democracies), arguing that the adoption of quotas is a consequence of "two causal pathways: directly, through postconflict peace operations, and indirectly, by encouraging countries, especially those that depend on foreign aid, to signal their commitment to democracy by adopting quotas" (Bush 2011, 103). Event history analysis shows the presence of liberalizing UN peacekeeping operations, aid dependence, and the presence of international election monitors influences the adoption of quotas. She performs an in-depth case study of Afghanistan, which is an on-line (1, 1) case: "A case study can check the results' robustness through process tracing. Since the preliminary large-N analysis generated satisfactory results for my theory, I chose Afghanistan—a country that was well-predicted by the statistical model ... Afghanistan adopted a gender quota on 4 January 2004, as part of a new constitution. The constitutional process began on 5 December 2001, after the

U.S. invasion, with the Bonn Agreement, which called for 'the establishment of a broad-based, gender sensitive, multiethnic and fully representative government' " (Bush 2011, 126).

Afghanistan is an on-line case, but is it representative or an extreme (1, 1) case? One does not need to look at the data to know that Afghanistan must be an extreme case of foreign aid, as well as extreme on "postconflict peace operations."

It will then not be surprising that anything more complicated, like the use of matching, is nowhere to be seen. Weller and Barnes (2014) have a whole chapter devoted to matching in their methods book, which exclusively looks at case studies *given* strong large-N statistical results. They do an extended example of matching using Ross's work on oil-dependent states (Ross 2004; Ross 2012). Weller and Barnes give a list of 46 matched pairs (total number of $Y = 1$ cases) in their table 6.1. However, there is little specific guidance about exactly which or how many of these could or should be explored.

All this indicates that case selection in statistical multi-method research relies on folk wisdom and conventional practices. Of course, there might be unpublished work—notably PhD dissertations—but based on what is in the major journals and university press books, it is certainly not the norm to connect the selection of the case study to the statistical analyses.

If there are two case studies and no statistical analyses then the paired comparison of (1, 1) against (0, 0) has a strong following. As Tarrow (2010; see also Slater and Ziblatt 2013) has noted, paired comparisons are very popular in comparative-case-study research.

Once one gets to 4+ case studies the odds of getting non-(1, 1) case studies go up significantly, but they remain relatively rare in statistical multimethod work, in contrast, say, to comparative historical work.

In summary, the statistical approach to multimethod research presented in this appendix finds little echo in research practice. If a study includes a statistical analysis plus case studies, the methodological logic presented in chapter 3 does a much better job—though far from perfect—in describing how research has been conducted over the last 10 years.

Focusing on statistical multimethod research—i.e., statistical analyses plus case studies—research practice patterns are quite clear, in political science at least:

- Scholars rarely use statistical analyses to choose cases.
- There is no matching on Z variables. Informal arguments about similar systems are not uncommon.
- Scholars overwhelmingly choose extreme (1, 1) cases.
- Researchers almost never select representative cases in the sense of $(\overline{X}, \overline{Y})$.
- Researchers rarely select (0, 0) cases.
- Random selection of cases is rare.

Statistical Multimethod Issues

Few are those who actually use statistical models (e.g., logit) to select cases. In this section I outline some of the issues involved if one were to use estimated statistical models to select case studies.

It is generally assumed that a case study should come from the data set used for the statistical analyses.[9] However, this need not necessarily be the case. A common bit of statistical advice is that one fit the model with some of the data and then confirm it with other parts of the data. One could apply this to multimethod work as well. The case study could be chosen from outside the data used to fit the statistical model. In practice, most scholars use all the data to estimate statistical models, but it is worth thinking about out-of-sample case studies. For example, Johnson (2014) chooses out-of-sample case studies in her statistical multimethod analysis of IGOs.

Another obvious problem is which model to use. The standard article normally presents five or six, or even more, statistical models. Which one should be used for selecting case studies?

---

[9] For example, "A second issue, which has been extensively discussed in the multi-method literature, is that the regression-type study must be carried out on a set of cases from the same population as the case study, relative to the causal effect of interest" (Seawright 2016, 195).

In some situations there is one model that is the centerpiece, and the others are variations on this central model. In the few existing cases of multimethod work using the estimated statistical model, it is sometimes not clear exactly which model is used. For example, Bush says that Afghanistan "was well-predicted by the statistical model." In her table 3, there are five models. Model 4 is the "full model," so presumably that was the one used. But model 5 does include one additional variable.

One of the most important issues is the potential tension between "the model" and the one or two X variables that are the centerpiece of the research. Sticking with Bush, she has three hypotheses in the theory section, but her statistical model has nine substantive variables. It could well be that the reason why Afghanistan fits is more because of the six other variables than the three variables of interest to her.

This problem can easily be compounded when researchers include a lot (often hundreds) of "nuisance" variables. For example, fixed effects are popular in cross-national studies. In conflict research, peace-year splines (Beck, Katz, and Tucker 1998) are quite standard practice. In a democratic peace analysis with peace-year splines—essentially lagged dependent variables—the spline variables might cover as much of the variance explained, as all of the substantive variables combined.

In short, there are three kinds of variables that determine whether a case is on-line: (1) substantive variables under examination, (2) confounders and control variables, (3) nuisance variables such as fixed effects and lagged dependent variables.

One possibility is to do the statistical analysis with *only* the substantive variable(s) of interest. Then on-line would really be those determined by the core independent variables. If the core-variables-only analysis roughly corresponds to the full model in substantive terms, this might be a way to avoid many of the problems of the full model and its potentially large number of variables.

In short, using an estimated statistical model to choose case studies involves a number of quite important decisions. Ideally, scholars should present them all, discuss them all, and justify them all.

Conclusions

Much of the discussion of qualitative methods focuses on *comparative* case studies. For example, for many, Alexander George defined the standard with his methodology of focused case comparisons (George and Bennett 2005). King, Keohane, and Verba famously argued that qualitative methods should follow the logic of statistical analyses.

Thus if *only* case studies are being conducted, then one more or less mimics the statistical logic of comparison. The recent statistical literature on small-N case selection (see above) generally follows the potential outcome framework. This often leads to paired comparisons of $X = 0$ and $X = 1$ cases and matching, exactly the logic of large-N statistical methods.

This comparative emphasis for case studies becomes more problematic in a statistical multimethod setting. Given that one is doing statistical analyses, that are comparative by definition, what is the value or point of doing comparative case studies? The unclear role of comparative case studies in statistical multimethod work explains perhaps the popularity of the pathway, i.e., causal mechanism, case study in applied research.

This book offers a different approach to multimethod scholarship. The research triad includes cross-case analyses, so the value of case studies lies elsewhere, notably within-case causal inference and exploring causal mechanisms.

REFERENCES

Abadie, A., et al. 2015 Comparative politics and the synthetic control method. *American Journal of Political Science* 59:495–510.

Acemoglu, D., and J. Robinson. 2006. *Economic origins of dictatorship and democracy*. Cambridge: Cambridge University Press.

Agrawal, A., and A. Chhatre. 2011. Strengthening causal inference through qualitative analysis of regression residuals: explaining forest governance in the Indian Himalaya. *Environment and Planning A* 43:328–46.

Aktürk, S. 2011. Regimes of ethnicity: comparative analysis of Germany, the Soviet Union/Post-Soviet Russia, and Turkey. *World Politics* 63:115–64.

Alford, R. 1998. *The craft of inquiry: theories, methods, evidence*. Oxford: Oxford University Press.

Angrist, J., and J.-S. Pischke. 2015. *Mastering metrics*. Princeton: Princeton University Press.

Ansell, B. 2010. *From the ballot to the blackboard: the redistributive political economy of education*. Cambridge: Cambridge University Press.

Ansell, B., and D. Samuels. 2014. *Inequality and democratization: an elite-competition approach*. Cambridge: Cambridge University Press.

Babbie, E. 2001. *The practice of social research*, 9th edition. Belmont: Wadsworth.

Back, H., and P. Dumont. 2007. Combining large-N and small-N strategies: the way forward in coalition research. *West European Politics* 30:467–501.

Back, H., H. Meier, and T. Persson. 2009. Party size and portfolio payoffs: the proportional allocation of ministerial posts in coalition governments. *Journal of Legislative Studies* 15:10–34.

Bara, C. 2014. Incentives and opportunities: a complexity-oriented explanation of violent ethnic conflict. *Journal of Peace Research* 51:696–710.

Bardsley, N., R. Cubitt, G. Loomes, P. Moffatt, C. Starmer, and R. Sugden. 2010. *Experimental economics: rethinking the rules*, Princeton: Princeton University Press.

Bartels, L. 1996. Pooling disparate observations. *American Journal of Political Science* 40:905–42.

Bates, R., et al. (eds.). 1998. *Analytic narratives*. Princeton: Princeton University Press.

Beach, D., and R. Pedersen. 2012. *Process-tracing methods: foundations and guidelines*. Ann Arbor: University of Michigan Press.

———. 2016. *Causal case studies: foundations and guidelines for comparing, matching and tracing*. Ann Arbor: University of Michigan Press.

Beach, D., and I. Rohlfing. 2015. Integrating cross-case analyses and process tracing in set-theoretic research: strategies and parameters of debate. *Sociological Methods & Research*. DOI: 10.1177/0049124115613780.

Beck, N. 2010. Causal process "observation": oxymoron or (fine) old wine. *Political Analysis* 18:499–505.

Beck, N., J. Katz, and R. Tucker. 1998. Taking time seriously: time-series-cross-section analysis with a binary dependent variable. *American Journal of Political Science* 42:1260–88.

Bennett, A., and J. Checkel (eds.). 2014. *Process tracing in the social sciences: from metaphor to analytic tool*. Cambridge: Cambridge University Press.

———. 2014. Process tracing: from philosophical roots to best practices. In A. Bennett and J. Checkel (eds.), *Process tracing in the social sciences: from metaphor to analytic tool*. Cambridge: Cambridge University Press.

Blatter, J., and M. Haverland. 2012. *Designing case studies: explanatory approaches in small-N research*. London: Palgrave.

Boix, C. 2003. *Democracy and redistribution*. New York: Cambridge University Press.

Boix, C., and S. Stokes. 2003. Endogenous democratization. *World Politics* 55:517–49.

Brady, H. 2004. Data-set observations versus causal-process observations: the 2000 US presidential election. In H. Brady and D. Collier (eds.), *Rethinking social inquiry: diverse tools, shared standards*. New York: Rowman & Littlefield.

Brady, H., and D. Collier (eds.). 2010. *Rethinking social inquiry: diverse tools, shared standards*, 2nd edition. New York: Rowman & Littlefield.

Brambor, T., W. Clark, and M. Golder. 2006. Understanding interaction models: improving empirical analyses. *Political Analysis* 14:63–82.

Braumoeller, B. 2004. Hypothesis testing and multiplicative interaction terms. *International Organization* 58:807–20.

Braumoeller, B., and G. Goertz. 2000. The methodology of necessary conditions. *American Journal of Political Science* 44:844–58.

Brehm, J., and S. Gates. 1977. *Working, shirking, and sabotage: bureaucratic response to a democratic public.* Ann Arbor: University of Michigan Press.

Bueno de Mesquita, B. 1981. *The war trap.* New Haven: Yale University Press.

———. 1990. Pride of place: the origins of German hegemony. *World Politics* 43:28–52.

———. 2000. Popes, kings, and endogenous institutions: the Concordat of Worms and the origins of sovereignty. *International Studies Review* 2:93–114.

———. 2007. Leopold II and the selectorate: an account in contrast to a racial explanation. *Historical Social Research [Historische Sozialforschung]* 32:203–21.

———. 2009. *The predictioneer's game.* New York: Random House.

———. 2013. *Principles of international politics: war, peace, and world order,* 5th edition. Newbury Park: Sage Publications.

Bueno de Mesquita, B., and Y. Feng. 1997. Forecasting China's political and economic future. *Problems of Post-Communism* 44:14–27.

Bueno de Mesquita, B., and D. Lalman. 1992. *War and reason: domestic and international imperatives.* New Haven: Yale University Press.

Bueno de Mesquita, B., R. McDermott, and E. Cope. 2001. The expected prospects for peace in Northern Ireland. *International Interactions* 27:129–68.

Bueno de Mesquita, B., and A. Smith. 2011. *The dictator's handbook.* New York: PublicAffairs.

Bueno de Mesquita, B., A. Smith, R. Siverson, and J. Morrow. 2003. *The logic of political survival.* Cambridge: MIT Press.

Bueno de Mesquita, B., et al. 1985. *Forecasting political events: the future of Hong Kong.* New Haven: Yale University Press.

Bush, S. 2011. International politics and the spread of quotas for women in legislatures. *International Organization* 65:103–37.

Camerer, C. 2015. The promise and success of labfield generalizability in experimental economics: a critical reply to Levitt and List. In G. Fréchette and A. Schotter (eds.), *Handbook of experimental economic methodology.* Oxford: Oxford University Press.

Cammett, M. 2014. *Compassionate communalism: welfare and sectarianism in Lebanon.* Ithaca: Cornell University Press.

Campbell, D., and J. Stanley. 1963. *Experimental and quasi-experimental designs for research*. Chicago: Rand McNally.

Caren, N., and A. Panofsky. 2005. A technique for adding temporality to qualitative comparative analysis. *Sociological Methods & Research* 34:147–72.

Carrubba, C., and M. Gabel. 2014. *International courts and the performance of international agreements: a general theory with evidence from the European Union*. Cambridge: Cambridge University Press.

Cheibub, J., J. Gandhi, and J. Vreeland. 2010. Democracy and dictatorship revisited. *Public Choice* 143:67–101.

Cioffi-Revilla, C., and H. Starr. 2003. Opportunity, willingness, and political uncertainty: theoretical foundations of politics. In G. Goertz and H. Starr (eds.), *Necessary conditions: theory, methodology, and applications*. New York: Rowman & Littlefield.

Clarke, K., and D. Primo. 2012. *A model discipline: political science and the logic of representations*. Oxford: Oxford University Press.

Coleman, J. 1990. *Foundations of social theory*. Cambridge: Harvard University Press.

Colgan, J. 2013. *Petro-aggression: when oil causes war*. Cambridge: Cambridge University Press.

Collier, D. 2011. Understanding process tracing. *PS: Political Science & Politics* 44:823–30.

Copeland, D. 2015. *Economic interdependence and war*. Princeton: Princeton University Press.

Craver, C. F. (2007). *Explaining the brain: what a science of the mind-brain could be*. New York: Oxford.

Cusack, T., T. Iversen, and D. Soskice. 2007. Economic interests and the origins of electoral systems. *American Political Science Review* 101:373–91.

Dafoe, A., and N. Kelsey. 2014. Observing the capitalist peace: examining market-mediated signaling and other mechanisms. *Journal of Peace Research* 51:619–33.

Demeulenaere, P. 2011. Introduction. In P. Demeulenaere (ed.), *Analytical sociology and social mechanisms*. Cambridge: Cambridge University Press.

Díez, J. 2013. Explaining policy outcomes: the adoption of same-sex unions in Buenos Aires and Mexico City. *Comparative Political Studies* 46:212–35.

Dion, D. 1998. Evidence and inference in the comparative case study. *Comparative Politics* 30:127–45.

Downing, B. 1992. *The military revolution and political change: origins of democracy and autocracy in early modern Europe*. Princeton: Princeton University Press.

Druckman, J., and C. Kam. 2011. Students as experimental participants: a defense of the "narrow data base". In J. Druckman et al. (eds.) *Cambridge handbook of experimental political science.* Cambridge: Cambridge University Press.

Druckman, J., et al. (eds.), 2011. *Cambridge handbook of experimental political science.* Cambridge: Cambridge University Press.

Dunning, T. 2012. *Natural experiments in the social sciences.* Cambridge: Cambridge University Press.

Elman, C. 2005. Explanatory typologies in qualitative studies of international politics. *International Organization* 59:293–326.

Elster, J. 1989 *Nuts and bolts for the social sciences.* Cambridge: Cambridge University Press.

Ertman, T. 1997. *Birth of the leviathan: building states and regimes in medieval and early modern Europe.* Cambridge: Cambridge University Press.

Esping-Andersen, G. 1990. *The three worlds of welfare capitalism.* Cambridge: Polity Press.

Falleti, T. 2005. A sequential theory of decentralization: Latin American cases in comparative perspective. *American Political Science Review* 99:327–46.

Favretto, K. 2009. Should peacemakers take sides? Major power mediation, coercion, and bias. *American Political Science Review* 103:248–63.

Fearon, J. 1991. Counterfactuals and hypothesis testing in political science. *World Politics* 43:169–95.

———. 1992. Threats to use force: costly signals and bargaining in international crises. PhD dissertation. University of California, Berkeley.

———. 1994. Domestic political audiences and the escalation of international disputes. *American Political Science Review* 88: 577–92.

———. 1995. Rationalist explanations for war. *International Organization* 49:379–414.

Fearon, J., and D. Laitin. 2005. Civil war narratives. Manuscript. Stanford University.

———. 2008. Integrating qualitative and quantitative methods. In J. Box-Steffensmeier, H. Brady, and D. Collier (eds.), *The Oxford handbook of political methodology.* Oxford: Oxford University Press.

Fink, S. 2008. Politics as usual or bringing religion back in? The influence of parities, institutions, economic interests, and religion on embryo research laws. *Comparative Political Studies* 41: 1631–56.

Fortna, V. 2009. Where have all the victories gone? Peacekeeping and war outcomes. Paper presented at the annual meetings of the International Studies Association.

Frankfort-Nachmias, C., D. Nachmias, and J. DeWaard. 2014. *Research methods in the social sciences*, 8th edition. New York: Worth Publishers.

Fréchette, G., and A. Schotter (eds.). 2015. *Handbook of experimental economic methodology.* Oxford: Oxford University Press.

Freedman, D. 1991. Statistical models and shoe leather. *Sociological Methodology* 21:291–313.

Friedman, M. 1953. *Essay in positive economics.* Chicago: University of Chicago Press.

Fuhrmann, M. 2012. *Atomic assistance: how "atoms for peace" programs cause nuclear insecurity.* Ithaca: Cornell University Press.

Gartzke, E., and D.-J. Jo. 2009. Bargaining, nuclear proliferation, and interstate disputes. *Journal of Conflict Resolution* 53:209–33.

Geddes, B. 1990. How the cases you choose affect the answers you get: selection bias in comparative politics. In J. Stimson (ed.), *Political analysis*, vol. 2. Ann Arbor: University of Michigan Press.

———. 2003. *Paradigms and sand castles: theory building and research design in comparative politics.* Ann Arbor: University of Michigan Press.

Geertz, C. 1973. *On the interpretation of cultures.* New York: Basic Books.

George, A., and A. Bennett. 2005. *Case studies and theory development.* Cambridge: MIT Press.

Gerring, J. 2006. *Case study research: principles and practices.* Cambridge: Cambridge University Press.

———. 2008. The mechanismic worldview: thinking inside the box. *British Journal of Political Science* 38:161–79.

———. 2010. Causal mechanisms, yes, but.... *Comparative Political Studies* 43:1499–526.

———. 2012. *Social science methodology: a unified framework*, 2nd edition. Cambridge: Cambridge University Press.

———. 2017. *Case study research: principles and practices*, 2nd edition. Cambridge: Cambridge University Press.

Gerring, J., and L. Cojocaru. 2016. Selecting cases for intensive analysis: a diversity of goals and methods. *Sociological Methods & Research* 45:392–423.

Glennan, S. 1996. Mechanisms and the nature of causation. *Erkenntnis*, 44:49–71.

———. 2002. Rethinking mechanistic explanation. *Philosophy of Science* 69:342–53.

———. 2010. Ephemeral mechanisms and historical explanation. *Erkenntnis* 72:251–66.

Glynn, A., and N. Ichino. 2015. Using qualitative information to improve causal inference. *American Journal of Political Science* 59:1055–71.

Goemans, H., and W. Spaniel, W. 2016. Multi-method research: the case for formal theory. *Security Studies* 25:25–33.

Goertz, G. 1994. *Contexts of international politics.* Cambridge: Cambridge University Press.

———. 2003. *International norms and decision making: a punctuated equilibrium model.* New York: Rowman & Littlefield.

———. 2005. *Social science concepts: a user's guide.* Princeton: Princeton University Press.

———. 2008. A checklist for constructing, evaluating, and using concepts or quantitative measures. In J. Box-Steffensmeier, H. Brady, and D. Collier (eds.), *The Oxford handbook of political methodology.* Oxford: Oxford University Press.

———. 2012. Descriptive–causal generalizations: "empirical laws" in the social sciences? In H. Kincaid (ed.), *The Oxford handbook of philosophy of social science.* Oxford: Oxford University Press.

Goertz, G., P. Diehl, and A. Balas. 2016. *The puzzle of peace: the evolution of peace in the international system.* Oxford: Oxford University Press.

Goertz, G., T. Hak, and J. Dul. 2013. Ceilings and floors: Where are there no observations? *Sociological Methods & Research* 42: 3–40.

Goertz, G., and J. Levy (eds.). 2007. *Explaining war and peace: case studies and necessary condition counterfactuals.* London: Routledge.

Goertz, G., and J. Mahoney. 2005. Two-level theories and fuzzy set analysis. *Sociological Methods & Research* 33:497–538.

———. 2012. *A tale of two cultures: qualitative and quantitative research in the social sciences.* Princeton: Princeton University Press.

Goertz, G., and A. Mazur (eds.). 2008. *Politics, gender, and concepts: theory and methodology.* Cambridge: Cambridge University Press.

Goodwin, J. 2001. *No other way out: states and revolutionary movements, 1945–1991.* Cambridge: Cambridge University Press.

Granato, J., and F. Scioli. 2004. Puzzles, proverbs, and omega matrices: the scientific and social significance of empirical implications of theoretical models (EITM). *Perspectives on Politics* 2:313–24.

Granato, J., et al. 2010. A framework for unifying formal and empirical analysis. *American Journal of Political Science* 54:783–97.

Grzymała-Busse, A. 2007. *Rebuilding leviathan: party competition and state exploitation in post-Communist democracies.* Cambridge: Cambridge University Press.

Guala, F. 2005. *The methodology of experimental economics.* Cambridge: Cambridge University Press.

Haggard, S., and R. Kaufman. 2012. Inequality and regime change: democratic transitions and the stability of democratic rule. *American Political Science Review* 106:1–22.

———. 2016. *Dictators and democrats: masses, elites, and regime change.* Princeton: Princeton University Press.

Haggard, S., et al. 2013. Inequality and regime change: the role of distributive conflict. *Comparative Democratization: APSA newsletter* 11:1, 4–7.

Harding, D., and K. Seefeldt. 2013. Mixed methods and causal analysis. In S. Morgan (ed.), *Handbook of causal analysis for social research.* New York: Springer.

Harvey, F. 2011. *Explaining the Iraq War: counterfactual theory, logic and evidence.* Cambridge: Cambridge University Press.

Hedström, P., and R. Swedberg (eds.). 1998. *Social mechanisms: an analytical approach to social theory.* Cambridge: Cambridge University Press.

Helfer, L., and E. Voeten. 2014. International courts as agents of legal change: evidence from LGBT rights in Europe. *International Organization* 68:77–110.

Hempel, S. 2007. *The strange case of the Broad Street pump: John Snow and the mystery of cholera.* Berkeley: University of California Press.

Hensel, P., G. Goertz, and P. Diehl. 2000. The democratic peace and rivalries. *Journal of Politics* 62:1173–88.

Herron, M., and K. Quinn. 2016. A careful look at modern qualitative case selection methods. *Sociological Methods & Research* 45: 458–492.

Holland, P. 1986. Statistics and causal inference (with discussion). *Journal of the American Statistical Association* 81:945–60.

Imai, K., et al. 2011. Unpacking the black box of causality. *American Political Science Review* 105:765–89.

Iversen, T. 2005. *Capitalism, democracy, and welfare.* Cambridge: Cambridge University Press.

Johns, L. 2007. A servant of two masters: communication and the selection of international bureaucrats. *International Organization* 61:245–72.

———. 2012. Courts as coordinators: endogenous enforcement and jurisdiction in international adjudication. *Journal of Conflict Resolution* 56:257–89.

Johnson, J. 2013. Models among the political theorists. *American Journal of Political Science* 58:547–60.

Johnson, T. 2014. *Organizational progeny: why governments are losing control over the proliferating structures of global governance.* Oxford: Oxford University Press.

Katzenstein, P. (ed.). 1996. *The culture of national security: norms, identity, and world politics.* New York: Columbia University Press.

Kiewiet, D., and M. McCubbins. 1991. *The logic of delegation: congressional parties and the appropriations process.* Chicago: University of Chicago Press.

Kim, D. 2013. International nongovernmental organizations and the global diffusion of national human rights institutions. *International Organization* 67:505–39.

King, G., R. Keohane, and S. Verba. 1994. *Designing social inquiry: scientific inference in qualitative research.* Princeton: Princeton University Press.

Kingdon, J. 1995. *Agendas, alternatives, and public policies*, 2nd edition. Boston: Little, Brown.

Koromenos, B., C. Lipson, and D. Snidal. 2001. The rational design of international institutions. *International Organization* 55:761–779.

Kreuzer, M. 2010. Historical knowledge and quantitative analysis: the case of the origins of proportional representation. *American Political Science Review* 104:369–92.

Krook, M. 2010. Women's representation in parliament: a qualitative comparative analysis. *Political Studies* 58:886–908.

Kruskal, W., and F. Mosteller. 1979a. Representative sampling I: non-scientific literature. *International Statistical Review* 47:13–24.

———. 1979b. Representative sampling II: scientific literature excluding statistics. *International Statistical Review* 47:117–27.

———. 1979c. Representative sampling III: current statistical literature. *International Statistical Review* 47:245–65.

———. 1980. Representative sampling IV: the history of the concept in statistics, 1895–1939. *International Statistical Review* 48:169–95.

Kupchan, C. 2010. *How enemies become friends: the sources of stable peace.* Princeton: Princeton University Press.

Kurizaki, S., and T. Whang. 2015. Detecting audience costs in international disputes. *International Organization* 69:949–80.

Kydd, A. 2006. When can mediators build trust? *American Political Science Review* 100:449–62.

———. 2007. *Trust and mistrust in international relations.* Princeton: Princeton University Press.

Lake, D. 2010. Two cheers for bargaining theory: assessing rationalist explanations of the Iraq War. *International Security* 35:7–52.

Lange, M. 2009. *Lineages of despotism and development: British colonialism and state power.* Chicago: University of Chicago Press.

Lazarsfeld, P., and A. Barton. 1951. Qualitative measurement in the social sciences: classification, typologies, and indices. In D. Lerner and H. Lasswell (eds.), *The policy sciences: recent developments in scope and method.* Stanford: Stanford University Press.

Levitsky, S., and L. Way. 2010. *Competitive authoritarianism: hybrid regimes after the Cold War.* Cambridge: Cambridge University Press.

Levitt, S., and J. List. 2015. What do laboratory experiments measuring social preferences reveal about the real world? In G. Fréchette and A. Schotter (eds.), *Handbook of experimental economic methodology.* Oxford: Oxford University Press.

Levy, J. 2008. Counterfactuals and case studies. In J. Box-Steffensmeier, H. Brady, and D. Collier (eds.), *The Oxford handbook of political methodology.* Oxford: Oxford University Press.

———. 2012. Coercive threats, audience costs, and case studies. *Security Studies* 21:383–90.

Levy, J., and W. Thompson. 2005. Hegemonic threats and great power balancing in Europe, 1495–1999. *Security Studies* 14:1–30.

———. 2010. Balancing at sea: do states ally against the leading global power? *International Security* 35:7–43.

Levy, J., et al. 2015. Backing out or backing in? Commitment and consistency in audience costs theory. *American Journal of Political Science* 59:988–1001.

Lieberman, E. 2005. Nested analysis as a mixed-method strategy for comparative research. *American Political Science Review* 99: 435–52.

———. 2015. Nested analysis: toward the integration of comparative-historical analysis with other social science methods. In J. Mahoney and K. Thelen (eds.), *Advances in comparative-historical analysis.* Cambridge: Cambridge University Press.

Lijphart, A. 1969. Consociational democracy. *World Politics* 21: 207–25.

———. 1975. The comparable-case strategy in comparative research. *Comparative Political Studies* 8:158–77.

Lipset, S. M., M. A. Trow, and J. S. Coleman. 1956. *Union democracy: the internal politics of the International Typographical Union.* Free Press.

Little, D. 1991. *Varieties of social explanation: an introduction to the philosophy of social science.* Boulder: Westview Press.

Lorentzen, P., M. T. Fravel, and J. Paine. 2016. Qualitative investigation of theoretical models: the value of process tracing. *Journal of Theoretical Politics.* DOI: 10.1177/0951629816664420.

Luebbert, G. 1991. *Liberalism, fascism, or social democracy: social classes and the political origins of regimes in interwar Europe.* Oxford: Oxford University Press.

Luetgert, B., and T. Dannwolf. 2009. Mixing methods: a nested analysis of EU member state transposition patterns. *European Union Politics* 10:307–34.

Lyall, J. 2014. Process tracing, causal inference, and civil war. In A. Bennett and J. Checkel (eds.), *Process tracing in the social sciences: from metaphor to analytic tool.* Cambridge: Cambridge University Press.

Machamer, P., et al. 2000. Thinking about mechanisms. *Philosophy of Science* 67:1–25.

Madrigal, R., et al. 2011. Determinants of performance of community-based drinking water organizations. *World Development* 39: 1663–75.

Mahoney, J. 2003. Strategies of causal assessment in comparative-historical analysis. In J. Mahoney and D. Rueschemeyer (eds.), *Comparative historical analysis in the social sciences.* Cambridge: Cambridge University Press.

———. 2008. Toward a unified theory of causality. *Comparative Political Studies* 41:412–36.

———. 2010. *Colonialism and postcolonial development: Spanish America in comparative perspective.* Cambridge: Cambridge University Press.

———. 2012. The logic of process tracing tests in the social sciences. *Sociological Methods & Research* 41:570–97.

Mahoney, J., and G. Goertz. 2004. The possibility principle: choosing negative cases in comparative research. *American Political Science Review* 98:653–69.

Mahoney, J., E. Kimball, and K. Koivu. 2009. The causal logic of historical explanation. *Comparative Political Studies* 42:114–46.

Mansfield, E., and J. Snyder. 2005. *Electing to fight: why emerging democracies go to war.* Cambridge: MIT Press.

Marchi, S. de. 2005. *Computational modeling and mathematical modeling in the sciences.* Cambridge: Cambridge University Press.

McAdam, D., and H. Boudet. 2012. *Putting social movements in their place: explaining opposition to energy projects in the United States, 2000–2005.* Cambridge: Cambridge University Press.

McBride, D., and A. Mazur. 2010. *The politics of state feminism.* Philadelphia: Temple University Press.

McGuire, J. 2010. *Wealth, health, and democracy in East Asia and Latin America.* Cambridge: Cambridge University Press.

Mello, P. 2012. Parliamentary peace or partisan politics? Democracies' participation in the Iraq War. *Journal of International Relations and Development* 15:420–53.

———. 2014. *Democratic participation in armed conflict.* London: Palgrave.

Milgram, S. 1974. *Obedience: an experimental view.* New York: Harper & Row.

Milner, H. 1997. *Interests, institutions, and information: domestic politics and international relations.* Princeton: Princeton University Press.

Mintz, A., S. B. Redd, and A. Vedlitz. 2006. Can we generalize from student experiments to the real world in political science, military affairs, and international relations? *Journal of Conflict Resolution* 50:757–76.

Mitchell, S., and B. Prins. 1999. Beyond territorial contiguity: issues at stake in the democratic militarized interstate disputes. *International Studies Quarterly* 43:169–83.

Møller, J., and S.-E. Skaaning. 2015. Explanatory typologies as a nested strategy of inquiry: combining cross-case and within-case analyses. *Sociological Methods & Research.* DOI: 10.1177/0049124115613778.

Moore, B. 1966. *The social origins of dictatorship and democracy: lord and peasant in the making of the modern world.* Boston: Beacon Press.

Morgan, S., and C. Winship. 2015. *Counterfactuals and causal inference: methods and principles for social research*, 2nd edition. Cambridge: Cambridge University Press.

Morton, R. 1999. *Methods and models: a guide to the empirical analysis of formal models in political science.* Cambridge: Cambridge University Press.

Morton, R., and K. Williams. 2010. *Experimental political science and the study of causality: from nature to the lab.* Cambridge: Cambridge University Press.

Most, B., and H. Starr. 1989. *Inquiry, logic, and international politics.* Columbia: University of South Carolina Press.

Nalepa, M. 2010. Captured commitments: an analytic narrative of transitions with transitional justice. *World Politics* 62:341–80.

Narang, V., and R. Nelson. 2009. Who are these belligerent democratizers? Reassessing the impact of democratization on war. *International Organization* 63:357–79.

Nash, J. 1950. The bargaining problem. *Econometrica* 18:155–62.

Nielsen, R. 2016. Case selection via matching. *Sociological Methods & Research* 45:569–97.

Norris, P. 2012. *Making democratic governance work.* Cambridge: Cambridge University Press.

North, D. 1990. *Institutions, institutional change and economic performance,* Cambridge: Cambridge University Press.

North, D., et al. (eds.). 2013. *In the shadow of violence: political science, economics, and the problems of development.* Cambridge: Cambridge University Press.

Ornston, D. 2013. Creative corporatism: the politics of high-technology competition in Nordic Europe. *Comparative Political Studies* 46:702–29.

Pahre, R. 2005. Formal theory and case study methods in EU studies. *European Union Politics* 6:113–46.

Paine, J. 2016. Still searching for the value-added: persistent concerns about set-theoretic comparative methods. *Comparative Political Studies.* 49:793–800.

Pearce, L. 2002. Integrating survey and ethnographic methods for systematic anomalous case analysis. *Sociological Methodology* 32: 103–32.

Pearl, J. 2009. *Causality: models, reasoning, and inference,* 2nd edition. Cambridge: Cambridge University Press.

Pearl, J., et al. 2016. *Causal inference in statistics: a primer.* New York: John Wiley & Sons.

Pevehouse, J. 2005. *Democracy from above: regional organizations and democratization.* Cambridge: Cambridge University Press.

Pierson, P. 2004. *Politics in time: history, institutions, and social analysis.* Princeton: Princeton University Press.

Przeworski, A., and H. Teune. 1970. *The logic of comparative social inquiry.* New York: John Wiley & Sons.

Przeworski, A., et al. 2000. *Democracy and development: political institutions and well-being in the world, 1950–1990.* Cambridge: Cambridge University Press.

Ragin, C. 1987. *The comparative method: moving beyond qualitative and quantitative strategies.* Berkeley: University of California Press.

———. 2000. *Fuzzy-set social science.* Chicago: University of Chicago Press.

———. 2008. *Redesigning social inquiry: fuzzy sets and beyond.* Chicago: University of Chicago Press.

Ragin, C., and G. Schneider. 2012. Comparative political analysis: six case-oriented strategies. In E. Amenta et al. (eds.), *The Wiley–Blackwell companion to political sociology.* New York: John Wiley & Sons.

Ragin, C., and S. Strand, 2008. Using qualitative comparative analysis to study causal order: comment on Caren and Panofsky (2005). *Sociological Methods & Research* 36:431–41.

Ray, J. 1993. Wars between democracies: rare or nonexistent? *International Interactions* 18:251–76.

Rodrik, D. (ed.). 2003. *In search of prosperity: analytic narratives on economic growth.* Princeton: Princeton University Press.

Rohlfing, I., and C. Schneider. 2013. Combining QCA with process tracing in analyses of necessity. *Political Research Quarterly* 66:220–35.

Rommetvedt, H., et al. 2013. Coping with corporatism in decline and the revival of parliament: interest group lobbyism in Denmark and Norway, 1980–2005. *Comparative Political Studies* 46: 457–86.

Rosen, J. 2013. Explaining women's parliamentary representation: political institutions, development thresholds, and gender equality in national politics. PhD Dissertation, Northwestern University.

Ross, M. 2004. How does natural resource wealth influence civil war? Evidence from thirteen cases. *International Organization* 58:35–67.

———. 2012. *The oil curse: how petroleum wealth shapes the development of nations.* Princeton: Princeton University Press.

Roth, L. 2006. *Selling women short: gender inequality on Wall Street.* Princeton: Princeton University Press.

Rudra, N. 2011. Openness and the politics of potable water. *Comparative Political Studies* 44:771–803.

Rueschemeyer, D., E. Stephens, and J. Stephens. 1992. *Capitalist development and democracy.* Chicago: University of Chicago Press.

Russett, B. 1995. The democratic peace: "and yet it moves." *International Security* 19:164–75.

Salmon, W. 1998. *Causality and explanation.* Oxford: Oxford University Press.

Sambanis, N. 2004. Using case studies to expand economic models of civil war. *Perspectives on Politics* 2:259–80.

Samford, S. 2010. Averting "disruption and reversal": reassessing the logic of rapid trade reform in Latin America. *Politics and Society* 38:373–407.

Schelling, T. 1978. *Micromotives and macrobehavior.* New York: W. W. Norton.

Schneider, C., and I. Rohlfing. 2013. Combining QCA and process tracing in set-theoretic multi-method research. *Sociological Methods & Research* 42:559–97.

———. 2016. Case studies nested in fuzzy-set QCA on sufficiency: formalizing case selection and causal inference. *Sociological Methods & Research* 45:526–68.

Schneider, C., and C. Wagemann. 2006. Reducing complexity in qualitative comparative analysis (QCA): remote and proximate factors and the consolidation of democracy. *European Journal of Political Research* 45:751–86.

———. 2012. *Set-theoretic methods for the social sciences: a guide to qualitative comparative analysis.* Cambridge: Cambridge University Press.

Schultz, K. 2001. Looking for audience costs. *Journal of Conflict Resolution* 45:32–60.

———. 2012. Why we needed audience costs and what we need now. *Security Studies* 21:369–75.

Seawright, J. 2016. *Multi-method social science: combining qualitative and quantitative tools.* Cambridge: Cambridge University Press.

Sekhon, J. 2004. Quality meets quantity: case studies, conditional probability, and counterfactuals. *Perspectives on Politics* 2:281–93.

Shepsle, K. 1995. Statistical political philosophy and positive political theory. *Critical Review* 9:213–22.

Sherif, M., et al. 1988 (1961). *The Robbers Cave experiment: intergroup conflict and cooperation.* Middletown: Wesleyan University Press.

Simmons, B., and Z. Elkins. 2004. The globalization of liberalization: policy diffusion in the international political economy. *American Political Science Review* 98:171–90.

Singer, J., and M. Small. 1974. Foreign policy indicators: predictors of war in history and in the state of the world message. *Policy Sciences* 5:271–96.

Skocpol, T. 1979. *States and social revolutions: a comparative analysis of France, Russia and China.* Cambridge: Cambridge University Press.

Slantchev, B. 2012. Audience cost theory and its audiences. *Security Studies* 21:376–82.

Slater, D. 2010. *Ordering power: contentious politics and authoritarian leviathans in Southeast Asia.* Cambridge: Cambridge University Press.

Slater, D., and D. Ziblatt. 2013. The enduring indispensability of the controlled comparison. *Comparative Political Studies* 46: 1301–27.

Slater, D., et al. 2014. Economic origins of democratic breakdowns? The redistributive model and the postcolonial state. *Perspectives on Politics* 12:353–74.

Small, M. 2009. How many cases do I need? On science and the logic of case selection in field-based research. *Ethnography* 10:5–38.

Snyder, J., and E. Borghard. 2011. The cost of empty threats: a penny, not a pound. *American Political Science Review* 105:437–55.

Soifer, H. 2012. The causal logic of critical junctures. *Comparative Political Studies* 45:1572–97.

———. 2015. *State building in Latin America.* Cambridge: Cambridge University Press.

Starr, H. 1978. "Opportunity" and "willingness" as ordering concepts in the study of war. *International Interactions* 4:363–87.

Steel, D. 2008. *Across the boundaries: extrapolation in biology and the social sciences.* Oxford: Oxford University Press.

Stokke, O. 2012. *Disaggregating international regimes.* Cambridge: MIT Press.

Sugden, R. 2009. Credible worlds, capacities and mechanisms. *Erkenntnis* 70:3–27.

Tannenwald, N. 1999. The nuclear taboo: the United States and the normative basis of nuclear non-use. *International Organization* 53:433–68.

———. 2005. Stigmatizing the bomb: origins of the nuclear taboo. *International Security* 29:5–49.

Tarrow, S. 2010. The strategy of paired comparison: toward a theory of practice. *Comparative Political Studies* 43:230–59.

Teorell, J. 2010. *Determinants of democratization: explaining regime change in the world, 1972–2006.* Cambridge: Cambridge University Press.

Themner, L., and P. Wallensteen. 2013. Armed conflict, 1946–2012. *Journal of Peace Research* 50:509–21.

Thiem, A., M. Baumgartner, and D. Bol. 2016. Still lost in translation: a correction of three misunderstandings between configurational comparativists and regressional analysts. *Comparative Political Studies* 49:742–74.

Toft, M. 2003. The geography of ethnic violence: identity, interests, and territory. Princeton: Princeton University Press.

———. 2009. Securing the peace: the durable settlement of civil wars. Princeton: Princeton University Press.

———. 2010. Ending civil wars: A case for rebel victory? International Security 34:7–36.

Tomz, M. 2007. Domestic audience costs in international relations: an experimental approach. International Organization 61:821–40.

Trachtenberg, M. 2012. Audience costs: an historical analysis. Security Studies 21:3–42.

Tsai, L. 2007. Accountability without democracy: solidary groups and public goods provision in rural China. Cambridge: Cambridge University Press.

Tsebelis, G. 1999. Veto players and law production in parliamentary democracies: an empirical analysis. American Political Science Review 93:591–608.

———. 2002. Veto players: how political institutions work. Princeton: Princeton University Press.

Veenendaal, W., and J. Corbett. 2015. Why small states offer important answers to large questions. Comparative Political Studies 48: 527–49.

Vinten-Johansen, P., et al. 2003. Cholera, chloroform, and the science of medicine: a life of John Snow. Oxford: Oxford University Press.

Waldner, D. 2012. Process tracing and causal mechanisms. In H. Kincaid (ed.), The Oxford handbook of philosophy of social science. Oxford: Oxford University Press.

———. 2015. What makes process tracing good? Causal mechanisms, causal inference, and the completeness standard in comparative politics. In A. Bennett and J. Checkel (eds.), Process tracing in the social sciences: from metaphor to analytic tool. Cambridge: Cambridge University Press.

Wallensteen, P. 2015. Quality peace: peacebuilding, victory and world order. Oxford: Oxford University Press.

Walsh, D. 2012. Does the quality of democracy matter for women's rights? Just debate and democratic transition in Chile and South Africa. Comparative Political Studies 45:1323–50.

Waltz, K. 1979. Theory of international relations. Boston: Addison-Wesley.

Weiffen, B., et al. 2011. Democracy, regional security institutions, rivalry mitigation: evidence from Europe, South America, and Asia. Security Studies 20:378–415.

Weinstein, J. 2006. *Inside rebellion: the politics of insurgent violence.* Cambridge: Cambridge University Press.

Weller, N., and J. Barnes. 2014. *Finding pathways: case selection for studying causal mechanisms in mixed-methods research.* Cambridge: Cambridge University Press.

Wood, E. 2000. *Forging democracy from below: insurgent transitions in South Africa and El Salvador.* Cambridge: Cambridge University Press.

———. 2003. *Insurgent collective action and civil war in El Salvador.* Cambridge: Cambridge University Press.

Yin, R. 2012. *Case study research: design and methods,* 5th edition. Newbury Park: Sage Publications.

Ziblatt, D. 2006. *Structuring the state: the formation of Italy and Germany and the puzzle of federalism.* Princeton: Princeton University Press.

———. 2009. Shaping democratic practice and the causes of electoral fraud: the case of nineteenth century Germany. *American Political Science Review* 103:1–21.

Zorn, C. 2005. A solution to separation in binary response models. *Political Analysis* 13:157–70.

INDEX

(0, 0) cases, 59, 65–66, 70–73; constraint causal mechanisms and, 89–101, 104–105, 107–108, 113–114, 121; counterfactuals and, 76–78; interactive causal mechanisms and, 157; in large-N qualitative testing, 197, 203, 208; paired comparisons and, 87, 186, 235, 255, 266; in the statistical approach, 251–252, 254, 267; typologies and, 74. *See also* case selection

(0, 1) cases, 59, 68–73; constraint causal mechanisms and, 99, 102–105; counterfactuals and, 77; interactive causal mechanisms and, 138; in large-N qualitative testing, 198, 203; in the medium-N paradigm, 237, 239; in the statistical approach, 252, 254. *See also* case selection

(1, 0) cases, 59, 66–68, 71–73; constraint causal mechanisms and, 99, 103–105; counterfactuals and, 76; interactive causal mechanisms and, 138; in large-N qualitative testing, 210–211; in the medium-N paradigm, 221, 233, 237; in the statistical approach, 251–252, 254. *See also* case selection

(1, 1) cases, 59, 63–66, 71–73, 89; constraint causal mechanisms and, 99–102, 104–105; counterfactuals and, 76–79; in game theoretic research, 186–187; generalization and extrapolation from, 221, 224, 231, 236–239; interactive causal mechanisms and, 136, 141–142; in large-N qualitative testing, 196–199, 203–204, 208–210, 215; paired comparisons and, 87, 235, 255, 266; in the statistical approach, 251–252, 267; sufficient conditions and, 103–104. *See also* case selection

Abadie, Alberto, 260
Acemoğlu, Daron, 10, 49–50, 180, 185, 193
additive models, 69, 117, 127–128
AIDS, 61–62, 71
Aktürk, Şener, 82, 138–139
analytic narratives, 3, 166n
Ansell, Ben, 127–130
audience costs, 166–167, 171, 174–178, 182–185, 199–207, 222–223
average treatment effect (ATE), 10, 34, 41, 226, 247, 251, 258
Avoid Overdetermination Guideline: for case studies, 78–81, 86; for necessary conditions, 91, 99, 105–109, 118; in the medium-N paradigm, 234; in pathway cases, 262; for sufficient conditions, 156–157, 161

Bardsley, Nicholas, 230
Barnes, Jeb, 34, 255, 258–259, 266
Beach, Derek, 42, 135
Bennett, Andrew, 134
Bibliographies, multimethod, 21–23, 85, 177, 239
biology, 12, 18n, 83. *See also* cholera
Boolean algebra. *See* fuzzy logic; Qualitative Comparative Analysis (QCA)
Borghard, Erica, 185, 200

136–137, 141–143, 147, 173;
mechanism overlap and, 54; and
overdetermination, 106–108;
research practice on, 95, 119–121,
146–150, 206; and scope, 46,
110–111; the statistical approach
and, 117–118; and subset
robustness, 226; sufficient versus,
111–112; trivialness of, 100–101,
114, 122. *See also* sufficient
conditions
Nelson, Rebecca, 195–199
nuclear weapons: deterrence and, 12,
80, 96, 108, 110; proliferation of,
181, 197, 215, 224

observational studies, 5, 31, 243, 247
Orston, Darius, 88
overdetermination. *See* Avoid
Overdetermination Guideline

paired comparisons, 14, 87, 162, 186,
235, 254–258, 266, 269
pathway case methodology, 16,
259–267. *See also* case selection;
causal mechanisms
Pedersen, Rasmus, 42
permissive conditions, 106, 159–160.
See also constraint causal
mechanisms; necessary conditions
Pevehouse, Jon, 7–8, 35–36, 39,
41, 72
physics: laws of. *See* covering laws
political opportunity structure,
150–152. *See also* constraint causal
mechanisms
political parties, 37–38, 44–45,
153–154, 158, 241
population, 13, 60, 83, 151, 189,
195, 219–222, 226, 233, 242,
247–248. *See also* scope
potential outcomes approach, 5n, 10,
75, 208, 245, 252; and case
selection, 16, 254–255, 260–262.
See also statistical approach
Primo, David, 3, 167, 175

process tracing: causal mechanisms
in, 8–9, 42, 168; in relation to the
research triad, 2, 164, 232;
within-case causal inference in, 4,
8, 49, 100, 139, 189, 194, 243,
255. *See also* detective metaphor
Przeworski, Adam, 74, 221, 234
psychology, 17, 229, 263

qualitative methods: equifinality in,
69; game theory and, 166–168;
generalization and scope in, 183,
219, 230; quantitative versus, 29,
64, 176, 190, 246, 253, 262, 269;
in relation to the research triad, 2,
5, 61. *See also* large-N qualitative
testing; QCA
Qualitative Comparative Analysis
(QCA): the (1, 0) cell in, 67, 221;
casual asymmetry and, 122, 140;
constraint causal mechanisms and,
46, 47–49, 92, 154; the
contributing factor model and, 155;
counterfactuals and, 120;
equifinality and, 69, 80, 153, 161,
226; interaction terms and, 10–11,
124–125, 130; necessary conditions
and, 12, 95–100, 115–117, 206;
overdetermination in, 55–56,
78–79, 87; regularity and
significance in, 26, 42, 206–208; in
relation to the research triad, 1–2,
5, 16–17, 164, 232; robustness,
225–227; scope in, 60; sequencing
and, 160; typological theories and,
134–135. *See also* necessary
conditions; sufficient conditions;
INUS condition; SUIN condition
quantitative methods: causal
mechanisms in, 29; in relation to
the research triad, 2, 5, 176.
See also statistical approach
Quinn, Kevin, 247–249, 258

Ragin, Charles, 16–17, 67, 83, 164,
217

counterrevolutionary, 54–55;
exploitation, 37–39, 41, 44–45,
109; military-absolutist, 132–133;
oil-dependent, 67–68,
162
statistical approach: average
treatment effects in the, 247–248;
case selection in the, 249–250,
258–262, 264–268; casual
complexity and the, 10; causal
mechanisms and the, 4, 6n, 7–9,
31, 34–36, 255, 259; control
variables in the, 246, 268; game
theory and the, 166–169, 172–175;
inference in the, 245–247;
interactions in the, 124–130;
compared to large-N qualitative
testing, 13–14, 190, 192, 208–210;
matching in the, 255–258;
compared to the medium-N
paradigm, 218, 224–226; necessary
conditions in the, 117–119;
potential outcomes and the,
254–255; representativeness in the,
248–251; in relation to the research
triad, 1–4, 15–16, 232, 262–263;
scope considerations in the, 13,
257; X-Y configurations and the,
251–254; variation on X and Y in
the, 253–254
statistical multimethod. See statistical
approach
Stokke, Olav, 120–121
substitutability, 102–104, 111.
See also (0, 1) cases
sufficient conditions: case selection
for, 99–105; in causal mechanisms,
31, 34, 41–47, 88–89; constraint
causal mechanisms, 93–95; in the
contribution factors model,
155–158; falsification and, 146;
game theory and, 172–174;
necessary versus, 92–93, 99–105,
107, 111–112, 122; in QCA, 116,
206–207, 226; the statistical
approach and, 92, 118, 121;

and subset robustness, 226.
See also necessary conditions
Sugden, Robert, 183–184, 188
SUIN condition, 103, 111, 163.
See also set theory

Tannenwald, Nina, 80, 97
Tarrow, Sidney,
Thompson, William, 204–207
Toft, Monica, 211–214
trade, 26, 116, 154, 161, 163, 241
trade-off: external-internal validity,
221, 227, 231; scope selection, 111
Tratchenberg, Mark, 178
trivialness, 100–102, 104, 114, 122,
207
Tsebelis, George, 97–98, 168
Tversky, Amos, 229
two cultures, 15, 133
typical case, 100, 247–253
typological theories, 131–136

validity, 82, 227–229, 249. See also
generalization
variables Z: case selection and, 59;
defined, 59; matching on, 255–257;
necessity/sufficiency and, 94,
99–100, 107–108; scope and, 81,
234–235; within-case causal
inference and, 70, 79–81
Verba, Sidney, 29, 115
veto players, 12, 96–98
Voeten, Erik, 8

Waldner, David, 32, 41–42, 56, 126
Wallensteen, Peter, 211–214
Walsh, Denise, 161
Weinstein, Jeremy, 74, 241, 253
Weller, Nicholas, 34, 255, 258–259,
266
Williams, Kenneth, 228
within-case casual inference: casual
mechanisms and, 6, 8, 49–52, 66,
81; counterfactuals and, 72, 75–78,
120, 142, 153; game theory and,